Brutal Valour
The Tragedy of Isandlwana

Book One of the Anglo-Zulu War

James Mace

Legionary Books
Meridian, Idaho 83642, USA
http://www.legionarybooks.net

First eBook Edition: 2016

Published in the United States of America
Legionary Books

Cover Images by Radoslav Javor, copyright © 2016 by Radoslav Javor and Legionary Books

All photography and maps are used with the generous permission of the Royal Welsh Museum, and from the collection of Ian Knight

The Works of James Mace

Note. In each series or combination of series', all works are listed in chronological sequence

The Artorian Chronicles
Soldier of Rome: The Legionary
Soldier of Rome: The Sacrovir Revolt
Soldier of Rome: Heir to Rebellion
Soldier of Rome: The Centurion
*Empire Betrayed: The Fall of Sejanus
Soldier of Rome: Journey to Judea
Soldier of Rome: The Last Campaign
*Centurion Valens and the Empress of Death
*Slaves of Fear: A Land Unconquered

The Great Jewish Revolt and Year of the Four Emperors
Soldier of Rome: Rebellion in Judea
Soldier of Rome: Vespasian's Fury
Soldier of Rome: Reign of the Tyrants
Soldier of Rome: Rise of the Flavians

Napoleonic Era
Forlorn Hope: The Storming of Badajoz
I Stood With Wellington
Courage, Marshal Ney

The Anglo-Zulu War
Brutal Valour: The Tragedy of Isandlwana
Crucible of Honour: The Battle of Rorke's Drift
Lost Souls: The Forgotten Heroes of Eshowe
Cruelty of Fate: The Fight for Khambula

* Stand-alone novel or novella

There are not enough tears to mourn the dead.

\-   King Cetshwayo kaMpande

Foreword by Ian Knight

In 1879 Great Britain was the world's greatest super-power, and its influence was nearing its height. Her possessions stretched across the continents, from the Americas to Asia, Australasia and Africa, and it was said that as the world turned the sun never set on her Empire. Since the young Queen Victoria had come to the throne in 1837 the British Army had faced Canadian rebels, Maori warriors, Afghan hillmen, Russians guns, and many of the impressive military cultures of India – and whilst it had lost many a battle, it had lost few enough wars. Yet, in January 1879, beneath a distinctive rocky outcrop in the southern African veldt known as iSandlwana, a part-time militia army of Zulu cattle-farmers inflicted upon it the greatest defeat the British Army would endure in a single action throughout the whole of the Victorian period – over 1,300 British soldiers and their African allies were killed, a butcher's bill greater than any other in the doleful litany of contemporary British military failures, greater than 'the Charge of the Light Brigade', greater than Majuba, or Colenso, or Magersfontein, or Spioenkop.

The image of dead redcoats scattered across the green summer grass at iSandlwana deeply shocked the Empire at the time and has become an enduring symbol, since, of the perils of Imperial adventuring. Historians continue to debate the events of 1879, books continue to be written and movies and television documentaries made. It's not hard to see why – the story has an almost Shakespearean air of grandeur and tragedy to it, of high strategic folly, of the hubris of generals, of lives needlessly squandered, of the tragic destruction of an ancient way of life - and yet all of this redeemed, if such things can be, by the courage of those who met each other in battle.

In *Brutal Valour* James Mace has chosen to explore the conflict through the lives of the ordinary men involved, a newly recruited soldier in the ranks of the British 24th Regiment and a Zulu warrior, both of whom are pushed by forces beyond their understanding into a bloody confrontation at iSandlwana.

James tackles the story with the same verve, commitment to historical accuracy, and insight into the universal experience of soldiers across the ages that he brought to his *Soldier of Rome* and Napoleonic novels.

Brutal Valour offers a vivid insight into the human cost of one of the most dramatic and intriguing incidents in Britain's colonial past in Africa.

- Ian Knight (author of *Zulu Rising*)

Table of Contents

Preface

It is December 1878, and war looms on the horizon in South Africa. British High Commissioner Sir Henry Bartle-Frere seeks to dismantle the powerful neighbouring kingdom of the Zulus and uses an incursion along the disputed border as his justification for war. He issues an impossible ultimatum to the Zulu king, Cetshwayo, demanding he disband his armies and pay massive reparations. With a heavy heart, the king prepares his nation for war against their former allies.

Leading the invasion is Lieutenant General Sir Frederic Thesiger, Baron Chelmsford, a highly experienced officer fresh off a decisive triumph over the neighbouring Xhosa tribes. He and Frere are convinced that a quick victory over the Zulus will negate any repercussions from the home government for launching what is, in essence, an illegal war.

Recently arrived to South Africa are newly-recruited Privates Arthur Wilkinson and Richard Lowe; members of C Company, 1/24th Regiment of Foot under the venerable Captain Reginald Younghusband. Eager for adventure, they are prepared to do their duty both for the Empire and for their friends. As Frere's ultimatum expires, the army of British redcoats and allied African auxiliaries crosses the uMzinyathi River at Rorke's Drift into Zululand. Ten days later, the British and Zulus will meet their destiny at the base of a mountain called Isandlwana.

Cast of Characters

The British:

Private Arthur Wilkinson – A new soldier recently assigned to C Company, 1/24th Regiment of Foot soon after completing recruit training at The Depot in Brecon, Wales
Private Richard Lowe – Arthur's childhood friend who enlists with him

Men of C Company, 1st Battalion, 24th Regiment of Foot (1/24th)

Captain Reginald Younghusband – Officer Commanding; an experienced and venerable officer who has held his commission for over sixteen years
Lieutenant the Honourable George Hodson – Subaltern under Younghusband, very young yet already experienced from the Xhosa War
Colour Sergeant Thomas Browne – Company's senior-ranking non-commissioned officer (NCO) and former instructor from The Depot
Sergeant John Edwards – Arthur and Richard's section leader
Corporal John Bellhouse – NCO in charge of the company's sharp-shooters
Lance Corporal William Johnson – A sharp-shooter who befriends Arthur
Privates James Trainer, Harry Grant – Fellow new recruits, who came with Wilkinson and Lowe from The Depot
Private Jason Bray – A much older veteran and mentor to Arthur and Richard

Officers and Other Soldiers of the Regiment

Colonel Richard Glyn – Regimental Commander, assigned as commanding officer of the centre No. 3 Column
Brevet Lieutenant Colonel Henry Pulleine – Commanding Officer, 1st Battalion, 24th Foot (1/24th)

Lieutenant Colonel Henry James Degacher – Commanding Officer, 2nd Battalion, 24th Foot (2/24th)

Captain George Wardell – Officer Commanding, H Company, 1/24th and friend of Captain Younghusband

Lieutenant Teignmouth Melvill – Adjutant, 1/24th

Lieutenant Neville Coghill – Aide-de-Camp to Colonel Glyn

Lieutenant Charlie Pope – Officer Commanding, G Company, 2/24th

Lieutenant Gonville Bromhead – Officer Commanding, B Company 2/24th, who's left to guard the depot at Rorke's Drift

Colour Sergeant Frank Bourne – Senior NCO of B Company, 2/24th. At just 24 years of age, he is the youngest colour sergeant in the entire British Army

Colour Sergeant Frederick Wolfe – Senior NCO of H Company, 1/24th

Senior Officers

Lieutenant General Sir Frederic Thesiger, Lord Chelmsford – General Officer Commanding (GOC) of all British military forces in Natal

Colonel Henry Evelyn Wood, VC – Commanding Officer of the northern No. 4 Column and previous recipient of the Victoria Cross

Colonel Charles Pearson – Commanding Officer of the southern No. 1 Column

Lieutenant Colonel John North Crealock – Chelmsford's acting military secretary

Lieutenant Colonel Anthony Durnford – Royal Engineer and Commanding Officer of the No. 2 Column of African auxiliaries and cavalry troops

Major Francis Clery – Aide-de-Camp (ADC) to Colonel Glyn

The Zulus:

Cetshwayo kaMpande – King of the Zulus. Came to power during a terribly bloody civil war between he and several of his own brothers more than twenty years prior

Ntshingwayo kaMahole – A Zulu *inkosi*, close friend of the king and one of his closest advisors

Sihayo kaXongo – One of Cetshwayo's closest friends, he is baron of the land nearest the river crossing into Natal at Rorke's Drift

Mehlokazulu kaSihayo – Sihayo's eldest son and heir. He takes matters into his own hands when his mother and one of the other wives betray his father and flee into Natal with their lovers

Mkhosana kaMvundlana – A senior *inkosi* in command of several regiments of younger warriors

Sikhotha kaMpande – Brother of Cetshwayo, who opposed his ascension to the throne. His faction, the iziGqoza, were expelled by Cetshwayo and now look to the British to help them exact their revenge

Dabulamanzi kaMpande – Another of the king's brothers. He is fiercely loyal to Cetshwayo, yet very eager for personal glory

Prologue: Heirs of Blood

Ndondakusuka, near the Thukela River
Zulu Kingdom, South Africa
2 December 1856

Cetshwayo kaMpande

"It should not have to end this way," the young warrior said as he clutched his shield close to his body, while huddling beneath a blanket in the early morning mist. His name was Cetshwayo kaMpande, eldest son of Zulu King, Mpande kaSensangakhona. He now found himself disowned as the heir apparent, in favour of one of the king's younger sons, Mbuyazi, and there was only one way left to reclaim what was rightfully his.

The night had been unexpectedly cold, and it bit into him as he glanced over his shoulder. In the soft glow of predawn, he could make out the slumbering forms of his numerous warriors. A few were starting to stir. It would not be long before the entire valley was awakened by the mass of men readying for battle.

"It is by our father's actions, constantly pitting brother against brother in return for his favour, that it has come to this," his brother, Dabulamanzi, remarked. Dabulamanzi was fiercely loyal to

Cetshwayo, as were a number of his other siblings. Yet five of their brothers now stood with the pretender. Cetshwayo found it a bitterly ironic tragedy that a squabble between the sons of Mpande had led to civil war engulfing the entire Zulu Kingdom.

Conflict between siblings and other family members within the Zulu royal house had become all-too-frequent since the reign of the king's brother, the legendary Shaka. It was he who had expanded the humble kingdom of cattle farmers into a vast empire now covering much of southeast Africa, with more than a quarter-of-a-million total subjects from various assimilated tribes. His twelve-year reign was a contrast of brilliance, particularly in the revolution of the Zulu style of warfare, and abject terror via ruling through authoritarian fear. It was still spoken of about how upon the death of his mother, Nandi, he'd ordered the deaths of over seven thousand of his people for not mourning with enough reverence. Whether this was truth or embellishment brought on by his successors was impossible to say. Cetshwayo had been just two years old when Shaka was murdered. He had no memory of his uncle.

Though Shaka had no recognized sons, viewing them as potential threats, he still found his position precarious due to the ambitions of his own brothers. One of the few he trusted, Dingane, had him assassinated. The usurper, in turn, met his end after a reign of twelve years. Their younger brother, Mpande, rebelled and overthrew Dingane with the help of over four hundred Dutch mercenaries.

Mpande broke from the tradition set by the paranoid and childless Shaka and Dingane. He married numerous wives and sired twenty-nine sons and twenty-three daughters. Though tradition stated the king's heir would be the eldest son from the chief wife, this was by no means absolute. The king could also change who the chief wife was at any given time. This was something Mpande did quite frequently, thus deliberately pitting his sons against each other. It was his ultimate weapon of control over his children and, by extension, the kingdom.

Since reaching the age of manhood, there had been constant tensions between Cetshwayo and his father. As the eldest of his siblings, he was convinced the throne of the Zulus was his by right, not some cheap prize his father could toss about. Mpande, in turn, began to view his eldest son as an entitled upstart who threatened the king's divine authority. Their quarrels culminated when the king took a former wife of Shaka's as one of his own, with the intent of siring a rival should Cetshwayo prove too powerful. Adding to this insult, Mpande had recently directed Mbuyazi and many of his followers to occupy the lands in the south that belonged to Cetshwayo. When Cetshwayo refused to yield so much as a scrap of land to his brother, war became inevitable. And though he had pitted his sons against each other in order to make his own position more secure, that the nation was now at war with itself had undermined Mpande immensely. There were many whispers among the *amakhosi* that the king was weak and unable to so much as control his own household. Many of these powerful barons had subsequently sided with Cetshwayo.

"Many of the *izikhulu* support your claim," Dabulamanzi said, in reference to the king's inner council. "Only the *iziGqoza* faction remain loyal to Mbuyazi."

"And this will prove to be their downfall," Cetshwayo said calmly, as he palmed the wide blade of his stabbing spear. "Those who escape the slaughter will be banished from the lands of the Zulu."

The iziGqoza, a subsect of the Zulus, were devoted followers of Mbuyazi. They varied considerably from Cetshwayo's own supporters, the Usuthu, in both culture and traditions. Many of the European settlers in Natal viewed all Africans contemptuously as simple-minded barbarians. In reality, there were vast cultural differences between the many different tribes in southern Africa, just as there were between the various white peoples of Europe. This was especially true within the Zulu Kingdom. Only a single generation had passed since many such tribes were annexed, oftentimes violently, by King Shaka. For Cetshwayo, the pending battle would not be just to secure his place as the heir to Mpande, but to bring about unity and cohesion before the kingdom fractured further. He would unite his people through love if possible, or fear if necessary.

"Our father is weak," he lamented to his brother. "He continues to grant more and more of the king's royal powers to the regional *amakhosi*. If this is not stopped, there won't be a royal household or a Zulu nation. Remember, my brother, the blood we spill this day is not just for ourselves but for survival of the kingdom."

Prince Mbuyazi rose long before the first glow of dawn. He knew his position was precarious and he hadn't been able to sleep at all during the long night. His iziGqoza numbered just seven thousand warriors with about twice as many women and children. Cetshwayo's reaction to the proposed usurpation of his lands was one of violence. Mbuyazi had proved ill-prepared to face him. And their father, who in theory ruled with absolute authority over the realm, was powerless to stop what he knew would be a savage blood-letting. Mbuyazi had become the king's favourite son in recent years, yet there was nothing he could do to protect him from his elder brother's wrath.

"My brother's forces number nearly three times ours," the prince said quietly. He scanned below the ridge, through thick mist, towards Cetshwayo's encampment.

"That may be," a voice said behind him. "But, we do have something that may even the odds a bit."

Mbuyazi turned, giving a tired smile at the sight of the one of the few white men on the field.

His name was John Dunn. Of Scottish descent and orphaned at a young age, he had been forced to find rather eccentric means of supporting himself or starve to death. Over the years, he became an efficient tracker, guide, and hunter, as well as a very shrewd trader in firearms. His exploits into Zululand had given him a far greater understanding of the region than one would expect of a twenty-two year old European. And when the Cape authorities put out a moratorium on the trading of firearms with the Zulus, Dunn simply had his weapons shipped in via the Portuguese colony of Mozambique to the north.

Speaking fluent Zulu and having befriended many of the local chiefs, including King Mpande, Dunn was asked to help find a solution to the struggle between the king's rival sons. Once it became clear that Cetshwayo and Mbuyazi would only be able to

18

settle their differences through bloodshed, Dunn declared his allegiance to Mbuyazi. He subsequently used his connections with white traders in Natal to secure a number of firearms for the iziGqoza, with many sneaking their shipments across the uMzinyathi River. He further brought with him thirty-five members of the Natal Border Police; white settlers who acted as a volunteer force along the Natal / Zulu border, to serve as advisors. Ironically, they were supposed to have prevented the sale of arms to the Zulus. Now, a number of them were fighting beside them in an inner-kingdom civil war.

"Your fire staffs are well known to our people," Mbuyazi said. "Shaka dismissed them. Only recently has my father been more accepting of their potential."

"And we will demonstrate their effectiveness to your brother soon enough," Dunn said. His confidence was waning with the knowledge of the size of Cetshwayo's army. He'd hoped to secure sufficient arms for at least half of Mbuyazi's warriors, but had only been able to procure a couple hundred total weapons. Most were outdated smoothbore muskets; many of which were hundred year old firelocks modified with flints in the hammer. Their accuracy was minimal, even in the hands of trained professionals, which the iziGqoza were not. Ammunition was scarce. Still, they were eager to learn. Dunn and his border policemen had trained them as best as they were able regarding loading and firing. He hoped a few volleys would disperse Cetshwayo's warriors who, as far as he knew, were devoid of firearms.

Prince of the Zulus and leader of the iziGqoza faction, Mbuyazi stood dressed in full regalia with elaborate plumes of feathers and cow tails protruding from his headband. Most warriors only donned their loincloth and minimal headdress prior to battle. The prince wanted to set an example to his own followers, as well as his brother's warriors. The sun was rising behind them, and he seemed to shimmer as the light danced off the dissipating mist. He was soon joined by his five brothers who had vowed to fight to the death, rather than submit to Cetshwayo.

"Fear not," one of them said quietly into Mbuyazi's ear. "Our enemies are many, but let us not forget that when our father fought against Dingane, he too was outnumbered."

"The lineage of the Zulu kings will once again be decided in blood," Mbuyazi lamented. As they looked down the gentle slope, they could now see the mass of their brother's warriors advancing, their war chants growing ever louder.

"Burn a line in the grass between us and our women and children," the prince ordered one of his warriors. "Beyond that line, we do not retreat. We will stand and fight. And if need be, we will die for our people, as true sons of Zulu!"

Within minutes, the sounds of burning grass crackled in the distance behind them down a reverse slope. This resonated with the war chants and banging of weapons on shields by Cetshwayo's rapidly approaching army. Their force was huge. It covered the landscape as far as Mbuyazi could see, like a great black shadow.

A few dozen yards to their front, Dunn had formed his marksmen into a skirmish line. His white troops were armed with modern rifled carbines, with percussion caps instead of flints. He regretted they had no horses, though he reminded himself there was a boat waiting for them, should things turn for the worst.

"Such discipline," a carbineer said nervously. He was filled with both admiration and dread at the sight of the massive Zulu horde.

"These are no mere barbarians," Dunn replied, his voice surprisingly calm despite the terror that welled up within him. "They do not simply rush forward as a disorganized rabble. Each regiment advances in company lines, not unlike European armies."

"Thankfully they don't have these!" the carbineer said, holding up his weapon. He let out a deep breath to try and settle his nerves.

Cetshwayo's army was now within four hundred yards and quickening their pace. Though still well out of range of the archaic muskets borne by his ill-trained skirmishers, Dunn surmised it was time to test the psychological effects of volley fire. His own carbineers would have better luck with their superior weapons and training. He figured with the uSuthu massed so close together, at least some of the iziGqoza shots would find their marks.

"Lungile!" he shouted, telling his men to make ready.

Some of his European volunteers spoke Zulu, and Dunn decided it was best to issue fire commands in the local tongue.

"Khomba!" At his next command, iziGqoza and white volunteer alike aimed their weapons at their foe.

20

Cetshwayo's warriors had now quickened their pace to a jog, the cadence of their war chants growing louder and faster.

Dunn hoped his African troops would remember their drills and prove able to reload their muskets quickly enough before the uSuthu closed the final distance. He swallowed hard before issuing his next command. *"Dubula!"*

The noise of several hundred muskets and carbines firing at once broke the stillness of the morning. It was impossible to tell just how effective their first volley was, although Dunn was able to see numerous clots of dirt kick up well in front of the uSuthu, telling him many of his men had aimed far too short. Terror now gripped the iziGqoza. Many of them froze in place, either forgetting how or simply unable to reload their weapons. Some of their muskets had misfired and they knew not what to do.

Plenty remembered what they'd been taught, however, and quickly primed the pans of their flintlocks, pouring the remaining powder down the barrel, and then ramming the ball home. For the Europeans it was a similar drill. Some wishing they had some of the experimental brass cartridge firearms they'd heard rumours about, which could fire ten to fifteen rounds per minute.

"Carbineers, fire at will!" Dunn shouted in English.

Sporadic shots reverberated from the white men as they fired their weapons as fast as they could reload. The uSuthu advance had not slowed. In fact, it had quickened to where they now moved at a full sprint, shouts of *'Uzulu!'* echoing from their ranks. A handful of iziGqoza marksmen managed to get off a second volley, though most threw down their firearms and fled towards the main battle line.

"Fall back!" Dunn shouted.

His men turned and fled up the slope, anxious to reach the perceived safety of the friendly army. Several were not fast enough, and along with a number of iziGqoza, they were felled by throwing spears or knocked down by Zulu shields. Some of these hapless men were brutally stabbed. Others had their brains bashed in with heavy clubs. Their screams of pain made the hair on Dunn's neck stand up.

His heart was threatening to pound out of his chest, and he sprinted the last few feet before lunging between the files of Mbuyazi's warriors, who stood ready behind their shields. Their own war chants countered those of their foes as they stood ready for the killing to commence in earnest.

John Dunn

Had their enemies possessed more firearms, it may have been enough to turn back Cetshwayo's army long enough to give the iziGqoza some breathing space. Fortunately, their numbers were few. Most of the shots fired by their traitorous adversaries had landed short or flown wildly in various directions. The white men on the left of the skirmish line inflicted the most damage. Their high-powered slugs blasted clean through cowhide shields, slamming into the bodies of warriors with a sickening thud. So powerful were these newer weapons, the Zulus struck down by them screamed uncontrollably; their guts ripped asunder, arms and legs shattered. However, rather than intimidating the uSuthu, it only enraged them. As they fell upon the stragglers who failed to flee up the hill fast enough, there was no mercy. Nearly every warrior who passed over a fallen white carbineer or iziGqoza skirmisher would plunge his stabbing spear into them or give them a smash with their knobkerrie clubs, as they bounded by. This left corpses of little more than pulpy masses of blood and gore, with splintered bones protruding grotesquely through torn flesh.

As a warrior prince who always led by example, in what he proclaimed as 'the spirit of Shaka', Cetshwayo ran at the head of his massive army. He was also as tactically cautious as he was personally brave. He understood the advantage Mbuyazi possessed with the high ground. Therefore, he kept his best regiments in reserve, preferring to let those he viewed as expendable soften up the enemy. With a final shout of *"Uzulu!"* his front ranks charged into the wall of iziGqoza shields. Warriors on both sides carried at least one or two *assegai* throwing spears, which they now unleashed on each other. Several embedded themselves in Cetshwayo's shield, as the defenders tried to slay the hated usurper. Another grazed his cheek, leaving a deep gash that oozed blood down the side of his face. Yet on the uSuthu came.

Where the killing began in earnest was up close. Another innovation of Shaka's was the short stabbing spear, possessing a longer and wider blade than the throwing assegai. It was called the *iklwa*, for the sound it made when being pulled from a victim's wound. Many such resonances were heard as the men battled. Another prominent weapon, depending on a warrior's personal preference, was the club known as the *knobkerrie*; a staff with a ball on the end used to smash in an enemy's brains. This was Cetshwayo's weapon of choice this day. As he hooked the outside of an opponent's shield with his own, he jerked hard. The prince was a large and exceptionally strong man, and he caused the man to stumble forward, where he smashed him hard across the top of the head with a loud snap as the skull ruptured. Cetshwayo bludgeoned him three more times, hastening the warrior's death as the skull caved in.

Having achieved his first kill of the battle, Cetshwayo slowly backed away, waving the companies of his lead regiments into the fray. It was a bloody slog as they tried to breach the wall of shields and bristling spears of Mbuyazi's warriors. Men on both sides fell dead or badly injured. And as the bodies became an obstacle, it was impossible to tell just who held the advantage.

On the right of the iziGqoza line, the white carbineers fired sporadic shots between the files of their allies. Tactically this would have little impact, given the thousands of warriors involved in the savage fray. For those amongst the uSuthu who watched their friends' brains splattered and bodies torn asunder by the close-range

23

lifeless eyes of Mbuyazi, before snapping the spear in half and plunging the long blade into his heart. This elicited a further shout of praise to Cetshwayo. In one battle, he had become the most powerful man within the Zulu kingdom.

"I want that man, Dunn," he said, nodding towards the boat in the distance.

"Inkosi, it would be dangerous for us to cross into Natal to hunt one man," a warrior replied.

"Oh, I don't want him dead," Cetshwayo remarked with a grin. "I want him as a friend. He can get the weapons my people need. And besides, I need someone who can be my eyes and ears regarding the whites on the other side of our border."

At the king's kraal, Mpande took the news of Mbuyazi's death, and that of his other sons, very hard. A month long period of mourning followed, and the king was now a broken man. He had forbidden Cetshwayo from returning to the royal court, even though his son tried to return all of the cattle taken from the defeated iziGqoza. Mpande also understood that, if Cetshwayo chose to ignore this directive, there was little he could do about it. Word of the defeat and wholesale slaughter of the iziGqoza faction spread quickly, with many of the regional chiefs now pledging their allegiance to Cetshwayo. Whether out of loyalty or fear that the king's son would unleash a new reign of terror in the spirit of Shaka, one could only guess.

In the early months of 1857, a messenger from Cetshwayo came to the royal court. Mpande received word that his son was on his way with a number of elite regiments and he feared usurpation. The king was partially relieved when he saw the messenger was an old friend named Siganada.

Siganada was a well-respected warrior and leader with the *amabutho*, the regiments of the Zulu armies. Now in his early forties, his father was a contemporary of Shaka. Siganada held the title of *inkosi* and had served as a royal advisor to Dingane and Mpande, as his father had to Shaka. This lifelong association and friendship with the Zulu royal house was the reason the king reacted with anger and sorrow when he first heard of Siganada's defection to Cetshwayo.

The king sat upon his throne, on a raised platform in the centre of the kraal. He wore his ceremonial headdress with a long spear resting on his lap. Years of inactivity had rendered him rather obese, and he used his regalia to mask his girth. Siganada wore no regalia, just his loin covering and the black head band that signified him as a married man. He carried only his shield and a single assegai. He set down his weapons, bowed deeply, while averting his gaze and ensuring he remained below eye level of the king, as was expected. He also held his hands up by his face, palms facing each other in a form of salute and reverence, as he approached the throne.

"*Ndabazitha*," he said, addressing Mpande in a form of reverence much the same as 'Your Majesty' to the British. "I bring news from your son."

"Indeed," Mpande replied. "So the usurper has come to claim what he thinks is his?"

"He comes not to usurp you, Ndabazitha, but he does come to claim what is rightfully his. Please understand, he wants peace with you, his father, for the good of the Zulu nation." The *inkosi* remained hunkered low, only scarcely daring to chance a quick glance to gauge his sovereign's reaction.

"And what does he demand in return?" the king asked after a rather long and uncomfortable pause.

"That you publicly acknowledge him as your undisputed heir," Siganada replied. "That he act as co-regent, sharing with you the burdens of ruling the kingdom."

"In other words, he will become king in all but name with myself little more than an old figurehead." Vexed by the outcome, Mpande knew he had little choice. To stand defiant against his son would only lead to more needless bloodshed, and he simply did not have the strength to oppose Cetshwayo and the uSuthu. "So be it. Cetshwayo may return to the Zulu royal kraal. But you, Siganada, are hereby banished from my kingdom. Go and beg for scraps from the Swazi and the Xhosa, who welcome traitors such as you!"

Chapter I: Gone for a Soldier

The Depot, Brecon, Wales
May 1878

Soldiers on Parade at The Depot in Brecon, Wales

The bugle sounding reveille came all-too-early for the young soldier. After all these weeks, everything came instinctively to him. He and his fellow recruits, crammed into a small barracks that gave them less personal space than the poverty-stricken workhouses in the industrial cities, hurriedly roused themselves. They quickly pulled on their dark blue trousers and shoes, buttoned up their red tunics, buckled their belts, donned their blue home service helmets, and grabbed their rifles as they rushed out onto the parade ground.

"Let's hope we don't get pissed on today," he grumbled to himself. While his home in Stratford-upon-Avon, England got plenty of precipitation, one could still reasonably expect a few days of decent weather for every one of rain. Wales, on the other hand, felt perpetually damp, especially in the spring. On this particular morning the air smelled of the rains from the night before, yet the skies were relatively clear. The gentle breeze was cool and biting as the men found their places in the company formation.

"Fall in at the double!" the sergeant-instructor shouted. *"Her Majesty does not have time to wait on your fucking lollygagging!"*

The past weeks had been nothing but a tedium of repetition, and the recruits who'd been at The Depot for more than a few days knew the drill. They would be on parade for the next hour, where the sergeants and corporal-instructors would conduct a thorough inspection of their uniforms, weapons, and kit. Deficiencies brought a swift verbal assault and, possibly, a sharp slap across the face with the sergeant-instructor's staff. After breakfast would be recruit training; marching, extensive rifle fighting and bayonet drill, military regulations, more marching, section manoeuvre and tactics, as well as weapons maintenance. This would be followed by company drill. Day after day they had been drilled to the point that the recruits could fall into any type of battle formation instinctively, while able to follow both verbal orders and bugle calls. Occasionally there was even a chance to fire their Martini-Henry rifles at the range, though training ammunition was disappointingly sparse. There were also numerous fatigue details meant to keep The Depot looking pristine, usually doled out to recruits as punishment for failing to meet certain standards. Afternoon meal would be followed by more parade, marching, and more recruit training. Evenings were spent cleaning and servicing kit, making certain everything was up to standard before lights-out. The following day it all started again.

There was no set timeline for a soldier's basic training completion. Once the commandant, at the recommendation of the instructors, determined a recruit had met the necessary standards, he was sent across barracks to the holding company from where he would be shipped off to join the regiment. Those who learned fast could expect to finish in as little as six to eight weeks; those requiring more extensive remedial training, often brutally enforced by the instructors with verbal and physical chastisement, would take as many as ten to twelve weeks before being deemed fit for service. This particular prospective soldier, who nearly stumbled as he hurried onto the parade ground, had been at The Depot for seven weeks.

His name was Arthur Wilkinson. And like most of the lads who now stood shivering in the cold spring morning, he was very young. At 5'6" he was average height, with a build that was neither too large nor too slender. His hair was dark brown, almost black.

His face was attractive and smooth, despite never having shaved a day in his life. Arthur had turned eighteen just prior to enlisting, though his boyish face made him look even younger. He had joined the army despite the vehement protestations of his father, who'd hoped to secure his son an apprenticeship with a local farrier in Stratford.

During some of the more savage days of training, particularly those when the freezing rains chilled them to their very bones as they were berated and struck by the instructors, Arthur wondered if he'd made a cocked-up life decision. He quickly learned that drill happened regardless of the weather. Having arrived in mid-March, the days were cold and wet. The company's senior trainer, Sergeant-Instructor Brown, was a brutal teacher bordering on sadistic. Every day he seemed to find something new to berate and punish each recruit. It became a struggle for Arthur not to wince whenever he saw Brown and his stick.

Standing next to him on this morning, as always since the day they arrived, was an equally young private named Richard Lowe. Slightly taller than Arthur with a more slender build, he had a thick mop of sandy blonde hair that sometimes fell into his eyes. The first time this happened, his ears were left ringing from the screaming rebuke he'd received, along with a hard cuff across the head from one of the corporals. Arthur later told him, *at least it wasn't Sergeant-Instructor Brown!* While they may have looked like young schoolboys, Arthur and Richard had endured weeks of vigorous, brutal training which earned them the right to wear the uniform of Queen Victoria's army. Their coats were the traditional red with green facings on the cuffs, as well as on the front of the high collar. The collar also bore a brass insignia of a sphinx that was awarded to their regiment, the 24th Foot, during its service in Egypt. The epaulets were red with a white border and a brass *24* on each side. Their trousers were dark blue with a thin, red stripe on the outside seam. While home in garrison, each wore the dark blue home service helmet bearing the regimental crest in the centre with a protruding metal spike out the top, in the German fashion.

Richard was also smooth in the face, though he too had never shaved a day in his life. His hope was to have a worthy moustache growing by the time they left recruit training. Despite the Queen's Regulations stating that moustaches would be worn, Sergeant-

Instructor Brown's face was also devoid of whiskers. Lowe had joked one evening that perhaps he viewed his lack of a proper moustache as a blow against his manhood, and that's why he was always so malicious.

"Why in the bleeding hell is your top tunic button undone? The Queen, in her misplaced generosity, gave you this uniform. You will treat it with respect!"

The booming voice of Sergeant-Instructor Brown woke both men out of their early morning stupor. The guilty offender was one of the newest recruits at The Depot. Brown slapped him hard across the side of the neck with his stick, leaving an angry welt in its wake. "Two hours extra duty for shaming Her Majesty's uniform!" He gave the hapless recruit another sharp rap with his stick across the same spot on his neck, which would turn a nasty shade of purple before the day was done.

"Is that all?" Arthur whispered to Lowe.

"He's feeling a might benevolent today," his friend chuckled quietly, remembering the time Sergeant-Instructor Brown made him run around the parade ground for an hour with his rifle over his head for having a piece of his kit out of place. At one point he had fallen down and started vomiting, only to have Brown kick him swiftly in the backside and harangue him to keep moving. Four hours of extra duty had been added for having soiled the parade ground, as well as his uniform.

Both men quickly fell silent and kept their eyes straight ahead as the sergeant-instructor made his way down their line. At random he would grab a recruit's rifle and give it a quick inspection. On this day he chose Arthur. The recruit brought the weapon to port arms, opened the breach to ensure the rifle was clear, and then presented it to the instructor. Brown snatched it from him and spent a full minute going over the weapon. He ran his finger inside the breach block and over the bore of the barrel. He closed the breach and handed the rifle back to Arthur without a word. He stepped over to Richard and went through the same procedure with his weapon. Again not a word was spoken. Arthur breathed a sigh of relief for his friend. Silence from Sergeant-Instructor Brown was as good as a commendation.

As soon as he and the corporals finished their inspection, Brown briskly marched to the front of the formation. *"Company… 'shun'!"*

"Mark…time! *Left, right, left, right…halt!* Report!"

Arthur stopped, clicked his heels and came to attention. "Private Wilkinson reporting, sir."

The major was an older soldier in his mid-fifties, with a badly receding hairline and a grey moustache. His uniform, however, was immaculate. Arthur recognized the India General Service Medal, as well as the South Africa Medal from 1854, and the Second China War Medal of 1861 on his uniform. The man clearly had a long career of service and may have even been enlisted at one point.

"At ease," the major replied. His expression was stern. "I understand you have a rather personal request to make. Well, out with it, boy!"

"I request permission to marry, sir," Arthur said quickly, before nerves got the best of him.

"Indeed," the major replied, leaning back in his chair.

He'd been told everything by Sergeant-Instructor Brown but persisted in grilling Arthur with the same gamut of questions, cutting him off once the private confessed he did not know if his woman was waiting for him or if she would even accept his proposal.

There was a long pause before the major spoke again. "Normally, I would give a man five lashes for making such an absurd request and taking up my valuable time. Lucky for you, flogging has been prohibited on home service. Well, what have you to say for yourself?" His expression was unchanged, and from his harsh countenance, one would never guess he found the young private standing before him amusing.

"I had to make my request now, sir," Arthur answered. "I could not very well ask for Elisa's hand, only to have her wait until I join the regiment. It could be weeks, even months, before I could make my request to the colonel and get an answer to her."

"Ah, so the lass has a name," the major observed. He contemplated for a moment before answering offhandedly, "There is a draft of new soldiers headed to South Africa within the next couple months. Lucky for you, none of them are married. Fulfilling your request will not cause the regiment to go over its quota of other ranks' spouses. Normally, one has to serve a full term in Her Majesty's Armed Forces, with good conduct, to be granted such a request. However, like most things in the army, this can also be waived with the right signatures."

"I have your permission then, sir?" Arthur asked nervously.

"Isn't that what I said?" the major responded curtly "Now get out of my sight and submit your leave request to the orderly corporal, before I change my mind and assign you to shovelling out the horse stalls for the next two months."

"Sir!" He left the office, keeping in step with the shouted cadence of Sergeant-Instructor Brown, and made his way back to the reception desk. The other recruits had long since left to pack their kit and personal belongings before making their way over to the holding company. The orderly corporal seemed as irritated as before to see him. "What is it, private?"

"I've been ordered to submit my leave request, corporal." He then smiled broadly. "I'm going home to get married."

Chapter II: To a Bloody War or a Great Plague

Pietermaritzburg, South Africa
June 1878

Lieutenant Teignmouth Melvill
Adjutant, 1/24th Regiment of Foot

Thousands of miles away, in the southernmost reaches of the African continent, the soldiers of the 24th Regiment of Foot were in a celebratory mood. The lengthy hostilities against the Xhosa had at last ended in a crushing victory, bringing an end to the Ninth Cape Frontier War. The Xhosa had been a frustratingly elusive enemy, refusing for the most part to engage the British army in open battle. Only now, after a year of ambushes and bush-fighting, they had finally been routed. When forced to face off against the power of the imperial redcoats, the murderous firepower wrought by the Martini-Henry Rifle proved unstoppable.

At an army camp about twenty miles from Pietermaritzburg, the 1st Battalion's adjutant, Lieutenant Teignmouth Melvill, was making his way over to the tent serving as the officers' mess. He had a bottle of claret he'd been saving for such an occasion, and he sought out one of his closest friends to share it with him.

While a number of lieutenants were young men in their late teens to early twenties, Melvill was fast approaching his thirty-sixth birthday. He'd received his commission nearly ten years earlier and served with 1/24th in Ireland, Malta, and Gibraltar before coming to the Cape. An officer of much intelligence, tactical and strategic savvy, to say nothing of his personal bravery, he was highly regarded by his fellow officers as well as the men in the ranks. A family man, he was married and the proud father a young son. His wife, Sarah, was expecting their second child in September.

One of the walls of the large white tent was rolled up with several camp tables and chairs laid out. Due to logistics difficulties, there was none of the fine regimental silver or copious amounts of spirits normally available. The conditions were quite austere by officers' standards, although far more comfortable than the enlisted rankers. Oddly enough, there was only one officer in the mess this afternoon, and he was just the man the adjutant sought.

"Gunny, old man!" Melvill shouted to his friend, who was reading a procured newspaper brought in by courier.

The man was Lieutenant Gonville Bromhead, often called 'Gunny' by his friends. Though Bromhead was a member of 2nd Battalion, friendships between officers stretched across the regiment. It was standard practice when one battalion of a regiment was posted overseas, the other remained on home service duties. However, when unusual circumstances led to the 2nd Battalion joining the 1st in South Africa, it had been a joyous reunion of old friends for the officers, as well as a number of the senior NCOs and other ranks. Many had served within both battalions, and Melvill had that rare gift of being universally liked by all.

"Ah, Melvill," Bromhead replied, standing and clasping his hand. He tended to speak loudly, as he was hard of hearing. This sometimes made him shy and reserved, although he still made friends readily enough. Some senior officers questioned just how effective a man with his hearing impediment could be, but 'Gunny' was well-liked by both his peers and subordinates. His courage in battle, particularly after the unfortunate circumstances that led to his assuming command of B Company, 2/24th, had endeared him to the enlisted men.

"Look what I brought," Melvill said as he presented the bottle.

"Delightful!" Bromhead replied boisterously. He signalled for one of the soldier servants in the mess to bring them cups. With the regimental silver locked away at Fort Napier, they had to settle for tin mugs.

"What shall we drink to?" Melvill asked, pouring generously. "Shall we toast the end of the Xhosa uprising?"

"Hmm…how about we stick with the usual?"

"Very well."

Both men then raised their cups, *"To a bloody war or a great plague."*

This rather morbid toast was quite common among officers of Queen Victoria's army. It had come about due to the stagnation of promotion brought on by decades of relative peace. Unless there was a 'bloody war or a great plague', there simply weren't any vacancies for ambitious young officers seeking promotion.

The last major conflict fought by the British Empire, against a viable enemy who could actually fight back, had been the Crimean War against Russia. Even that ended more than twenty-two years earlier. Before that, one would have to go all the way back to the horrific slaughter of the Napoleonic Wars. Colonial wars were common enough during the Victoria Era, though they amounted to little more than minor skirmishes against disorganized barbarians armed with archaic weapons and with minimal casualties. The last Sikh War ended with the dissolution of the Sikh Empire in 1849, while the Indian Rebellion had been violently suppressed nine years later. Even the recent war against the Ashanti had been terribly one-sided, with Sir Garnet Wolseley butchering the forces of Chief Amanquatia in a pair of lopsided victories in 1874. Such conflicts filled the imperial army with a sense of invincibility; however, the lack of casualties led to few officer vacancies. Those with commissions and still on home service were reluctant to give them up, even when they were beyond the age of viable active service. This left many subalterns and captains languishing for years, even decades, because there was simply no room for promotion.

Gunny's father, Sir Edmund de Gonville Bromhead, 3rd Baronet—who had children much later in life—fought beside Wellington at Waterloo in 1815. His father before him a lieutenant general, and his father had stood beside General Wolfe at the Battle of Quebec. Such a lineage left a powerful military legacy to live up to. But for Gonville, the youngest of Baron Bromhead's four sons, such opportunities were denied. He was now thirty-three years old and felt he was long overdue for his captaincy, especially in light of his recent elevation to officer commanding of B Company.

"Fighting tribesmen armed with spears is not exactly the same as facing Bonaparte's Imperial Guard," Bromhead said, his voice etched with frustration. He angrily shook his head. "Damn it all! Did you know my father was a major when he was ten years younger than I?"

"You expect too much of yourself, old boy," Melvill remarked. "We live in a different time than our fathers and grandfathers. The British Empire extends to every continent; there is no one left to fight except savages armed with spears." He chuckled and added with a wink, "Perhaps we should have given those damned Kaffirs a few Martini-Henrys to even the odds a bit."

They shared a laugh at the assessment. While they respected the courage and tenacity of their latest adversaries, the Xhosa had been compelled to fight a guerrilla-style war of hit-and-run tactics in the heavily forested mountains. In the end, they were overwhelmed by sheer brutal force and unable to answer the hellish onslaught of British firepower.

"And how are you assimilating to company command?" Melvill asked.

"All the responsibility and none of the extra pay," Bromhead grumbled. "I may be in command, but Captain Godwin-Austen still holds the billet."

"Well, don't be too harsh on him. He did get shot in the back by one of your own men, accident or not. He's lucky it was a glancing shot; otherwise it would have blown him in half. Besides, a number of companies in the regiment are commanded by lieutenants who are overdue for their captaincy. Charlie Pope comes to mind."

"As do you," Bromhead observed. "I apologise for my selfishness, for you've held your commission three years longer than I. You would likely be a captain by now had you not dropped out of Staff College to return to the regiment."

"Couldn't let you lot battle these savages without me." Melvill shrugged. "My loyalty is to the Regiment before myself."

"Very noble of you, sir," Bromhead replied with a trace of sarcasm, as both men took a long drink. "Mmm, good claret, this.

twenty-year old ensign at the time, though he was *mentioned in despatches* for heroism during one assault.

"Make no mistake," Thesiger said. "If our civilised allies are capable of making war on us, is it any surprise that a supposed friend who walks around naked, carries a spear, and made rivers run red with the blood of his own people might also become our enemy?"

Most of the officers accepted the GOC's analogy. It was not for them to question why they might be called upon to make war in Queen Victoria's name. All that mattered was they did their duty with valour and conduct befitting gentleman officers. Only Richard Glyn harboured doubts as to a future conflict with the Zulu. He knew Sir Henry Bartle-Frere was obsessed with the idea of turning South Africa into a confederacy under British control. It was no coincidence that his close friend, General Thesiger, now commanded all British forces in the Cape. Frere was a shrewd politician, who was used to getting his way. If need be, he would call upon his friend, with his army of redcoats, to bring the Zulus, and any other tribes or belligerent European settlers who tried to resist, to heel.

Chapter III: Homecomings and Reunions

Sergeants on home service

"Home," Arthur said quietly. He and Richard stepped off the train platform, their packs slung over their shoulders. They'd elected to wear their glengarry caps instead of the cumbersome blue helmets that Arthur found silly looking, especially with the protruding spike atop. They left their rifles, bayonets, and most of their kit at The Depot, taking only their personal hygiene kits, a change of pants and socks, plus a few personal items.

The station was unusually busy this evening. Passengers paid little attention to the two young redcoats as they disembarked onto the crowded platform. With their boyish faces, both looked like they should be studying for school exams, rather than serving in Her Majesty's armed forces.

"We've only been away for a couple months, and yet it feels like a lifetime," Richard observed. "This place won't have changed, but by God we have."

fortune overseas, enabling him to give his wife and numerous children a very comfortable lifestyle and education. Thomas was delighted to have his son and new daughter-in-law stay with them a few months before Reginald returned to the Regiment.

He wife still sleeping, Reginald rose early. The sun shone brightly, penetrating through the haze which hung over the industrialised city. He finished breakfast, intending to take a stroll in the gardens before spending the afternoon playing billiards with some old friends. His plans were interrupted, however, by a knocking at the front door. A moment later, Thomas' butler escorted a young soldier into the dining room. He wore the blue frock with red trim, white waist and shoulder belts, and high boots of the 1st Life Guards, part of the Queen's Household Cavalry.

"Captain Younghusband?" the trooper asked.

Reginald nodded and the young man came to attention.

"You are to report to Major Davies at Horse Guards, sir."

"Splendid," the captain said, standing up. "Tell the major I will see him presently."

"Sir!" The trooper stamped his foot, did a quick about turn, and followed the butler to the front door.

"Your orders come through?" Thomas Younghusband asked, joining his son in the dining room. In his late seventies and completely grey of hair, Thomas was still in surprisingly robust health. He had joined Reginald on many a horse ride during the past few months, and the old man swore he could still best any of the young men at polo.

"Only reason for me to be summoned to Horse Guards," Reginald replied. He had grown tired of the tedium from being on leave and his excitement was obvious.

He followed his father's valet to his bedroom, where the servant helped him into his uniform. On this day, he wore his blue patrol jacket and service cap. By the time he came downstairs and stepped out the front door, his horse was saddled and waiting for him. A twelve-year old mare named Nikki, she'd been with him since his first tour in India.

Before leaving, he turned to the valet. "Be a good man and, after she's woken, let Mrs Younghusband know we will be off on another adventure soon."

"Of course, sir." The valet, an older gentleman who'd known Reginald since he was a small boy, paused for a moment before asking, "Do you think it's wise for her to travel in her condition, sir?"

"Hmm, yes...alright then. Please inform my lady, then, that *I* will be off on another adventure soon."

"Very good, sir."

It was still early morning as the captain made the three-mile ride from Regent's Park to Horse Guards. His horse's hooves clattered on the cobblestone road as he passed the magnificent British Museum; first founded by King George II over a hundred years before. He rounded the National Gallery at Trafalgar Square, pausing for a few moments to gaze up at the impressive monument that was Nelson's Column. Completed in 1843, the 170-foot column, topped with its 18-foot statue of Lord Nelson himself, commemorated his decisive victory at the Battle of Trafalgar in 1805. Many would lament that Nelson was killed at Trafalgar and never able to enjoy the spoils of, arguably, the greatest naval victory in history.

Reginald Younghusband saw it differently. "In death, he achieved immortality," he said quietly, a trace of envy in his voice.

Horse Guards Parade

Horse Guards Parade was an old tiltyard that had been used to host jousting tournaments during the time of King Henry VIII. Now, it was a drill field for the Household Cavalry. The large white building served as the office of the Commander-in-Chief of the Army who, at the time, was Field Marshal Prince George, Duke of Cambridge.

The entrance to the courtyard was flanked by a pair of troopers in ceremonial uniform on horseback. They saluted Reginald with their sabres as he rode between them. The same trooper who delivered the message was waiting for him in the courtyard, with another soldier who took the captain's horse.

"Right this way, sir." The trooper led him into a wing of offices and knocked on an oak door.

A voice inside bellowed, *'Come!'*

The trooper opened the door. "Captain Younghusband to see you, sir."

The staff officer, Major Archibald Davies of the Coldstream Guards, was a man Captain Younghusband was relatively familiar with. A veteran of the Crimea, he now served as a personnel officer on the staff of the Duke of Cambridge. The two had met at several formal functions over the course of the captain's leave in London.

"Reginald, good to see you, old man!" The major clasped his hand, as he entered the office. "I trust you've had a pleasant leave?"

"Delightful, sir. Miss Evelyn Davies became Mrs Reginald Younghusband in February. I'm pleased to say we are already expecting our first child."

"Good man." Archibald handed him a glass of claret. "Here's hoping for a fine strapping son!" He then waved Reginald to take a seat. "I take it you are aware of the troubles in our province of Natal."

"From what I understand, the Xhosa have been roundly beaten," the captain replied. "There may be some mopping up to do, but surely they're not anxious to start trouble again."

"Not the Xhosa," the major responded, his expression grim. "The High Commissioner for South Africa and General Thesiger are concerned about a possible conflict with the Zulu."

This gave Younghusband pause, as he finished his claret. "The Zulus have been our friends and trading partners for decades. I find it hard to believe, sir, that they've turned against us."

"Things change," Davies countered. Ironically, he used the same analogy that General Thesiger had used with his officers. "The Russians were our friends when we fought Bonaparte, only to become our enemies a generation later. You need not concern yourself with *why* the Zulus might become our enemies, only with what an officer of the Crown is expected to do should war come."

"I am ready to return to my regiment at any time, sir."

"Unfortunately," the major continued, "Whitehall is reluctant to send reinforcements to South Africa, despite the urgent requests from the High Commissioner and General Officer Commanding. Her Majesty's government would have us use diplomacy, rather than force to placate the Zulus. In my mind, one often equals the other."

"Sometimes the bayonet is as good as a diplomat," the captain conceded. He thought back to many such situations he'd encountered over the years, where a settlement was only achieved through coercion brought on by rifle and bayonet.

"Yes, well, while the government has refused to send any fresh regiments to the Cape, there is no bar on Home Service volunteers being attached to fill vacancies within the 24th."

"We'll definitely need them," Reginald observed. "My own company lost a number of men due to injuries during the Xhosa uprising, and I know several who were getting close to the end of their enlistments before I went on leave. But what about officers? I have only one subaltern, and some companies have none at all. And last I knew, both of our battalion major billets were vacant."

"Unfortunately, we have none to send with you," the major said. "I know your whole regiment is a bit short on officers at the moment. I myself was roundly chastised by the Duke of Cambridge himself for offering to volunteer my services to the 24th. And for reasons I have yet to comprehend, many a young gentleman with the Queen's Commission has been released by his regiment to serve with the colonial forces, yet not with the understaffed regulars in Natal."

"So it's a handful of other ranks volunteers I'll be taking with me," Reginald remarked.

"Many of the volunteers have already left for Natal. No, my good man, most of your charges are men of your own regiment; eighty total, fresh from The Depot in Brecon."

"A bunch of smooth-faced babies," Reginald laughed, though it was devoid of humour. If most of his time-expired veterans had opted to take their discharge, as expected, he needed at least some men of experience to replace them, not inexperienced recruits who could scarcely march and shoot.

"Smooth-faced babies who may soon face the spears of forty-thousand blood-thirsty barbarians," the major added, his expression grim. "I've already sent orders to the holding company in Brecon. The new soldiers will meet you in London at Paddington Station. You sail from Portsmouth aboard the newly-commissioned HMS Tyne in three weeks. If we're lucky, I might be able to scratch together a few veterans for you before then."

It was not just Captain Younghusband who would be accompanying the draft of new soldiers to South Africa. On a drizzly day in Brecon, Sergeant-Instructor Thomas Brown was summoned to see The Depot's commandant. Raised on a farm and slightly taller than average, he possessed a large, powerful chest and arms. His size and booming voice made him an intimidating force, hence why he had served two full tours as an instructor. Though the Queen's Regulations stated that moustaches would be worn, few had ever given him grief over his smooth face. He had recently turned thirty years old and was coming to the end of his long-service enlistment of twelve years. His life was about to undergo a substantial change, and he'd given months of thought as to what he would decide on this day.

"Sergeant-Instructor Brown reporting, sir!" he said as he came to attention.

"At ease," the major replied, pointing to a chair. "Have a seat, sergeant."

"Sir." Brown sat with his hands gripping the arms of the large leather chair. His enlistment was set to expire in two days, and he had his suspicions about where the army would send him to serve Queen and Country, should he decide to re-enlist.

"You've been with us for three years now," the commandant observed, glancing at some papers on his desk. "I also see this is your second time posted at The Depot."

"Yes, sir," Thomas replied. "I was appointed corporal-instructor two years after I joined the ranks."

"And those previous two years were spent in Burma where you made corporal in just under twelve months. You did a three-year standard tour here before returning to active service in India for four years, during the third of which you made sergeant. You've now completed your obligations as a sergeant-instructor, quite admirably I might add."

"Thank you, sir."

"You are also at the end of your long-service enlistment, so you have two options. Accept your discharge and return to civilian life with the full thanks of Her Majesty for your service to the Crown. Or you can reenlist and join the regiment on active service, where you belong."

Thomas silently contemplated.

"How would your wife feel about a return to overseas service?" the commandant asked.

"Eleanor was born into the army," the sergeant answered. "Her father was my sergeant major in India. To be honest, sir, I think she finds Brecon to be insufferably boring. South Africa might be a good change of pace for us both."

"Do you know a Captain Reginald Younghusband?"

"I do, sir," Thomas replied. "He was the commandant of musketry when I was first a corporal-instructor."

"He's now Officer Commanding, C Company, 1/24th," the major explained. "His colour sergeant is retiring from the ranks, and Sergeant Major Gapp recommended you to Colonel Glyn as his successor; provided you choose to re-enlist, of course."

"Sergeant Major Gapp was my mentor when I served here," Thomas stated while attempting to mask his feelings of elation. He suspected he was returning to active service, but not once did he anticipate a promotion.

"Captain Younghusband is currently on leave in England," the major continued. "He'll be returning with a draft of new soldiers and volunteers from other regiments, to serve as replacements for time-expired soldiers who are set to return home. You will take charge of

the men in the holding company and join up with him in London."
He then stood. Thomas was quickly out of his chair, accepting the
major's extended hand.

"It's been an honour to serve with you, *colour sergeant*," the
commandant said. "I wish you and the lads all the best in Natal."

"Thank you, sir." Thomas came to attention and left the office.

The quartermaster sergeant met him outside and handed him a
thin package wrapped in brown paper.

"You'll be wanting these," the man said with a knowing grin.

Inside was the insignia of two crossed flags and a crown to go
above his three gold chevrons; the symbols of Colour Sergeant
Thomas Brown's new rank.

It was a sunny, yet windy day when Arthur and Elisa Wilkinson
became husband and wife. They had to formally give notice and
wait the required two Sundays before they could legally marry. It
was therefore only on the day prior to Arthur's return to Brecon that
they were able to sanctify their union. The wedding was a small
affair at the Church of the Holy Trinity, nestled on the banks of the
River Avon. Dating from 1210, it was sometimes referred to as
Shakespeare's Church, the place of his baptism. In addition to
Arthur's father and Elisa's family, Richard Lowe attended in full
dress uniform. He was accompanied by his favourite consort, Molly
McCormick, who also happened to be a friend of Elisa's. At Elisa's
request, Arthur was also wearing his formal dress uniform.

His father, dressed in a modest suit and bowler hat, seemed
nervous; a stark change from his usual brusque demeanour. About
twenty minutes before the ceremony, he pulled Arthur aside, near
the small graveyard that overlooked the river.

"I have something for you," he said as he fumbled in his pocket.
"Or rather, it is for Elisa." He pulled out a small, well-worn wooden
box. His face filled with emotion as he opened it, revealing a ring.
"This was your mother's. I have not looked at it in almost eighteen
years. I almost had it buried with her. I'm glad now that I did not."

Arthur took the box, fighting to remain stoic. His face was
taught, and he struggled to speak. "I...I don't know what to say."

"You don't have to say anything, son. I know your mother is looking down from Heaven. Her soul is glad that the symbol of our love can now be that of yours and Elisa's." They shared a brief embrace which, despite its brevity, was the most profound expression of affection Arthur's father had ever shown him.

Both men then stood tall.

His father smiled, finally giving his approval. "That uniform suits you."

Since he didn't have enough money left after paying for the train ticket home and all the stoppages taken out for his uniform and kit, Arthur thought he'd have to wait to buy Elisa a proper ring. He wasn't concerned about a ring for himself. He would just as soon wear a copper band, so his mates would at least know he was a proper married gentleman. What he didn't know was his father had met with Elisa earlier and given her his own ring to give to Arthur. The only other person privy to the elder Wilkinson's plan was the vicar, who coyly played along when Arthur and Elisa self-consciously explained they'd not been able to purchase rings of their own. The ceremony itself was surreal. Arthur couldn't even recall all the words said between him, Elisa, and the vicar. It was with nervousness and rapt anticipation when he took his wife into his arms and kissed her passionately. Elisa's mother had wept tears of joy, as had Molly McCormick. Richard Lowe whispered a few words of congratulation, laced with rude humour, to Arthur as the newlyweds walked down the aisle together.

That night as they lay in bed, having made love multiple times, the cold reality of what lay ahead came over Arthur. The overwhelming joy of Elisa becoming his wife was severely tempered, knowing they would now be abruptly separated again. Neither slept a wink, clinging to make the moment last as long as possible, and dreading the early glow of the rising sun. That morning they left for the train station, walking silently hand-in-hand. It was cloudy with a slight drizzle; a contrast to the joyful sunniness of their wedding day.

They stood waiting for the train, eyes fixed on the station clock and holding each other close. Elisa rested her head against her husband's shoulder, fighting to hold back tears, her fingers fumbling with the buttons on his coat. "A strange thing," she said, her voice trembling, "to be filled with both sadness and pride."

could slaughter him and his friends in a matter of seconds. Still, he refused to give up his charge just yet.

"It is not I or my friends you must concern yourselves with," he stressed, keeping his voice calm and confident. "But if you commit murder on Natal soil, it will be nothing short of an act of war. Will your king risk war in order to settle a simple family quarrel?"

Mehlokazulu's eyes narrowed, his nostrils flaring as rage nearly consumed him. He shouted some quick orders to his men, twenty of whom swarmed the nearest huts. Within moments, a woman's screams were heard. The young *induna* reeked of malicious satisfaction as his mother was forcibly dragged from the hut. She thrashed about as the men threw her onto her back. One of them cried out when she bit him hard on the forearm. Enraged, the warrior took his knobkerrie and bashed her about the face and mouth. Her lips were split and covered with blood, and both her eyes were already swollen. She rolled onto her side, spitting her front teeth onto the ground. The *induna* shouted more orders, and the men dragged her away, tying a rein around her waist. The policeman and his friends could only watch helplessly.

His rage giving way to satisfaction, Mehlokazulu's demeanour changed to one of haughtiness and triumph. "Rest easy, my friends. No crimes will be committed on Natal soil. The traitor will be lawfully executed on Zulu land. You would also do well to refrain from using your friends, the swallows in redcoats, as a threat…"

"Mehlokazulu…my son!" MaMtshali shrieked through her bloodied mouth. "Please! Show mercy to your mother!"

The border policeman was horrified. He knew the woman about to be drug away and murdered was one of Sihayo's wives, yet he did not know she was this maddened warrior's own mother. Despite the sickening feeling that knotted in the pit of his stomach, he now understood. Loyalty to his father, an *inkosi*, as well as his king, took precedence over all… even the love for one's mother. MaMtshali was punched hard in the stomach by one of the warriors, and the young *induna* finished his speech.

"King Cetshwayo bears no ill will towards his British friends. He cherishes the friendship of his noble sister, Queen Victoria. We hope her government in Natal understands the absolute and sacred honour of our king, which every last Zulu would gladly defend with his life. Our encounter this day has been unfortunate, but know that the sons of Zulu are still loyal friends of the British."

Without waiting for further reply, he turned his horse about and shouted a few orders to his men. They raised their weapons high and gave an affirmative shout before setting off at a run towards the river. Only the older of his two uncles looked back and made eye contact with the policeman, giving him a stern nod of warning before joining his nephew.

MaMtshali was dragged, kicked, and sometimes carried across the river, to a spot within Zulu territory, near the banks of a stream called the Cumbeza. Mehlokazulu halted his party, and several of his warriors raised their spears, ready to eviscerate the adulterous and treacherous wife of their beloved *inkosi*.

Her son stopped them. "No." He dismounted his horse and walked over to his mother.

She was battered and whimpering, tears streaming down her face as her eyes pleaded with him.

He remained cold and defiant. "Traitorous whore she may be, but as the wife of an *inkosi* she is entitled to a bloodless death."

The reins wrapped around her waist were quickly removed and tied around her neck.

Her breathing quickened as panic consumed her. *'Please'*, she wordlessly pleaded.

Her son sliced his fingers across his throat. With a quick jerk on the leather straps, her neck snapped and she collapsed to the ground. All two hundred warriors gave a shout of triumph. Those with muskets fired into the air in celebration. Mehlokazulu stood in silence, staring at her corpse as it gave a few last convulsions before lying still.

"She should count herself fortunate these aren't the days of Shaka," remarked his uncle, who was still seated on his horse. "Impaling would have been a fitting punishment."

The young *induna* said nothing, but instead turned his gaze back towards the west. He'd been mildly concerned his incursion would rile up the white government in Natal; yet surely they understood that an insult to the king's *inkosi* could not be tolerated. And after all, he had barely crossed the border. The British would not risk losing five decades of trade and friendship over the death of a single disloyal whore.

Natal Border Policemen

It was a cloudy day when Arthur and Richard arrived back in Brecon. The Depot was a buzz of activity, especially at the holding company billets. A dozen newly-graduated privates had been added to the ranks during their absence. Though these men were a bit disgruntled at being denied the chance to go on leave, the thought of their upcoming adventure overwhelmed any sense of disappointment.

As the two returning soldiers dropped their packs onto their bunks, they saw some of their mates playing cards, smoking copious amounts of shag, and talking excitedly amongst themselves.

"Hey, look who's back!" Private Trainer said, as he looked over his shoulder, a rolled cigarette protruding between his teeth.

"Good to see you, too, James," Richard replied as he slapped him on the back.

"We thought we was going to the Cape without you lot," another soldier, Samuel Grant, remarked.

"So we have our orders, then?" Arthur asked, as he removed his belt and unbuttoned his tunic.

"We leave for London in three days." The booming voice behind them caused Arthur's blood to chill.

The soldiers were immediately on their feet, and the young private turned to find himself face-to-face with Colour Sergeant Brown. He stood with his hands on his hips.

"Wilkinson, Lowe, welcome back."

"Thank you, sergeant-instruc…I mean, *colour sergeant*," Arthur stammered, noticing Brown's new rank insignia.

"I see by the ring on your finger that your lady said 'yes'," Brown observed. He gave a nod of approval. "Good. Full inspection tomorrow, lads. Any issues should have already been submitted to the quartermaster, so I don't want to hear any fucking excuses over missing or broken kit!"

"Yes, colour sergeant," the men replied in unison.

"Also, you'll be turning in your home service helmets tomorrow and issued your Foreign Service head gear." He gave a curt nod before leaving the barracks.

"Oh, bugger me," Lowe said quietly. "Does that mean he's coming with us?"

"Sure does," Trainer replied. "He's the new colour sergeant for C Company, 1st Battalion."

Three days later, the eighty or so new privates of the 24th Regiment stood crammed together on the train platform. Arthur, for the first time, felt like he was finally off on an adventure. The sight of their pearly white helmets and gleaming brass plates contrasted sharply with the odd Home Service helmets they'd been wearing up until this time. Their rifles were slung over their shoulders, their packs full of all sundry items, personal belongings, and various pieces of kit. Their bedrolls were rolled tight and strapped to the tops of their packs.

Collectively, they looked like a group of valiant heroes, whose images Arthur had seen splashed across various books and newspapers. Yet now he was part of the story; off on an adventure in a remote province to serve Queen Victoria and the Empire. It would be he and his mates who the papers wrote stories about, even if the public at times seemed to spurn the redcoat.

The thought of the heat and open grasslands of southern Africa, with its exotic bevvy of wild animals and savage natives, contrasted with the light drizzle and cool breeze blowing in his face. The weather during the summers in Wales was wildly unpredictable, ranging from days of endless showers to warm, sun-filled days. Arthur naively assumed the weather in South Africa would be more consistent.

In addition to all the fresh-faced privates, a lance sergeant and a pair of corporals, including the irritable orderly NCO whose name Arthur learned was Harry Markham, accompanied them. All stood shoulder-to-shoulder, while Colour Sergeant Brown paced in front of the formation, his stick tucked under his arm. The loud whistle and rumbling of a train's engine caught their attention. Arthur grinned broadly as the hulking locomotive and its long line of cars squealed to a halt with a belch of thick smoke from its smokestack.

"Alright, you lot!" Colour Sergeant Brown shouted. "Get your arses aboard the train, fill it from back to front. Shove in cheek-to-cheek, and I don't want to hear any grumblings from any of you who forgot to piss! Now move!"

The excited soldiers quickly, and with surprising order, scrambled aboard the train, forcing their way as far back as possible. Most of the men removed their packs and held them on their laps as they squeezed together on the short-backed bench seats. Arthur considered himself fortunate to have acquired a window seat, as two of his mates were scrunched in next to him. He laid his rifle against the window, set his helmet atop, and laid his hands on his pack, while resting his head against the glass. A few minutes later, with another whistle, the train lurched forward. His adventure had begun!

MaMtshali would not be the only victim of Mehlokazulu's rage. The day following the brutal slaying of his mother, he and a small band of warriors crossed into Natal once more. Another of Sihayo's wives, emboldened by MaMtshali's daring act of rebellion, had defected across the uMzinyathi River and taken up residence at the home of another border policeman. This incident followed almost exactly as the first, with the young woman forcibly dragged back into Zululand. She was slain next to MaMtshali's body, which was already drawing flies and mangled by wild animals. News of the rather disturbing border incidents involving the kidnapping and murder of Sihayo's wives caused a panic among the native blacks and white settlers within Natal. In the Zulu Kingdom there was much consternation and conflicting feelings. While the brutal manner in which the two women had been dragged away and killed caused a degree of sorrow, especially among their families, it was understood that betrayal of one of the king's most revered *amakhosi* could not be left unpunished. Perhaps the only person thrilled by the barbaric and unfortunate incidents was the High Commissioner of Southern Africa, Sir Henry Bartle-Frere, who now had political justification for defaming Cetshwayo as a murderous despot and removing him from power.

Sir Henry Bartle-Frere
High Commissioner of South Africa

The sun was warm on this July day in Pietermaritzburg, but the overhang on the long deck provided plenty of shade for the group of men gathered outside the office of the high commissioner. Black servants brought them iced drinks while the men smoked cigars and contemplated the pending fate of British Natal and the surrounding regions. Joining Sir Henry was Sir Theophilus Shepstone, the very man who had crowned Cetshwayo on behalf of the British government six years before. A lifelong resident of Southern Africa, he was multilingual, with intricate knowledge of the various tribes.

Chapter VI: Friends Become Enemies

Paddington Station, London
July 1878

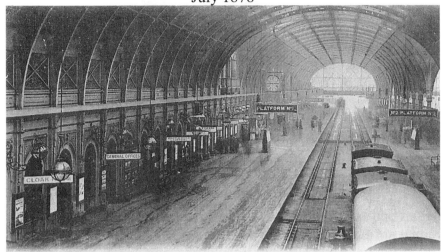

Paddington Station during the Victorian Era

It had been five hours since they departed Brecon before the train finally rolled into London. Though several of the cars had been acquisitioned as troop transport, the remainder took on their usual civilian passengers. After stops in Newport—where they were required to change trains—Bristol, Swindon, and Reading, the train finally lurched to a screeching halt at Paddington Station around midnight. And like every other soldier aboard the crowded train, the first thing Arthur needed to do was relieve himself.

"Empty your sodding bladders and then get into formation!" Colour Sergeant Brown shouted, as his soldiers frantically rushed to find the nearest toilets.

The station was practically deserted except for a couple of maintenance workers and the crewmen from the train, who were disembarking as this was their last call. There was one lone officer in a red tunic waiting for them. Thomas walked over to the man and stamped his foot, coming to attention.

"Captain Younghusband," he acknowledged.

"You must be Colour Sergeant Brown," Reginald replied. He extended his hand. "A pleasure to finally meet you."

"The pleasure is all mine, sir, though we have met before."

"Have we?" the captain asked.

"Yes, sir. I was a corporal-instructor under your command at The Depot."

Reginald's eyes lit up in realisation. "Of course. I do recall you now, though I remember your booming voice far more than your face."

"I'll take that as a compliment, sir," Thomas replied with a quick flash of a grin.

"All new recruits?" the captain asked, noting the very young faces emerging from the toilets.

"Mostly." Thomas then glanced over his shoulder. "Don't worry, I trained them all myself."

"We have a few volunteers waiting for us at King's Cross," Reginald explained. "There will be another handful to pick up in Winchester, Botley, and Hilsea."

"Very good, sir." Brown then bellowed over his shoulder, *"Fall in at the double!"*

Her Majesty's newest soldiers soon emerged from the station, squinting their eyes as they tried to see by the glow of the occasional gas lamp lining the road. They then began the three mile trek along Marylebone Road to King's Cross Station. Captain Younghusband walked just ahead of the formation, where the soldiers marched in a column four men wide. Colour Sergeant Brown walked behind the last rank. They were mostly silent except for the pounding cadence of their shoes on the cobblestone road.

Arthur had never been to London. Sadly, he found himself unable to take much of it in, what with the stifling darkness all around them. He knew the city was huge, one of the largest in the world, and he wondered where his brother might be in all this. He further surmised their extremely late arrival had been deliberate. During the day the streets would be filled with people and carriages. It was expedient, not to mention causing less of a stir, to have the column of armed soldiers make their way to the station in the middle of the night.

Yet despite the late hour, the street was still very much alive. Numerous tradesmen worked all hours, street vendors catered to the shadowy people of the night, while homeless slept in the gutters, curled up beneath newspapers or whatever rags they could find the fend off the cold. No one paid them any mind, as the thieves and footpads had liberated them of anything of value long ago. Few of these people even acknowledged the column of soldiers, except for the various 'ladies of the night' who lurked in many an open doorway.

"Oy! We got us a score of lovelies here!" shouted one rather buxom prostitute, who was somewhere in her mid-thirties and had likely been a member of 'the world's oldest profession' most of her life.

"I say, some tasty morsels, this lot," stated a much younger woman, who was wearing little more than her underclothes and what looked like an open vest with too many feathers. "Oh come on over here, dearies! No sense going off to die for Queen and Country without dipping your wick a bit first."

"Can you spot me a shilling or two?" Richard whispered to Arthur, while suppressing a chuckle.

"I'll go halves with you, if you like," James Trainer, who was marching directly behind him, added.

"Nobody's going 'halves' with anyone!" Colour Sergeant Brown snapped, the soldiers cringing at his uncanny sense of hearing. "The only thing you'll get from this lot is a glut of social diseases that'll rot your cock off and drive you mad. Not exactly worth a shilling, is it, Private Lowe?"

"No, colour sergeant," Richard replied glumly.

"Here, I ain't had no one's cock rot off!" the young prostitute retorted. "Me twat is as clean as the sodding Virgin Mary!" She then added with a laugh that sounded almost like a cackle, "That's why I cost *three* shillings!"

This caused a short laugh to come from the collective soldiery. Colour Sergeant Brown had to stifle a snort and a grin, and even Captain Younghusband allowed himself a quick smile of amusement.

About halfway to King's Cross they passed the world-famous Madame Tussauds wax museum. Founded by the French-born Marie Tussaud in 1835, it was renowned for the incredibly lifelike displays of famous persons. Among the more renowned was a replica of Napoleon Bonaparte on his death bed, which was said to have been visited quite frequently by the Duke of Wellington in later life.

However, for the soldiers of the 24th it was just another building before finally reaching King's Cross.

"Mark...time!" Colour Sergeant Brown shouted. *"Left, right, left, right...halt!"*

The soldiers took one additional step and stopped. They were then dismissed and told to remain on the platform.

"Don't want any of you monkeys wandering off and getting yourselves lost," he said. "And no sneaking off to catch a case of crotch rot either! You should have drained your bollocks before we left Brecon."

Having the platform all to themselves, the bevy of soldiers spread out and tried to make themselves comfortable. For the handful who sleep would deny, they huddled together under the glow of a gas light, quietly playing cards. The summer air was warm and pleasant, and Arthur found a place near the brick wall. He laid his blanket out on the ground and removed his shoes and jacket, which he used as a blanket. His pack served as a makeshift pillow and, while not the most comfortable arrangement, he was soon fast asleep.

For Lieutenant General Sir Frederic Thesiger, the writing was on the wall. The High Commissioner was determined to see Lord Carnarvon's dreams of a South African confederacy through to fruition. All that stood in the way was the threat of a despotic tyrant and his army of 40,000 blood-thirsty savages. It would fall to Thesiger to defeat this tyrant, yet it appeared he would have to do so with insufficient manpower and resources.

"Gentlemen," Sir Henry said to his cabinet members, Thesiger, and Shepstone. "I received word today from Sir Michael Hicks-Beach who, I am sad to say, has replaced Lord Carnarvon as Secretary of State for the Colonies. He states the troubles in India and Eastern Europe are so serious that we cannot afford a war against the Zulus."

"Wars do not start and stop at the Colonial Office's convenience," Shepstone stated indignantly. Despite his lifelong outward friendship with the Zulus, his true loyalties were being laid bare. "Would Sir Michael have us risk losing Natal?"

"If the government will not send us sufficient troops, we must look within the colony," Thesiger observed pragmatically. This was by no means the first time he had been required to use indigenous levies during a colonial war, and he knew that getting outwardly upset at the home government would not change the situation.

"The Basuto and Mponso tribes have a long standing animosity against the Zulus," Shepstone observed. "And of course there are the iziGqoza, who are no doubt most anxious to exact revenge after twenty years in exile. They are led by Cetshwayo's own brother, Sikhotha. He barely escaped with his life during the king's notorious blood-letting."

"But who to organize and lead them?" the GOC asked.

"There is one man who could get the job done in short order," Frere spoke up. "Lieutenant Colonel Anthony Durnford, Royal Engineers. I take it you are acquainted with him, Sir Frederic?"

"Mostly by reputation," Thesiger replied. "He's a good engineer and the current Garrison Engineer for Natal. I also do not doubt his bravery. However, his skills at leading men into battle are seriously lacking. He completely mucked up the pursuit of the renegade, Langalibalele, while getting himself stabbed twice at Bushman's Pass. Now he can't even use his left arm."

"A bad spot of luck, which is of no surprise when dealing with these damned native auxiliaries," Sir Henry replied. "Could have happened to anyone. Most of those filthy cowards fled. As I understand it, only the Basuto remain loyal. Sir Theophilus, I believe your son, George, was with Durnford at Bushman's Pass."

"That he was," Shepstone confirmed. No one else noticed the scowl on his face at the mention of Durnford's name.

George Shepstone was fiercely loyal to Durnford, who he viewed as both friend and mentor. His father, however, did not share these warm feelings. In fact, Sir Theophilus viewed Anthony Durnford as a renegade and self-seeker of martial glory. He was also far too prejudiced in favour of the African tribesmen, no doubt influenced by his friend, Bishop Colenso. This influence had affected George as well. Sir Theophilus recalled a rather unfortunate scrap between his sons, when 'Offy' dismissed Durnford as 'a damned nigger-lover'. The ensuing brawl left George with a bloody

90

nose and his brother with two black eyes. Even the debacle of Bushman's Pass could not assuage George's feelings of admiration for the engineer officer. Sir Theophilus decided if his younger son had a shortcoming, it was that he was loyal to a fault.

Frere continued, "Whatever his flaws, the Basutos' loyalty to Durnford remains strong. He's a fine horseman despite only having the use of one arm, has years of experience in South Africa, and he speaks Zulu."

"Fine," the GOC said, giving a dismissive wave. "Let him organize our native contingent. All that matters is whether he can get those damned apes to stand and fight."

While Sir Henry and the other political figures discussed some of the difficulties coming out of London, Thesiger began to wrap his mind around all the preparations to be made if he was going to launch an invasion of the Zulu Kingdom. Though he loathed and mistrusted the Natal natives as ill-disciplined cowards, he knew he would require large numbers of them to supplement his understrength regiments of redcoats. He was certain he could also call upon volunteers from the settler communities. After all, they had a stake in the outcome of any potential war. The issue with using European volunteers was that they were mostly rouges with little to no discipline who, at times, would be harder to manage in battle than their black counterparts. The General Officer Commanding for Natal had his work cut out for him, and likely only a short time to have his armies ready.

Lieutenant Colonel Anthony Durnford

A few days later, the High Commissioner and GOC continued planning for the inevitable, with a handful of replacements now en route from England. And yet, it had been a pleasant afternoon for Lieutenant Colonel Anthony Durnford, Royal Engineers. He'd received his orders from the General Officer Commanding and decided to spend the day in the company of his dear friend, Bishop of Natal John Colenso.

A staunch advocate for the welfare of the indigenous Africans, Colenso's teachings were considered radical, even borderline heresy. For example, he did not believe Adam and Eve were the sole founders of the human race, but rather one among many ethnicities God populated the earth with simultaneously. He further refused to teach that the pagan ancestors of his converted Africans were condemned to hell. He was also a frequent critic of the patronising and belittling attitude of the Cape authorities. Colenso was quick to berate any who referred to the natives as 'apes', 'niggers', or any other assortment of gross language that demeaned the indigenous peoples of South Africa. Instead, he viewed them as equals, deserving both dignity and respect. Durnford and Colenso thus became natural allies of compassion towards the African, in stark contrast to the overly hostile and racist attitudes that persisted within the Cape Authority.

"I'm sorry I will be leaving your company so soon," Anthony said. "We are two souls who differ greatly from our countrymen. But I take heart, seeing your daughters are passionate about continuing your work."

"Sir Henry is determined to have his war," Colenso speculated, his demeanour sombre. "Why else would he call upon you to resume command of your mounted natives, as well as a yet unknown number of auxiliaries? I fear for all of God's children subjected to the horrors wrought by Frere's ambition, including you, Anthony."

"General Thesiger has assured us that war is the absolute last resort," Durnford replied. "But we must always be prepared for any potential hostilities."

"You don't believe that any more than I do," the bishop replied, his expression one of sadness.

Durnford shook his head. "No. But I am a soldier, and I must follow my orders. I am also sad to say that I believe even Sir Theophilus Shepstone has turned on Cetshwayo. You, dear bishop, may be the only true friend the Zulu king has left."

"Anthony!" a woman's voice called from inside the house.

Durnford turned and smiled at the sight of Colenso's striking daughter, Frances Ellen. She walked briskly out into the garden and embraced him. She was always careful of his crippled arm, which he usually kept pinned inside his jacket.

"Always good to see you, Nell."

"Father tells me there are more troubles across the river."

Durnford simply nodded.

She shook her head in frustration. "Why? Why do the authorities think of nothing but killing?"

"This is a vast and great country," her father replied woefully. "If only the people loved each other as God loves them."

Frances composed herself, though she was clearly upset. Like her father, she and her elder sister had been staunch advocates for the welfare and treatment of the local peoples. Durnford was also very dear to her, and the two had grown close over the years. Any time the government called its soldiers to conflict, she feared greatly for his safety.

As he put together the contingency plan for a possible invasion of Zululand, Lieutenant General Thesiger was beginning to realize just how many indigenous and colonial troops he would require. His intent was to fight a quick, decisive war and have it concluded before any soft-bellied sorts who infested the home government could protest. Because of his recent experience against the Xhosa, who for over a year refused to face him in open battle, Sir Frederic reckoned the best way to prevent the Zulus from conducting such an evasive war was to launch multiple columns at various points along the border. Each of these would centre on a single regiment of professional British infantry, with companies of volunteers drawn from the settler community. However, if he was going to have any chance of drawing the Zulus into a brawl, while surrounding the king's kraal at Ulundi from multiple directions, then the need for African levies would grow exponentially. He would also need qualified Europeans to lead them, for the thought of black Africans leading themselves was absurd in his mind.

The quality of men available within the settler communities was slim at best. Many of these men had served in irregular units as junior officers and NCOs, but they had little regard for those they led, and almost none of them spoke any of the local languages. One man the GOC summoned for his assistance in sorting this matter was a former army officer named Rupert Lonsdale. Lonsdale had at one time served with the venerable 74th Highlanders and was now making a decent living for himself as a civilian magistrate along the frontier.

Having kept himself well informed of the pending crisis along the Natal-Zulu border, Lonsdale reckoned he would be asked to fight for his queen and country sooner rather than later. He arrived at Fort Napier late in the morning and was immediately taken to see the GOC. He'd familiarised himself with Lieutenant General Thesiger's military history and read in detail the accounts of his recent victory against the Xhosa.

"General, sir," he said, stamping his foot and coming to attention. Though he no longer held the Queen's Commission and was in civilian garb, some old habits died hard.

"Please stand easy, Mr Lonsdale," Thesiger said, standing and clasping his hand. "You know my secretary, Lieutenant Colonel Crealock?"

"I believe we have met," Lonsdale said as he offered his hand. "A pleasure to see you, sir."

"Indeed," the colonel responded with reservation.

The men were seated, and the GOC decided to open with some lighter talk first. "I trust you are well and keeping a handle on the settlers and natives in your district."

"The natives are little trouble," Rupert replied. "To be honest, it's the damned Boers and our own countrymen who cause me the most headaches. Not a day passes that I'm not having to solve some dispute between rival farmers over which scrap of land their cattle can eat and shit on...beg your pardon, sir. Years on the frontier have made my language decidedly coarser than when I wore Her Majesty's uniform as a proper officer."

"No need for apologies, Mr Lonsdale. It is coarse men, who are also proper soldiers and gentlemen, which I have most need of."

"You need officers to lead your natives," Rupert conjectured.

Thesiger confirmed with a slow nod.

"What I need are *proper* officers," he stressed. "Men who know what it is to command, and who understand the rather archaic workings of our natives."

"I am always at Her Majesty's service."

"Good, because I am offering you command of the 3rd Regiment of the Natal Native Contingent. You have a daunting task ahead of you, not much time to accomplish it, and with a minimal amount of resources. I had hoped to dress our local auxiliaries in proper uniforms; however, the quartermasters can scarcely keep our own men supplied, let alone provide tunics for several thousand natives."

"Just give me some red rags to tie around their heads so our lads don't shoot them as hostiles," Lonsdale recommended. "I take it they will have to fight using their own weapons?"

Thesiger nodded.

"Rifles are something we actually have in good supply," Crealock stated. "However, as I advised the general, it would be unwise to issue our best weaponry to a bunch of untested savages who may run at the first sight of the Zulus, or worse, turn on us. I've recommended we issue one rifle per ten men with five rounds of ammunition to each rifleman. I must say, I was a little unnerved to learn that Durnford's Basuto horsemen are each armed with a Swinburne-Henry carbine and full allotment of ammunition."

101

"Lieutenant Colonel Durnford has vouched for them," the GOC explained. "And I am willing to indulge him for the time being."

In truth, Sir Frederic did not trust the Basutos or Durnford's other mounted Africans, such as Zikhali Horse, any more than Crealock. However, what he was critically short on more than anything was cavalry. He had no units of professional British cavalry, and the bands of settler volunteers were mostly undisciplined renegades who were all but useless when it came to reconnaissance and mounted warfare.

"Your regiment will be strictly infantry," the GOC continued. "You will be in charge of all recruitment; natives as well as European officers and non-commissioned officers to lead them."

Crealock grumbled, "I heard Durnford addressing one of his black apes as 'sergeant' the other day. Damned improper if you ask me."

Though he said nothing, Thesiger gave an almost imperceptible nod of concurrence.

Lonsdale sought to reassure both men. "Rest assured, sirs, my officers and non-comms will be white Europeans, even if they are an ill-disciplined lot themselves who can't speak the language of our natives." He cocked a half grin and added with a touch of irony, "With so many damned Dutch and Germans amongst the settler communities, a number of them can't even speak English properly."

"Another challenge I am sure you will rise to," the general said. "Colonel Crealock has all the information you need; authorisations for recruitment, local officer commissions, and any equipment you may need to draw." He then stood and extended his hand. "Good to have you back, *Commandant*. Perform your duties well and Her Majesty will not be ungrateful."

Over the next few weeks, Lonsdale was given the considerable task of building an entire regiment of indigenous warriors, trained in European tactics, from scratch. Finding talented leaders for his battalions was proving even more problematic than raising the necessary levies of black warriors. Natal was notorious as a place for washed-up adventurers, men whose exploits had led to misfortune, debt, and other nefarious actions that made them either unwilling or unable to return home. One such man was George

Browne, a thirty-three year old 'soldier for hire' born in Cheltenham to Irish parents. A teller of tall tales, in his own words, he was,

"Arrested while a schoolboy from Cheltenham on his way to a shoot at Wimbledon on suspicion of being a Fenian; enlisted as a gunner; blew up his father with a squib cigar; shot a man in a duel in Germany; biked into the Lake of Geneva; went to New Zealand where for twelve years he fought the Maoris; ate a child while starving and afterwards hunted bushrangers in Australia; took a schooner in search of copper island, or anything else of value; next a Papal Zouave; under Colonel Dodge in America he fought the Sioux."

Though they had known each other for several years, Lonsdale had no way of disseminating the truth from fiction in Browne's flamboyant narrative about himself and his adventures. Even if most of what he claimed were deliberate falsehoods, George Browne—or 'Maori', as he was more commonly known—had certainly led an interesting life to say the least. He was as brave as he was boastful, he spoke the Zulu tongue, and he was extremely proficient at organizing large groups of men and leading them into battle. He'd served most recently with Lieutenant Colonel Henry Pulleine's frontier regiment, *Pulleine's Rangers*, during the latest Cape Frontier War and acquitted himself well. In short, he was the ideal man to lead the 1st Battalion of the 3rd Natal Native Contingent (1/3rd NNC).

And though they would share the title of 'Commandant', it was made plain that Lonsdale was Browne's superior officer. This all suited 'Maori' just fine. He was a biting and extremely racist man, but he did possess a certain level of respect for Cetshwayo's exiled brother, Sikhotha, and his iziGqoza Zulus. Sikhotha, who spoke passable English, had befriended Rupert Lonsdale who, as a token of his regard, gave the iziGqoza chieftain one of his uniform shirts. Sikhotha was a much bigger man than Lonsdale and could scarcely button the shirt. However, as he viewed the gift as a mark of honour, and he swore to never remove it.

George 'Maori' Browne
Commandant, 1/3rd Natal Native Contingent (NNC)

It was late in the afternoon on his second day of riding when Captain Reginald Younghusband rode into Fort Napier, home of the 24th Regiment of Foot. Reginald grinned broadly and took a deep breath. At last he was home! Though born in Bath and raised in London, for him, wherever the 24th went was his true home. He'd arrived just in time for supper. A fortunate circumstance, as he was famished after two days of hard riding and not a bite since breakfast.

Though both battalions of the Regiment were headquartered at the fort, which sat atop a hill overlooking Pietermaritzburg, only a portion of their actual troops were on hand. Within Younghusband's own 1st Battalion, only his own C Company, Lieutenant Francis Porteous' A Company, Lieutenant Charles Cavaye's E Company, and Captain George Wardell's H Company occupied the post. B Company was left to garrison southern Natal, while D, F, and G companies were dispersed throughout the Cape.

What companies were in garrison were terribly understrength. Though casualties inflicted by the Xhosa during the previous war had been relatively light, a slew of injuries and illnesses, as well as discharges for those whose enlistments had expired, took its toll on the ranks. The draft of new recruits and volunteers would help alieve this; however, it was not just within the other ranks that numbers were short. Each company was billeted a captain as commander and two lieutenant subalterns. In reality, only a couple of companies had their required billet of subalterns, and some had none at all. C Company had just one, a twenty-four year old baby-faced lieutenant named George Hodson. It was he who greeted his commander as he stepped into the officers' mess.

"Looks like we have a stranger in the mess!" George called out as he stood and extended his hand. "Welcome back, sir."

"Thank you, Mister Hodson," Reginald replied, clasping his hand. He leaned in slightly and scanned his subaltern's face. "Damn it, man, still can't sport a proper moustache."

"Not much I can do about it," George replied, with a somewhat uncomfortable shrug. "I guess I just have to fight that much harder to prove my manliness."

"That he did!" Captain Wardell said. He walked over to the men and put his hand on the lieutenant's shoulder. "Three times our Mister Hodson was *mentioned in despatches* during the Xhosa war, and Colonel Wood still berates him as a fresh-faced child."

"Well, Colonel Wood isn't our regimental commander, so I wouldn't let it bother you," Reginald said, bringing a smile from his subaltern.

Wardell then extended his hand to Reginald. "A pity you missed it, old boy…the fighting I mean. Once we finally got the Xhosa out in the open, the boys unleashed a splendid display of musketry on them. You, of all people, would have been proud."

"I would hope so, I trained many of them," Reginald said with a touch of sarcasm.

Wardell signalled for one of the soldier-servants to bring his fellow captain a cup. The two men sat near the head of the table, occupied by their current battalion commander, acting-Major William Degacher.

At thirty-six years old, with over eighteen years under the colours, Degacher was one of the oldest and most experienced officers in 1st Battalion. Yet with his substantive rank still that of captain, it was unlikely he would hold onto his position as commanding officer of 1/24th for much longer.

"Welcome back, Reginald," Degacher said, raising his cup in salute.

"Thank you, William." He then noted the insignia on his fellow officer's collar. "They're not letting you keep your majority, I hear. Pity, that."

"Sadly, all promotions, substantive as well as brevets, must come from Horse Guards," William said. "Even the GOC cannot authorise me to wear the major's collar laces and Bath star. But, Colonel Glyn has asked me to continue as acting commanding officer and to remain on staff, once I am replaced."

"Who would replace you?"

"Word has it Lieutenant Colonel Pulleine has grown tired of raising and training frontier troops in the Transkei," Degacher answered. "I hear his Frontier Light Horse, along with the *Pulleine's Rangers*, as his infantry fancies themselves, performed admirably during the Eastern Cape troubles. Be that as it may, I know from having been privy to his correspondence with Colonel Glyn that he is more than ready to return to the Regiment."

"Pulleine's a brilliant organiser, logistician, and staff officer," Reginald noted. "But he has little experience leading line companies. If rumours about the possibility of a war against the Zulu prove true, he won't have much time to learn."

"Don't worry," Degacher grinned. "I may not wear the rank, but I'll still be acting-major at the battalion. I'll keep an eye on him. Besides, we've got Mister Melvill here. Plus Sergeant Major Gapp can see to all the NCO affairs."

Over the remainder of their supper, all were keen to tell Reginald what a shame it was that he missed out on giving the Xhosa a damn good thrashing. In turn, they asked him about home and how his leave went. The conversation soon turned to his recent marriage and pending fatherhood.

Battalion adjutant Lieutenant Melvill quipped, "Not wasting any time, are you?"

"If troubles are brewing, I'm not sure if I want Evelyn anywhere near Natal," Reginald replied. "And since I may not see her for some time, at least she'll be giving me an heir. And what of you? I heard you and Sarah are expecting your second child any day now."

"Charles William Melvill was actually born three days ago. He and Sarah are doing well, thankfully. Though I think it might take my oldest boy some time to get used to having a little brother."

"They're only a couple years apart in age, I'm sure they'll get on just fine. And if not…well, brothers are known to be brawlers." Reginald refilled his cup and raised it to Melvill. "To our fine sons, may they carry on our legacy!"

After supper, Reginald accompanied Melvill to the battalion orderly room. The adjutant took the list of new soldiers and gave it to one of his clerks, directing him to check the company rolls and divide the replacements up accordingly.

"Your C Company is down quite a bit," Melvill noted. "Twenty of these new replacements you brought will be sent to 2nd Battalion, as they have far fewer vacancies than we do. I can give you fifteen of the rest. I see your new Colour Sergeant came with them as well."

"That gives me a little over eighty total. Still understrength, but we'll make due."

Lieutenant the Honourable George Hodson
Subaltern, C Company, 1/24th

Chapter VIII: The First Day

Fort Napier outside Pietermaritzburg
September 1878

Captain (acting-Major) William Degacher

Rifles slung and legs stretching to keep up with Colour Sergeant Brown's brisk pace, the draft of soldiers made remarkable time as they trekked along the winding road that led from Durban to Pietermaritzburg. They saw little in the way of exotic wildlife, mostly cattle herds being tended to by young African boys. Their first day proved relatively short, as it had been mid-afternoon by the time they left the harbour. They halted just beyond Pinetown, a small settlement founded twenty-eight years earlier and centred on the Wayside Hotel.

The road was hard-pack dirt, deeply rutted from its constant use by traders and other settler traffic. They saw a number of wagons bearing goods to and from Durban. These were quite large and hauled by teams of sixteen oxen. The drivers of these ponderous wagons were mostly white settlers, either British or Dutch, with thick heads of shaggy hair beneath wide-brimmed straw or slouch hats, scruffy beards, and burnt skin that fared poorly in the African sun. Keeping the pairs of oxen moving together as a single unit were young African boys called *voorloopers*. Controlling and guiding eight pairs of oxen was an art-form, which could be terribly frustrating and exhausting, especially when each of the beasts wished to go off on its own.

On their third night, the group was camped on a ridge just a few miles from Pietermaritzburg. Six men at a time were required to conduct one hour guard shifts both in and around the small camp, with orders to wake Colour Sergeant Brown immediately should anything be amiss. The sun was setting, and Arthur found himself with James Trainer on overwatch near the road. Though he was closer to Richard, due to their lifelong friendship, Arthur found he and James becoming better friends as time wore on. The two had shared many of the same hardships during recruit training, yet James' demeanour was almost always calm and good natured. As they paced back and forth, watching the sun slowly set, and glad they had first watch rather than one in the middle of the night, Arthur noticed a subtle change to Trainer's demeanour. He'd become more sombre lately, and he laughed even less than he had at The Depot.

"Something bothering you?"

"Just wondering if we're all going to be split up," James replied. "Spent so much time getting to know you, Richard, Harry Grant, and the other lads, I don't want to lose that. I have to confess, I was an only child and didn't have many friends growing up. When I joined the army, scarcely anyone back home in Birmingham even noticed. It was either work in one of the munitions factories or come here and get to fire those same bullets. It was an easy decision. You and Lowe have become my closest mates...and Grant, I suppose. I feel kind of stupid saying this, but you lot are the closest things to true friends I've ever had."

Arthur looked at his friend in the fading light and cocked a half grin, not sure if James was playing him for the fool. "That's bollocks. You're always so bloody chipper and full of laughs. Even the esteemed Colour Sergeant Brown never made you flinch."

"Believe me, it was all an act," Trainer explained. "Hell, with my acting skills I should have joined the theatre. I may have laughed and joked my way through recruit training, but I was damn near pissing myself every hour of every day. And if you don't mind

109

acting as padre for my most shameful confession, I cried every night for the first three weeks like a whipped orphan boy in one of Dickens' books. Not very manly, I know."

"Don't worry, your secret's safe with me," Arthur said, patting him reassuringly on the shoulder. He added with a wink, "Of course, it may cost you the occasional bottle of port or tobacco pouch."

The men shared quite a laugh at this.

"And yes, I'll act as your padre any time you need to confess something shameful, unqualified as I am."

The next morning, they were awoken just before dawn and told to get their backsides moving. A few miles into their march, they were approached by an officer on horseback. Arthur heard him introduce himself as Lieutenant Coghill, aide-de-camp to Colonel Glyn. Coghill informed Colour Sergeant Brown that they were just a few miles from Fort Napier, and representatives from companies in both battalions were waiting to take charge of their new soldiers. He handed a sheaf of papers to Brown before the two exchanged salutes, and the officer rode back the way he'd come.

By midmorning they reached a river known as the Msunduzi, which ran along the south-eastern edge of Pietermaritzburg. After crossing the river and up a gently sloping hill covered in palms and various other trees, they finally arrived at Fort Napier. Established thirty-five years before, it was one of the first garrisons built after the British established the Colony of Natal.

The temperature was already quite warm, as the sun beat down through wisps of clouds. Arthur and his companions found themselves sweating profusely by the time they reached the gates of the fort. Waiting for them were a handful of NCOs, along with a pair of lieutenants; the adjutants of each battalion. Colour Sergeant Brown halted the formation, walked over and saluted the officers, exchanged a few words with them, and turned to face the draft of soldiers.

"When I call out your name, you will fall out and fall in with the corporal from A Company, 1st Battalion! *099, Davies...799, Edwards...862, Freeman...*" and so it continued until twelve young men had formed up in front of the corporal from A Company, 1/24th.

Arthur and Richard exchanged looks as they recalled James Trainer's words from the night before.

"Next group, you will fall in with the lance corporal from C Company, 1ˢᵗ Battalion! *312, Ellis…474, Grant…841, Lowe…*"

Arthur swallowed hard as he watched his best friend sprint over to the lance corporal. He heard a few other names, including James Trainer. And because lists were usually alphabetical, the wait for Arthur Wilkinson was always maddening. He breathed a sigh of relief and almost let out a loud whoop, when he heard his name called for C Company.

"297, Wilkinson!"

He sprinted over to the band of recruits and halted next to Richard. His friend leaned over and whispered, "You know that means we're in Colour Sergeant Brown's company."

Arthur closed his eyes and tilted his head back slightly. He stifled an urge to laugh at the absurdity of it all.

The lance corporal, who stood looking at the sheet in his hands for a moment, appeared to be extremely bored with the task he'd been given. "Follow me, lads, I'll take you over to the company billets."

He led them away as Colour Sergeant Brown continued to call off names to the other companies in his booming voice. On their way into the fort, the first thing Arthur noticed about the men of the 24ᵗʰ was how rough they all appeared. Uniforms were mostly faded and patched. The relaxed grooming standards allowed on Foreign Service was evident. Beards were expressly forbidden while on home service, yet it appeared that just as many as not sported a full set of whiskers.

"By God, these men look hard," Richard said in appreciation, as well as a little bit of trepidation.

"They look like they've had the same uniforms since they got here," Arthur added.

"Uniforms are only reissued once a year, in April," the lance corporal replied. "You should have seen what we looked like after spending a year in the bush, fighting the Xhosa. That left us a little less than parade standard, to say nothing of the stench. My trousers were so tattered, I thought I'd be down to fighting the Xhosa in me underpants!"

He chuckled at this last remark, as his own red tunic was sun-faded, with patches of various colours used to cover up tears in both jacket and trousers. They reached the barracks block for

C Company, a long, single-story brick building that looked much the same as any other.

"Here we are, lads." The lance corporal directed each man to where their individual sections bunked until it was just Arthur and Richard. He then stepped back outside. "You two, come with me."

"Yes, sir," they replied together.

The lance corporal waved his hand dismissively. "Knock that shit off, I'm not no 'sir'. Hell, I ain't even a full non-comm! Name's Bill Johnson." He extended his hand, which Arthur and Richard clasped in turn as they introduced themselves.

"We are in your section, then?" Richard asked.

"Well it's not *my* section, exactly, but yes, we will be bunking and messing together." Johnson then added, "We've been short-handed for some time, so we're glad to finally get some replacements. But damn it all, did every last one of you have to be straight from The Depot? I see our new colour sergeant is fresh off the boat as well, judging by his lack of a beard and unblemished uniform."

"He was one of our instructors at The Depot," Richard noted with a slight grimace.

"Oh bugger me," Bill muttered, rolling his eyes. "A damned parade ground NCO! He'll probably expect us to look all smart and ready to march before the Queen each day. God help us if he demands we polish our helmet plates all nice and pretty, seeing as how most of us tossed ours."

Before the men could banter further, a loud voice shouted from across the way, *"Johnson!"*

The lance corporal let out a deep sigh and turned to face the sergeant who'd bellowed his name.

"Ah, Sergeant Edwards," he said with a forced grin. "Just finishing up sorting our newest replacements per Mister Hodson's orders. These two lads are in our section."

"I'll take them from here," the sergeant said, stern-faced. "You are to report to Corporal Bellhouse regarding musketry practice." He waved for Arthur and Richard to follow him.

"Don't sweat it, lads," Bill whispered. "Edwards is a bit of a hard-nose, and he hates dealing with new recruits, but he's fair enough. Just don't cock up too often or bombard him with questions, and he'll pretty much leave you alone. You have any questions or problems, me or Bray will sort you out."

The two new privates gave him a quick word of thanks before following after their section leader. Sergeant John Edwards appeared to be roughly thirty years of age. He sported a full moustache, though judging by the fresh nicks on his cheeks, it appeared he had shaved his side whiskers recently. He wore a faded blue forage cap, and his uniform was as worn and patched up as the others they saw. Arthur also noticed that his belt, which should have been white, appeared to have been deliberately stained a dark brown. The gold chevrons on his right arm were noticeably less faded than the rest of his uniform, meaning he'd likely achieved his rank fairly recently.

"Bray!" he shouted to an older private who sat on a camp stool outside the barracks, running a rag over his rifle with a pipe protruding from his teeth. "Got a couple of new mates for you."

"Well damn it all," the man replied. "I knew my being able to stretch out at night in the bush was too good to last." He eyed Arthur and Richard up and down, noting their white helmets and belts. "I'll get the tea brewing."

"Never mind that," Edwards stated. "We have parade in less than an hour. Get their kit stored and have them ready to fall in."

The private known as Bray simply nodded, and the sergeant left them. The old soldier said nothing for a few moments, simply puffing on his pipe while finishing running the rag over the barrel of his Martini-Henry. He set the rifle against the brick wall and stood while placing his pipe on the camp stool. As he stepped over to the new men they noted the strong smell of tobacco and dried sweat. His thick brown beard had a few traces of grey as did his mop of hair, which was starting to recede slightly.

"Well, come on, then," he said, waving them into the billets. "I'll show you where you'll be sleeping and storing your packs. Not much room in these, but we make due."

"Thanks," Arthur replied, fighting the urge the call the man 'sir'.

Though only a private like them, Bray appeared to have been in the army since before Arthur or Richard were even born. This was confirmed when they saw his red tunic hanging off the end of his bunk. It bore three long-service chevrons on the right cuff, with each signifying at least six years of service. Inside their section's room they noticed a number of rickety bunks and a small card table.

113

"Better than using my sodding pack," he said. "Damn thing has left a crick in my neck."

"Life is harsh enough when we're in the bush," Bray reasoned. "Might as well make yourself as comfortable as possible while in garrison."

The other soldiers in the section were mostly aloof, as Bray had said they would be. None had so much as introduced themselves to their newest mates. Arthur and Richard were sometimes referred to as *'Johnson's pets'*, since the lance corporal had essentially taken them under his charge.

"Don't sweat it," Bill told Arthur one morning after he asked when they'd be invited to play cards with the others. "Like I said, you've got to earn your place with this company. It takes much longer when we're in garrison and there's no war going on; not many opportunities to prove your mettle. Just give it time."

Arthur thought perhaps he would get the opportunity to prove himself to his mess-mates when Captain Younghusband was ordered to send half the company on a four-day patrol towards the town of Dalton, thirty miles to the northeast. There hadn't been any reports of unrest in the area, and they were at least a hundred miles from the troubles along the Zulu border. Colonel Glyn had stressed that the presence of Her Majesty's redcoats was always good for the locals. What exactly he meant by that, the young soldier could only speculate.

It was now October, and they were well into the South African spring. Given how dry and brittle the grasses were when he arrived, along with the withered trees and bushes, Arthur had been under the impression Southern Africa was always dry and hot. He soon learned that, despite the fact that the region had been in a drought during the past few years, spring and summer were very rainy. The dry, desolate landscape would slowly change to one of full green trees and lush grasses. On the morning that half the company departed Fort Napier, the skies were cloudy and a moderate drizzle was coming down from the heavens.

"Could be worse," Richard said as he adjusted his helmet. "At least it's not rainy *and* cold."

"Bah, this is nothing," Bill remarked. "We're still in a drought here. The grasses should already be green and thick. Last month we only had maybe three days of modest rainfall. Normally, we get a day of downpours for every two without. The summer is worse, as it will go from deluge to scorching heat, often over the course of a few hours."

"*Fall in!*" shouted Colour Sergeant Brown, who would be leading the patrol. "Un-sling your rifles, carry them with the barrels angled down. We've got seventeen miles to make today and will be camping near Albert Falls. Sergeant Edwards, your section will lead."

"Yes, colour sergeant." Edwards then called over his shoulder, "Section, on me!"

The rain continued at a drizzle as the forty soldiers from C Company followed the long traders' track north past Pietermaritzburg. Beyond the town, the land stretched into vast swaths of farm fields and grasslands. The ground had been tilled by hand or with ox-pulled plows. The fields, which grew mostly mealie, should have been covered in the fast-growing stalks. With the drought Bill had spoken of, the undersized shoots struggled to grow.

Aside from the soldiers, a single wagon accompanied them bearing their tents and cooking equipment. The driver was a Basuto who spoke passable English. He would sing and hum to himself most of the day as they plodded along at the agonisingly slow pace of his oxen. The voorlooper keeping the animals from straying was a young boy, possibly the driver's son.

The pace was slow, yet by mid-afternoon they reached Albert Falls. Arthur expected to find a town, but there were just a few brush huts. The falls themselves were quite pretty, albeit the numerous waterfalls were only flowing at a fraction of what they were capable of during the wet summers. The drizzle soon stopped and the sun was breaking through the clouds. As he leaned against his rifle, the young soldier grinned. He was finally seeing some of the first signs of exotic wildlife since he'd arrived in Natal. A trio of giraffes were lumbering slowly through the dry grasses not three hundred yards from where he stood. And near the water's edge were about twenty zebras drinking their fill.

"*Wilkie!*" Sergeant Edwards shouted. "Quick gawking at the fucking locals and get your arse over here to help unload the wagon!"

The patrol to Dalton proved uneventful and the band of forty redcoats made its way back towards Fort Napier. Dawn came too early on the fourth day, yet all were glad to know they would sleep in their bunks this coming night. Arthur was still bleary-eyed as he took his position with the rest of the section just outside their tents. He was surprised to see that Colour Sergeant Brown was conducting the morning inspection. Sergeant Edwards walked just behind him with a notebook in hand. The two NCOs stopped in front of every soldier, with Brown thoroughly inspecting each man's weapons and kit. Far be it from wanting his men 'parade ready', the colour sergeant cared less about appearance and more about the serviceability of their equipment. Arthur could overhear him telling Edwards whenever a soldier needed to patch his uniform or repair a pouch on his belt.

When they got to him, Arthur found himself staring eye-to-eye with Colour Sergeant Brown. Thankfully, the instincts drilled into him since his first day in the army overcame any nerves. He raised his rifle to port arms, opened the breach, inspected the chamber, and handed it to Brown. The colour sergeant ran his fingers inside the breach, as well as inside the end of the barrel, reminding the young private of his last day of recruit training. Brown checked the action on the rifle before handing it back to Arthur. He grabbed him hard by the shoulder straps, testing their durability, as well as his waist belt. He had Arthur open his ammunition pouch and checked to make sure it was sound and would not rip or allow bullets to fall out. Without a word, he stepped over to Richard.

The colour sergeant, who had been unnervingly quiet during this time, suddenly exploded. *"Why in hell is this man's waist belt unbuckled?"*

Sergeant Edwards' eyes grew wide. He slapped his notebook closed and stood beside Richard, shouting into his ear, *"Private, why is your belt unbuckled?"*

"Oh, shit," Richard swore, dropping his gaze and started to hook his belt together.

"Eyes front, damn you!" Edwards smacked him across the face with his notebook. He looked over at Arthur. "Private Wilkinson!"

"Sergeant," Arthur replied.

"Is this man not your mate?" the sergeant growled.

128

Arthur swallowed and paused for a second before replying. "Yes, sergeant."

"Then why in the bleeding fuck did you let him fall out with his kit undone?" Edwards snapped, cuffing him across the ear with his notebook. "I suppose next you'll be letting him go into battle with a faulty weapon?"

"N…no, sergeant."

"Bollocks!" Edwards barked, slapping him across the ear once more with his notebook.

"You were taught better than this, Private Wilkinson," Brown said. The calmness in his voice rattled Arthur far more than Sergeant Edwards' bellowing.

As the colour sergeant moved on to the next man, Edwards stood with his face barely a few inches from Arthur's ear. "Embarrass me like that again in front of the colour sergeant," he whispered sinisterly, "and I will make you wish you'd fallen off the ship and drowned before you ever got to Africa."

Though it was a cool morning with a hint of mist on the field, Arthur found he was sweating profusely as Sergeant Edwards dismissed the men to breakfast. He looked over at Richard, whose face was ashen white.

"I…I'm sorry, Arthur."

"Goddamn you!" Arthur snapped. "Why in the bloody hell am I taking the heat for your cockup?"

"Because you let your mate down," Bray spoke up. "If we let one of us fail, then we all fail with him. Don't worry, I'll be getting an earful from Sergeant Edwards later." Rather than seeming annoyed, the older private appeared to be smiling through his thick beard. "Now come on, lads, just shake it off. If you can't handle the stress of a brassed off non-comm slapping you around a bit, you won't be worth a pile of horse shit when facing a horde of black savages looking to spill your guts. You'll end up like Hughes, index the wrong range on your bundook, and lob your shots clear into Transvaal just before they skewer your knob off."

His last remark got a much-needed chuckle from the two young soldiers. Later, while the sections were on the march, Lance Corporal Johnson approached Arthur.

"How you holding up?" Bill asked. "You know Lowe feels bad enough that he got you in trouble with the colour sergeant. Probably makes him feel a bit less than worthy right now."

"I'll talk with him later," Arthur replied.

The two kept walking, eyes scanning trees and hillsides.

"Just so you know, I suspect I know why Edwards went off like he did," the lance corporal remarked. "Normally an unbuckled belt isn't something our non-comms get that pissed up about. A smack across the head and a few choice profanities about attention-to-detail will usually sort it out. But let me ask you this, can you read and write?"

"I can. But what has that to do with anything?"

"More than you realise," Bill said. "You've only been here a couple months, but Sergeant Edwards has been watching you closely. The fastest way to end up on the promotion ladder is by demonstrating literacy. Since we bloody rankers come from what the people back home view as the lowest scum of society, not many of us can read. Just look at the enlistment roles. See who actually signed their names or left an *X*, and you'll know what I mean. And a non-comm isn't worth a shit if he cannot so much as read the company's standing orders, or scrawl down the directives given to him, or write his own despatch. Hell, I've spent the last two years trying to teach myself to read; newspapers, the chaplain's Bible, even the first aid guide that Surgeon-Major Shepherd wrote. Edwards kept pushing me to learn to read, saying he saw potential in me beyond just shooting and stabbing darkies. It was only after I was able to sign my name to my pay chit last year that I was even given my lance corporal's chevron."

"You mean to tell me I'm being looked at for possible promotion?" Arthur asked. "I mean…already? I've only just arrived."

"Not for me to say," William chuckled as they continued on their way.

"A scholar who can recite Shakespeare still needs to be a solid soldier and prove his leadership potential. Don't be thinking you're going to end up sporting a pair of corporal's stripes within your first year in the army. Regimental high fliers exist, but they are extremely rare. Just know that Sergeant Edwards will be watching you, far more than he does Lowe, Bray, or any of the other lads in the section…except maybe Hughes, but that's only because I think he enjoys giving that hopeless twat extra duty. He sees potential in you, as do I. Give it enough time, take care of your mates, and you just might end up sporting the 'lance jack' stripe before you know it."

Chapter X: Sharp-shooters

Pietermaritzburg, Natal
Late October 1878
***

On what was otherwise a pleasant spring afternoon, Sir Henry Bartle-Frere was seething in anger. The government in London was constantly trying to hamstring him, and the local authorities in the Cape didn't help matters. As part of his scheme to justify war against the Zulus, he'd hoped to use the report from a border commission overseen by the Lieutenant-Governor of Natal, Sir Henry Bulwer, regarding a land dispute in Transvaal between the Boers and the Zulus. The results should have been a foregone conclusion, yet the commission's report was damning to Frere's intentions. In what was becoming a rather regular series of meetings, the High Commissioner sought the advice of the General Officer Commanding.

"I appreciate you coming, general, or I should say, *my lord*. My condolences to you on the death of your father, but I feel congratulations are in order for your recent elevation."

"Thank you, Sir Henry," Sir Frederic Thesiger, now known as *Lord Chelmsford*, replied.

A despatch from London had arrived the day before, informing him of the death of his father, the 1st Baron Chelmsford. Given his father was eighty-four years old and had been in poor health for some time, his passing was expected. Natal newspapers had already printed the story, with all soldiers briefed on the new term of address for the GOC.

A black servant brought a tray bearing a crystal decanter of claret, and the two men drank a toast to Chelmsford's father before commencing with their business.

"Now, Sir Henry, what vexes you this day?"

The High Commissioner handed him the report from Sir Henry Bulwer's boundary commission.

"Absurd, isn't it?" Bartle-Frere said when he saw Chelmsford had finished reading. The GOC's face was impassive.

132

"This changes nothing," he replied calmly. "It is a mere setback; another bureaucratic obstacle to overcome, nothing more."

"Damned treasonous is what it is," Sir Henry remarked with irritation. "Bulwer is Lieutenant-Governor of Natal and was tasked with settling the Transvaal border dispute. But instead of doing what one would find proper and reasonable, his commission has found almost entirely in favour of the blasted Zulus."

"Regardless, we still have our *casus belli* with the incursions by Cetshwayo's warriors across the Buffalo River. And because of that, we can use the border commission's findings, however poorly misguided they may be, to our advantage."

"I like the way you think, my lord." Sir Henry said with a relieved grin. The two men were indeed of one mind and had been so ever since the issue of the Zulus arose a few months earlier. "Neither Bulwer nor the colonial secretariat in London may see Cetshwayo as a threat, but you, my friend, possess a great deal of foresight. I think I shall make the results of the commission's findings…*conditional* to our friends across the river. How soon can you be ready to march into Zululand and end this farce once and for all?"

"I will need until the first of the year to have my columns organized. But it's not just sufficient fighting men, it's the matter of keeping them fed and supplied. I'm already having a nightmare of a time procuring sufficient wagons, draught animals, and drivers. The rates demanded by the ungrateful settlers, who should be thanking us for protecting them from Cetshwayo's spears, is downright robbery."

"See to it. It will give me enough time to draft up our terms and have a meeting with the king or his ambassadors. We'll see just how determined he is to have peace between our empires."

It was with much anticipation that Arthur and his mates looked forward to musketry qualifications. Over the previous few days they heard the echoing report of rifle fire coming from the ranges to the west of the fort, as the other companies conducted their live fire drills. In what had become a habit since their incident with Sergeant

"Quite a day for you, Wilkie," Bray said. Arthur then looked to Richard, who smiled weakly. He had performed adequately at the range, though like much of the company, he'd struggled with the three and four hundred yard targets, particularly while standing. Poor James Trainer and Harry Grant barely qualified with their weapons; their section leader berating them for being 'blind as fucking bat shit' and telling them they needed spectacles.

Arthur finish his supper and made his way to Corporal Bellhouse's billet. He saw other soldiers who'd been named company sharp-shooters meandering towards the corporal's room. He was happy to follow them since he wasn't sure where Bellhouse bunked. He was soon joined by Lance Corporal Johnson gruffly wrapping a burly arm around his shoulders.

"Glad to have you joining us!" he said boisterously.

"I forgot you were with the sharp-shooters," Arthur said.

"What? How could you forget this?" Bill pointed to the crossed rifles patch on his left cuff. "You've been staring at it ever since you arrived."

"Come on, damn it! I haven't got all sodding night," Bellhouse called, as they arrived where he sat on a camp stool outside the barracks block. He was in his shirtsleeves with his glengarry hat cocked to the side on his head. Corporal John Bellhouse was in his early twenties, sporting a pair of long, bushy sideburns and a thick mop of matted hair. A pipe protruded from his clenched teeth as he looked over the men who assembled near him.

"Connolly, Sharp, Hicks, Newberry, Murphy, Phillips, welcome back." Bellhouse then shook his head at Bill and chuckled, "Damn it, Bill, I thought I'd be rid of you by now!"

"Bollocks," the lance corporal retorted. "I can outshoot all of you with me eyes shut. You're stuck with me, John."

Everyone present had the same crossed rifles patch on his left cuff that Bill wore, for all had been company sharp-shooters before. It was then Arthur realized he was the only new soldier from The Depot to be selected for the sharp-shooters. Bellhouse saw Arthur staring and smiled as he tossed a similar patch to him.

"Here you go, Wilkie. Wear it with pride and make sure you continue to earn it. As the others will tell you, we serve as skirmishers and designated marksmen for the company. We still fall under our respective sections, only coming together when the captain orders us deployed as such. You can expect to be detached to the skirmish lines whenever the battalion is on the march, especially when enemy contact is imminent. Makes life a bit more interesting, believe me. I'll check with Sergeant Edwards and make certain your chit has been submitted for incentive pay. It isn't much, and they make sure we earn it. We're also given extra rounds during training, as well as on campaign. Colour Sergeant Brown has already put in the request with the quartermaster, so we should have our additional issue in the next day or so."

"Somebody at the top is itching for a fight," Bill speculated. "Otherwise, Quartermaster Pullen would be keeping the ammunition boxes hidden and locked away. And if Colonel Glyn is telling him to cough up a few extra rounds to the companies' sharp-shooters, I'd bet my cleanest pair of underpants that the order is coming from the GOC."

"Ah yes, *Lord Chelmsford*, as we're now to refer to him," Private Newberry remarked, giving a slight roll of the eyes. "Sod it, we thrashed the Xhosa. I'm sure we can handle the Zulus, or whoever his lordship tells us to place in our sights. One naked darkie with a spears falls when he's shot just as much as the next."

Corporal Bellhouse went on to explain to Arthur the extra training they would be expected to perform. The additional ammunition would only be enough for them to occasionally practice a few long-range shots once per month. Most of their training would focus on skirmishing tactics. The added benefit of the additional training was they were exempt from many of the more mundane fatigue details, as well as guard duty. They would still be required to attend all parades, drill, and duties as assigned by the officer commanding. However, when other soldiers were pulling weeds or performing menial labour, they would be roaming the hills away from the fort, practicing the tactics that would be expected of them as skirmishers. As he kept glancing at the crossed rifles patch in his hand, Arthur could not wait to begin.

The British and Zulu Empires were still at peace with no formal overtures made yet towards war, but Lord Chelmsford knew he had to begin preparations immediately, otherwise the Zulus would have time to organise and perhaps launch a counter-invasion of their own. And with the government in London still refusing to send any more reinforcements to the Cape, the GOC was compelled to rely more heavily upon local volunteers and African auxiliaries than he felt comfortable with.

In all, he had eight battalions of regular army infantry, yet no cavalry to speak of. As for artillery, he only had two batteries of seven-pounder Rifled Muzzle Loader (RML) guns. Relatively light and easy enough to transport, the RML cannon were only moderately effective at ranges up to roughly 1,000 yards. Beyond that, their efficacy dwindled considerably. There was an ongoing debate within the Royal Artillery as to whether the RML was even worth all the effort.

Chelmsford's greatest obstacle of all was logistics. Between rations, ammunition, tents, engineering tools, and all the various forms of equipment an army needed, he required a vast number of wagons and draught animals. And yet, there simply were not enough available. Resources of the Army Commissariat and Quartermaster Corps in Natal were insufficient, and local settlers and traders only had so many wagons, carts, and animals to part with. Those that did charged the British government disparate fees for their rental or purchase.

It was more due to these logistical concerns, rather than manpower shortages, that Chelmsford was compelled to reduce his initial plan of five invasion columns to three. He still kept five columns; however, the No. 5 under Colonel Henry Rowlands, VC would remain in the Transvaal to prevent any unrest or uprisings like the most recent with the Xhosa. The No. 2 Column under Lieutenant Colonel Anthony Durnford would be a mobile force, consisting almost exclusively of Natal auxiliaries, horsemen and infantry alike. They would remain near Middle Drift as a mobile reserve force to prevent Cetshwayo from launching a counterattack into Natal.

This left him with three assault elements that would spearhead the invasion. The southern, No. 1 Column, was commanded by Colonel Sir Charles Pearson of the 3rd Regiment of Foot (the Buffs). With two battalions of infantry and a strong contingent of both indigenous cavalry and NNC, he had roughly 4,700 men under his command.

Leading the northern, No. 4 Column, was the venerable Colonel Sir Henry Evelyn Wood, VC of the 90th Light Infantry. His forces were much smaller, however, with just his own 90th Light Infantry, along with 1/13th Regiment, and some African horsemen. This gave him a total strength of just over 1,500 men, and Chelmsford directed him to use his forces to conduct raids of the northern territories within the Zulu kingdom.

It was with the centre column, however, that the GOC intended to place the bulk of his fighting strength. Commanded by Colonel Richard Glyn of the 24th Regiment, he would have both of his battalions, along with N Battery, 5th Brigade, Royal Artillery, No.1 Squadron, Imperial Mounted Infantry (IMI), various pioneers, an engineer company, two battalions of NNC, and assorted troops of carbineers and volunteer cavalry. Overall, his strength was similar to that of Pearson's at roughly 4,700 men. While Chelmsford would be responsible for the overall conduct of the invasion, he had decided to personally accompany Glyn's No. 3 Column.

Since most of these forces were scattered throughout The Cape, it would take time for each column to muster its forces at their various staging points. Many of the units had hundreds of miles to cover, and progress along the dirt roads would be impeded by the spring and summer rains. With no trains available, it would be weeks before they arrived. Chelmsford's other concern was that Cetshwayo likely had spies scattered throughout Natal and would know when and where his forces were mustering.

Colonel Charles Pearson (No. 1 Column), and Colonel Henry Evelyn Wood, VC
(No. 4 Column)

One of Arthur's favourite places, where he found a large measure of peace, was the regimental library. A very small building, tucked away behind the canteen, he spent many of his off-duty hours reading and enjoying the relative solitude. The collection of books was sparse, yet he still found himself able to escape from the daily life on the Empire's frontier in the pages of Dickens or even a book of poems by Lord Byron that somehow had made its way to Southern Africa. At times he simply enjoyed reading newspapers from home, even when the events were several months old. And it was here that he could make good on a promise he'd been neglectful of.

He had purchased a pen set and bundle of writing paper from the commissary. The assistant commissary who helped him with his purchase was a gruff, grey-haired and bearded former NCO named James Dalton. When Arthur explained that he needed to send a letter to his wife, Dalton had winked and sternly told him to always make sure his spouse was well taken care of. And so, as he sat alone in the library, a small oil lamp providing light, and a small picture of Elisa lying next to the packet of papers. Arthur laid out the first sheet and slowly began to write:

My Dearest Elisa,

I am sorry for the long delays in my writing to you. You'll be proud to know that during musketry training, I was one of the best shots in the company and have been made one of the sharp-shooters. This also means an added stipend to my pay, which I intend to include in my stoppages sent to you. I have increased my stoppages to where I have just enough to purchase a few supplemental rations, especially vegetables, which are scarce in the mess, as well as these papers and a writing pen. My hope is that you will soon have enough from my pay to acquire passage to Natal, so that we may be together again. A few of the other married soldiers, including my section leader, Sergeant Edwards, live in a block of townhouses not far from the fort. They are pretty sparse, but we can fix them up proper once you arrive.

I think about you every day. Your picture, which sits on the table next to me as I write this, brings me comfort and joy. The only thing that will make me happier is when I hold you in my arms. I love you with all of my heart, and I look forward to the day when we are together again.

Your loving husband,
Arthur

He let out a melancholy sigh, set the pen down, and rubbed a cramp out of his hand. He'd made no mention of the political struggles between the Cape authority and the neighbouring Zulu kingdom, and he certainly wasn't going to say anything about the possibility of war with Cetshwayo, of which rumours abounded throughout Natal. It was not that he wished to keep anything from his wife; however, the last thing he wanted was to give her cause to worry needlessly. And besides, all the talk he'd heard about a pending conflict with the Zulus had been nothing more that gossip and speculation.

In mid-November, Frere called for a private meeting with Lord Chelmsford and Sir Theophilus Shepstone in order to discuss the language of his proposal. He read the following points to the two men, who waited until he finished before giving their thoughts:

- Surrender of Sihayo's three sons and brother to be tried by the Natal courts.
- Payment of a fine of five hundred head of cattle for the outrages committed by the above and for Cetshwayo's delay in complying with the request of the Natal Government for the surrender of the offenders.
- Payment of a hundred head of cattle for the offence committed against Messrs. Smith and Deighton.
- Surrender of the Swazi chief Umbilini and others to be named hereafter, to be tried by the Transvaal courts.
- Observance of the coronation promises.
- The Zulu army be disbanded and the men allowed to go home.
- The Zulu military system be discontinued and other military regulations adopted, to be decided upon after consultation with the Great Council and British Representatives.
- Every man, when he comes to man's estate, shall be free to marry.
- All missionaries and their converts, who until 1877 lived in Zululand, shall be allowed to return and reoccupy their stations.
- All such missionaries shall be allowed to teach and any Zulu, if he chooses, shall be free to listen to their teaching.
- A British Agent shall be allowed to reside in Zululand, who will see that the above provisions are carried out.
- All disputes in which a missionary or European is concerned, shall be heard by the king in public and in presence of the Resident.
No sentence of expulsion from Zululand shall be carried out until it has been approved by the Resident.

"Gentlemen," Sir Henry said as he removed his reading glasses. "Does this meet with the proper intentions for justifying our proposed annexation of the Zulu Kingdom under a confederacy administered by Her Majesty's government in Natal?"

146

"It does, Sir Henry," Chelmsford replied. He then read over the copy he'd been provided once more. "Most excellently."

"And your thoughts, Sir Theophilus?" Frere asked. "You are, after all, the one who oversaw Cetshwayo's coronation, and your influence among the Zulus is greater than any."

"Cetshwayo will never agree to any of this." Shepstone's blunt remark echoed the thoughts shared by all. "And if he wanted to, his barons, the *amakhosi*, would never allow it. Even Shaka, who ruled with far greater autocratic power than Cetshwayo does now, could never have subjected his people to such terms."

"Well," Frere shrugged. "That is his problem, not ours."

"Agreed," Shepstone concurred. "But I do not think that any one of us should deliver the ultimatum to Cetshwayo's representatives."

"Who do you have in mind?" Chelmsford asked.

Sir Theophilus sneered. "My brother."

In late November Elisa Wilkinson finally received the letter her husband posted to her five weeks before. It had taken a week for the letter to reach Durban, three more by steamship to England, and finally another week to make its way from Portsmouth to Stratford-upon-Avon. She had read the letter at least a dozen times, holding it close to her chest, as she could feel her heart pounding. A few days later, she received a postal order for a sizeable amount of money.

"This must be the better part of his wages since he joined the army," Elisa gasped in surprise as she showed the note to her parents.

"He loves you very much," her father replied. "And he wants you to be with him on this adventure."

It was overwhelming for the young woman, for she never ventured far from her home. About the furthest she had ever been was Cheltenham, and now she was looking at possibly joining her husband in Southern Africa. The prospect was both exhilarating and terrifying, in equal measure.

Fortune smiled upon her a few days later when there was an unexpected knock at the door. Elisa was home by herself, washing the linens for her mother. She quickly dried her hands and answered the door. She was greeted by a woman in a dark burgundy dress and hat. She looked to be in her late twenties and was, Elisa would consider, more handsome than pretty. Her countenance was one of a woman who was experienced far beyond her years.

"Mrs Wilkinson?"

"Yes." Elisa's expression betrayed her confusion.

"My name is Eleanor Brown."

"Elisa," she replied, taking her hand and curtseying. "Do I know you?"

"No, but I think we shall get to know each other very well over the next few months." Eleanor then smiled warmly as she explained, "My husband is Thomas Brown, your husband's colour sergeant. He told me about Arthur's brave gesture, asking the commandant in Brecon for permission to marry. A dashing young man, I am certain."

"Yes, he is…please, do come in." Elisa hurried into the kitchen and put the kettle on. She returned with a plate of biscuits, and the two women sat in the small drawing room. It was a cold December day, but the sun shone warmly through the window.

"It will be much warmer in South Africa, I assure you," Eleanor remarked. "As you may have guessed, Thomas asked me to find you and to accompany you to Natal."

Elisa let out an audible sigh of relief. "Please give him my thanks. I received the stoppages from Arthur so that I might book passage to come join him, yet I have no idea as to how I should go about it. I take it you've been through this before?"

"Ever since I was a little girl," Eleanor laughed. "I was born into the army. I spent most of my childhood in India, where my father was a sergeant major. Though I never told him, I hated the army and wanted nothing more than to return to England and live a 'normal' life; as if I knew what that was. Once I came of age, I was determined to return home and find a suitable husband. And then I met Thomas…"

148

In early December, a message was sent to King Cetshwayo to have his delegation meet with the British government's representatives on the Lower Thukela. In his response, the king stated he was willing to fully abide by the boundary commission's report. He further hoped this gesture of goodwill would demonstrate to Frere and the other British officials that the Zulus were of no threat to Natal and wished to continue living in peace, as friends and trade partners.

It had been a trying time for the king. Most troubling of all were the reports from his spies that British troops were staging at various points along the border. Several companies from Colonel Wood's own 90th Light Infantry had begun assembling at Utrecht, near the northwest boundary between the Zulu Kingdom and Natal. And now there was word that a very large force was slowly assembling near Jim Rorke's old homestead. In his distress, Cetshwayo sent an urgent letter, written and translated by John Dunn, to the lieutenant-governor of Natal, Sir Henry Bulwer, whose commission had been tasked with resolving the border dispute:

I hear of troops arriving in Natal, that they are coming to attack the Zulus, and to seize me. In what have I done wrong that I should be seized like an 'Umtakata', a name my people use for evil-doers? The English are my fathers, I do not wish to quarrel with them, but to live as I have always done, at peace with them. Cetshwayo says that he sees that His Excellency is hiding from him the answer that has returned from across the sea, about the land boundary question with the Transvaal, and only making an excuse for taking time so as to surprise him. I trust that this dispute will be brought to a conclusion soon, one which is fair to all concerned. Cetshwayo expects both prudence and justice from the representatives of his sister, Victoria.

What the king did not know was that Sir Henry Bartle-Frere had used Mehlokazulu's incursion as an excuse to stifle the findings of the boundary commission for the time, and Bulwer was powerless to stop him. While he sympathised with Cetshwayo, there was little he could do, as the matter was now in the hands of the High Commissioner. It was only now, at the end of the year, that Frere

"Cetshwayo has no quarrel with Britain," Frances Colenso said, before Sir Henry could speak. "He, like his father before him, have been our trading partners and friends. He would gain nothing by declaring war on us."

"My dear," Bartle-Frere replied. "One can never truly know the mind of a barbaric savage like Cetshwayo."

"My father knows him well." Frances tried not to glare at the high commissioner. "He may not dress like us, and their customs may appear strange, but he is no mindless barbarian."

The rest at the table silently watched this exchange. While cordial, it was filled with much tension. Sir Henry gave a gentle, yet patronising laugh, as if he were talking to a child. Frances found it infuriating.

"I need not remind you of Cetshwayo's bloody history," Sir Henry continued. "He slaughtered twenty thousand of his own people in order to make himself king."

"Many of our leaders did no less," Bishop Colenso finally spoke up. "And at much later periods in our history. We treat the Zulus as barbarians. Yet were we any better? I think the graves of the slaughtered left by Cromwell tell a very different story."

"Be that as it may," Chelmsford countered. "What happened in England two hundred years ago does not change the immediate threat that the Zulu possess to our citizens in Natal."

"We have delivered our terms to Cetshwayo," the high commissioner explained. "It is now up to him if there will be peace or war."

"This is a vast and great land," Colenso replied sadly. He then removed his glasses for a moment. "There should be room for all."

"But there is, my dear bishop," Sir Henry said. "And the sooner the Zulus disband their *impis* of war, the sooner all of South Africa can enjoy the privilege of civilisation under proper British authority and management."

The tenor of the discussion changed with the arrival of Anthony Durnford. With his slouch hat cocked slightly on his head, and left arm pinned inside his jacket, he still cut the rather dashing figure.

"A thousand pardons, my lord," he said to Chelmsford, as he removed his hat and took a seat. "I was conducting an inspection of one of my troops from Basuto Horse."

"And are they ready to do battle?" Chelmsford asked diplomatically.

Sir Henry's choice of words were far less cordial. "Or will they turn on us and fight beside their heathen brothers?"

"The Basutos and Zulus are age-old enemies, Sir Henry," Durnford explained. "My men are all Christian gentlemen. I know each man by name, and I can personally attest to their collective valour and loyalty."

"Anthony, would you be so kind as to walk with me in the garden?" Frances asked, rising up from her chair. The incessant talk of war upset her, and she wished to be away from it, at least for a while.

"Of course, my lady." Anthony stood and donned his hat before nodding to the GOC. "My lord."

As soon as the two were out of hearing, Sir Henry let out a chuckle. "A spirited little girl your daughter is, bishop."

"She needs a man," his wife, Catherine asserted. "One who will tame her properly."

"She is her own woman," Colenso said sternly. He then addressed Frere. "And she is almost thirty, Sir Henry. Scarcely a 'little girl'."

"Oh, I meant no offence," Catherine replied. "It's just that, such a beautiful creature as she, do you think it's wise to have kept her away from civilisation for so long? I worry she may have spent too much time with these dark savages."

Colenso forced a smile and tried to deflect the remark with nonchalance. "The Lord has blessed me with strong sons. However, I thank him every day for giving me even stronger daughters. Now if you will excuse me, gentlemen and ladies."

Sir Henry watched as the bishop left to join his daughter and Durnford in the garden. He took a drink off his cocktail and puffed his cigar in agitation. "I sometimes wonder which side that man is on."

"Like all men of the church, he believes he is on the side of God," Chelmsford replied dismissively. "Mind you, I did hear he got called before the High Church on charges of heresy a number of years ago."

"Yes," Sir Henry recalled. "And yet the Judicial Committee of the Privy Council overruled their attempts at removing him from office. I sometimes think he was acquitted just to keep him as far away from England as possible. What manner of man views the black savage as an equal in the eyes of God? Let us not allow ourselves to be fooled by such naïve idealism; the native African is a beast that needs to be tamed. And you, my lord, are the one who will pacify the Zulu."

All those present, with perhaps the exception of their wives, knew Sir Henry's ultimatum would come to nothing on the Zulu side. The terms were so damning that even if he were compliant, Cetshwayo was powerless to impose them on his people.

"Gentlemen," Chelmsford said, addressing the colonels. "I think the time has come to expedite moving your columns to their staging points. Once the ultimatum has expired, Cetshwayo must be drawn into battle as soon as possible. And if he refuses to engage us openly, then we will converge on his royal kraal and burn it to the ground."

The men at the table proceeded to beat their hands on the table, giving the occasional *'here, here'* in acknowledgment. As career soldiers, they cared little for the political reasons behind the pending conflict with the Zulus. Each had his duty to perform. If all went well, the Zulu kingdom would be conquered before anyone in London could raise a finger in protest.

Chapter XII: To Rorke's Drift

Helpmekaar, Natal
December 1878

Reverend Otto Witt

The ultimatum had yet to expire; however, every last British soldier in Natal knew that war with the Zulus was inevitable. For the 24th Regiment, who would form the nexus of the centre No. 3 column, theirs was a 115-mile trek from Fort Napier to the crossing point at Rorke's Drift. Named after an Irish trader named James Rorke, the small mission station served as the perfect place to stage an invasion force. Anticipating the army's need for the outpost as a supply depot and hospital, Lord Chelmsford personally negotiated a lease with the current tenant, a thirty-year old Swedish missionary named Otto Witt, who lived at the Drift with his wife and two young children.

"Damned murderous savages!" Witt said when Chelmsford came to visit the station. "When they're not threatening those who would bring them the word of God, they are crossing into Natal to commit murder. I cannot tell you how much I fear for my wife and children. I do hope you will take care of this naked barbarian who dares call himself a king."

"Rest assured, Mr Witt," Chelmsford comforted him. "Her Majesty's armed forces are the best trained and equipped in the world. We will deal with this 'naked barbarian' in due course."

Despite his expressed gratitude for now having the protection of British soldiers at his home, Reverend Witt asked an exorbitant fee from the colonial government for use of his home. Chelmsford decided not to argue despite the protestations from Lieutenant Colonel Crealock.

"Damned highway robbery, it is!" the colonel later complained.

"Well, he is having to move his entire family from their home," the GOC remarked. "Although, the good reverend has offered to stand and fight beside our boys should his home come under attack from the Zulus."

"Not very likely, that," Crealock chuckled with amusement. While the thought of Cetshwayo launching an attack on Natal seemed absurd to the outside observer, Chelmsford's conscience felt better knowing he had Durnford's highly mobile No. 2 Column acting as a buffer between Zululand and the settlements along the Natal border. If nothing else, it certainly set the minds of the settlers at ease.

One man whose position was becoming ever more tenuous was Cetshwayo's lone white advisor, John Dunn. Having negotiated a truce between the warring brothers of the Zulu royal house twenty-three years prior, he had become the king's chief advisor on white affairs. He had also built quite the trade network between the Zulus and the Portuguese colony of Mozambique to the north. He had a homestead near the coast but spent much of his time at Ulundi, advising the king. And while he had a British wife, he'd taken a number of Zulu wives as well and sired many children. Yet the colour of his skin alone now brought suspicion and hostility from the *amakhosi*.

During the early evening, soon after the return of the *izinduna* who received Frere's ultimatum, it became clear that Dunn's time in Zululand was growing short. After the 'White Zulu', as he was known on both sides of the border, retired to his camp for the night, Sihayo and a few other councillors held a private meeting with the king.

"The man is dangerous," the *inkosi* said. "He may have spent much of his life in our lands and taken the wives you so generously offered him, but he is still British. Let us not forget, he sided with your brother, the traitor Mbuyazi, at Ndondakusuka."

"That was more than twenty harvests ago," Cetshwayo replied. "John Dunn has been both an advisor and friend to the Zulus. We have gained much in the way of trade through him, particularly firearms."

"Garbage," another councillor retorted. "The weapons Dunn has sold us over the years are garbage! Your own spies have seen the rifles the white soldiers now carry, *Ndabazitha*. They are far more accurate and deadly than any gun Dunn sold us."

"You gave two wives to Dunn for a pair of such weapons," Sihayo added. "And he has acquired another forty-six over the last twenty years. Some he has converted to Christianity, as are all of his children. He subverts the ways of our people, and he will not hesitate to act as a spy for the British, should it come to war. If he remains at Ulundi, we cannot promise his safety."

In a coincidental emphasis of Sihayo's words of warning, a host of Zulu warriors from the king's personal guard rampaged through Dunn's camp that night. When he protested, they shouted that his time was over, and they would gut any white man who desecrated the land of the Zulus. The following morning, without any fanfare or even a farewell to Cetshwayo, John Dunn left for his home on the coast. A few days later he crossed into Natal.

Colonel Richard Glyn's column was beginning to grow, as the various units converged on Rorke's Drift. In addition to both battalions of his 24th Regiment, he had N Battery, 5th Brigade Royal Artillery with is six seven-pounder cannon; No. 5 Company, Royal

Engineers, though these had yet to arrive from Greytown. There was also No. 1 Squadron, Imperial Mounted Infantry (IMI); Rupert Lonsdale's 3rd Regiment of the Natal Native Contingent (NNC); No. 1 Company, Natal Native Pioneer Corps, as well as elements from the Natal Mounted Police, Natal Carbineers, Newcastle Mounted Rifles, and the Buffalo Border Guard. All told, he had 4,709 officers and men including local Africans, white settler volunteers, and professional imperial redcoats. To haul all of their rations, baggage, tents, ammunition, and artillery, there were 220 wagons, 82 oxcarts, 1,507 oxen, 49 horses, and 67 mules. However, as sixteen oxen were needed for each wagon, Glyn had less than half the number of draught animals necessary. This meant having to establish supply points along the way, with his ox teams constantly ferrying supplies forward to the column as it progressed.

It was indeed an impressive display of fighting man and beast, and it took no small amount of logistics and organizational skills to keep it all working efficiently. Colonel Glyn was more than up to the task; however, even though he was technically the column commander, it would not be he who gave the orders.

"A pity his lordship has chosen our column to accompany," Glyn's chief staff officer, Major Francis Clery, remarked with no small trace of disappointment one evening. While he had no personal qualms with Lord Chelmsford, he knew the GOC was a notorious micromanager. His presence would relegate Colonel Glyn to little more than an observer. Furthermore, there was no small amount of animosity between Clery and the man he viewed as Chelmsford's vile henchman, Lieutenant Colonel Crealock.

"Lord Chelmsford is commander-in-chief of all armed forces in Natal," Glyn observed rather glumly. He liked the thought of having the GOC constantly watching over his shoulder even less than Clery. "It is his prerogative which column he chooses to accompany."

Clery was uneasy about having to share responsibilities with Chelmsford's staff, who could simply override or ignore the column staff altogether, but he knew they were without choice. He hoped the Zulus would quickly give Chelmsford the battle he so desperately craved, so they could be done with it before things became too unpleasant between the staffs.

Major Cornelius Francis Clery
Chief-of-Staff, No. 3 Column

Rupert Lonsdale was given a bit of a reprieve when it came to finding capable men to serve as his officers. The steamship, Edinburgh Castle, had arrived on 2 December, carrying another batch of new recruits and volunteers, as well as a number of much needed officers. Among them was a regular army subaltern named Charlie Harford. He'd requested a leave-of-absence from his own 99th Regiment, in order to serve as a special service officer in South Africa.

Twenty-eight years old, he spent six years of his youth in Pinetown, Natal and was not only familiar with the land, but he spoke Zulu and several other local dialects. Harford was an extremely intelligent and well-spoken, albeit rather eccentric, young man. Lonsdale appointed him as Staff Officer with the local rank of acting-captain. As soon as he visited the pay office, drew his horse and carbine, and purchased a few personal necessities, Harford headed to Sandspruit. This was located just a few miles from Rorke's Drift, where the 3rd NNC Regiment was coming together.

For the officers and men of 1/24th, the rallying at Rorke's Drift become a reunion of many old friends. The companies had been mostly scattered throughout Natal and were only now converging on Helpmekaar, about fifteen miles from the Drift. The unfortunate lads in B Company were being left to garrison southern Natal, while D, F, and G Companies were en route to join A, C, E, and H Companies. It was a similar situation with 2nd Battalion, with several of their own companies still making the long journey to the drift. And while their B Company had arrived at Rorke's Drift, they would not be crossing into Zululand.

"Someone has to stay and guard the depot," Colonel Glyn explained to Lieutenant Colonel Henry Degacher and his staff. "With the shortage of wagons and oxen, the column will be constantly ferrying supplies to the front from here. And to be perfectly frank, I think it should be Bromhead's men who remain."

"Agreed," Degacher replied. "Up until last year 'Gunny' was languishing as a career subaltern. He's a likeable enough chap, but that does not make for an effective officer commanding. He's also deaf as a post and about as uninspiring of an officer as I've ever met."

"It doesn't help that there are no other officers in the company," Glyn added. "Not since you reassigned Lieutenant Godwin-Austen to G Company. Not to mention, Bromhead has the youngest colour sergeant in the entire damned army as his senior NCO. It's settled. B Company will guard our supplies and the drift. We may want to place a more competent officer in command of the overall garrison, just in case."

"How about Spalding?" Clery spoke up.

Major Henry Spalding of the 104th Regiment was the column's adjutant and Quartermaster-General.

"He's a competent officer who understands transportation and logistics," Glyn concurred. "Only makes sense that he sort out our supply issues and maintain communications between here and Helpmekaar. He will be in command of both stations, as well as responsible for the defence of the drift."

The news would come as a terrible disappointment to the men of B Company, 2/24th. Lieutenant Bromhead was especially distraught to be losing out on yet another opportunity to live up to his family's martial reputation. He said as much in a letter to his brother,

Major Charles Bromhead, who was on home service in England and had, thus far, an enviable military career of his own.

Dear Charles,

Opportunity to live up to our family's honourable name has been denied me once more. While the Regiment makes ready to invade the Kingdom of the Zulus, my company has been left behind to guard the stores at a remote mission station called Rorke's Drift.

I know that our father expected great things from both of us, as does now our brother, Benjamin, since he inherited father's baronetcy eight years ago. You have at least had some opportunity to test your mettle, whereas I have fought against flies and dysentery more than any human enemy. The Xhosa were not a worthy foe, and for the sake of the Regiment's reputation, I hope the Zulu prove a more stalwart adversary. Still, after our great-grandfather stood with General Wolfe at Quebec, our grandfather rising to lieutenant general, and our dear father standing with Wellington at Waterloo, my greatest fear is that I will never be worthy of the name 'Bromhead'.

I trust this finds you well, and please forgive me if my frustrations seem a bit unbecoming. You, of course, understand my dilemma far better than our brothers. Give my best to Benjamin and the rest of the family.

I have the honour of always being your brother,

Gonville

Lieutenant Gonville Bromhead
Officer Commanding, B Company, 2/24th Regiment

For Elisa Wilkinson, the past few weeks seemed like a blur. She was ever thankful to have Eleanor Brown with her, as otherwise she would have been completely lost and alone. For Eleanor, the British Army had been part of her life since the time she was born. She had thought to leave that lifestyle behind when the family eventually returned to England, but then she met Thomas Brown. At the time, he was a dashing young corporal so smitten by her that he chanced earning the wrath of his sergeant major for attempting to court his daughter.

"What father's soldiers never knew was just how big of a softie he really was," Eleanor said, with a light-hearted laugh as they rode the train from London to Portsmouth Harbour.

It was Elisa's first time to the capital, and she found the place both awe-inspiring and terrifying. She was amazed at how easily Eleanor found her way around, and it was with much relief they boarded the train bound for the southern coast.

"So your father didn't make life difficult for Thomas?" Elisa asked. She privately wondered just how much grief Arthur had been given by his officers and NCOs.

"Oh, he did, at least for a little while. The truth is, Thomas had a reputation for being both a fine soldier and gentleman. His captain told him on more than one occasion that, were he a man of means, he would have made a proper officer. But I did not care about any of that. He was the man I loved, and wherever he went I would follow."

"Do you ever regret that he stayed in the army?"

"Sometimes," Eleanor confessed. "There are many days when I wish we would settle down someplace nice and quiet, where he could find work a little less 'adventurous', and we might be able to start a family. But since he decided to re-enlist and join the Regiment in South Africa, we may just have to start our family there."

"That's not unheard of," Elisa remarked. "I know of a few people who were born overseas because of where their fathers were posted."

"True, but I always said I never wanted to give birth in an army hospital, or worse have to rely on the medicines and midwives of the natives. You are still very young, my dear, and you have plenty of time. I, on the other hand, am not far removed from thirty. So if we are going to have children, it may as well be now."

Elisa nodded and turned her attention to just outside the window, where the trees and rolling fields raced by. Having just been married, she had given little thought yet to children. While she longed for the day when she became a mother, she also knew it would be far less stressful on both she and Arthur if they waited a few years. Neither of them knew whether or not he would choose to re-enlist at the end of his six-year term. If he chose to take his discharge, they could return home and begin a family there. And if he decided that he loved the army life…well, they would sort that out when the time came.

Without knowing it, Elisa and Eleanor's journey would follow almost the exact same path as their husbands, including transport aboard the same steamship, the HMS Tyne. It would be another three to four weeks before they arrived in Natal, and both were blissfully unaware of the looming crisis and terrible dangers their husbands would soon face.

As the days passed, more men and supplies arrived at Rorke's Drift. Anticipation built as the men of C Company, 1/24th looked forward to the pending invasion of Zululand. No one understood why they were readying to make war on a former ally, and few bothered to ask, even amongst the officers. Only Chelmsford and a few of his senior staff officers knew the invasion did not have the sanction of the home government, and that they were making ready to instigate what was in fact an unlawful war. The GOC was certain a quick victory, the capitulation of Cetshwayo, and the incorporation of the Zulus into a South African confederation would bring accolades rather than a rebuke from Whitehall. His greatest fear was, like the Xhosa the year before, the Zulu would refuse to engage him in battle. Yet all the men in the ranks assumed they were doing their duty to Queen Victoria by bringing further conquest and glory to the British Empire.

Christmas came, and the men were allowed a day of rest. Colonel Glyn had purchased spirits and malt liquor for his men to celebrate, though he diplomatically stated that they came with the compliments of Her Majesty and Lord Chelmsford. New Year's soon followed, and the ultimatum was just days from expiring.

The drought that plagued southern Africa for the past few years also came to a rather abrupt and violent end, as the heavens opened up and unleashed a torrential downpour upon the encamped army. Drainage trenches had been dug around many of the tents, but flooding still occurred with many a soldier bickering endlessly about his soaked blankets and equipment.

"Bugger me," Arthur grumbled as he hunkered beneath their tent, his bottom wet from the pooling water, as he tried to find a dry rag with which to wipe down his rifle. "Sergeant Edwards will have my arse if this gets any rust pits on it."

"Here," Bray said, pulling a rag from his pack and tossing it to him. "Now you know why I hang my pack and bundook off the support poles."

Arthur gave a nod of thanks and began feverishly wiping down his weapon. He then made a mental to note to always make certain his pack and rifle were kept off the ground, lest the camp get flooded again. A soggy bottom he could deal with, a rusty Martini-Henry not so much.

It was late afternoon and the rains had ceased. Arthur finished with his rifle and stepped out of his tent, breathing in the smell of the recent rains. He had overheard that most of the column was now assembled, and it would not be long before they crossed the uMzinyathi River, which stretched out just beyond their camp. Once across the border, they would be at war with the Zulu. He was filled mostly with excitement, and just a touch of nervousness that was quashed by the cool confidence displayed by the company veterans. As he sat on a camp stool, watching a team of artillerymen struggle with heaving one of their cannon that had become stuck in the mud, he spotted his friend, Private James Trainer. The two had not seen much of each other, as they were in different sections and when he wasn't drilling with his own, Arthur was off training with the company's skirmishers. The young man was carrying his pack and rifle, his head stooped beneath his helmet, as if he were distraught.

"Oy, James!" Arthur called out, walking over to the distressed young man. "Why the sad face? And where are you off to with all of your kit?"

"I've been reassigned," James replied dejectedly.

"Reassigned? To where?"

"The damned rocket battery, Durnford's column. Apparently Major Russell doesn't have any of his own people. So me, Grant, and a few other lads from the battalion have all been attached to them. One major, one bombardier, and eight of us poor sods from the 24th."

"Bugger me." There was a trace of sympathy in his voice.

"Yeah, this whole thing sucks a giant bull's cock. Most of the veterans are thinking we'll get maybe one good fight out of the Zulus…if they bother to show up. Instead of battling them with you lot on the firing line, we get to lob goddamn fireworks at them. I wonder how proud I'll be getting my campaign medal at the end of all this, knowing that all I did was toss sodding party favours at the enemy."

"Eh, it could be worse." Arthur placed a reassuring hand on his friend's shoulder. "At least you're not one of those poor bastards from Bromhead's Company of 2nd Battalion. They drew the short stick and are stuck guarding the stores."

"Yeah," James chuckled. "Those buggers are going to miss out on all the fun."

Establishment of the depot at Rorke's Drift had fallen under the command of the column adjutant, brevet Major Henry Spalding. The garrison from B Company, 2/24th, plus a number of excess NNC warriors served as Spalding's labour force. Besides the two main buildings at the mission station, there was a small cookhouse and two kraals for livestock. The two large buildings, which until recently had been Reverend Witt's home and church, were now being converted into a hospital and commissariat store.

Overseeing the hospital was Surgeon James Reynolds, a thirty-four year old Irish doctor assigned to 1/24th. His counterpart from 2/24th, Surgeon-Major Peter Shepherd, would be accompanying the column into Zululand. Both men were highly-skilled doctors, yet it was Shepherd whose reputation as a pioneer and innovator in the field of medicine had made him a legend, both at home and abroad.

A thirty-seven year old Scotsman and the son of a humble farmer from Aberdeenshire, Peter Shepherd graduated from Aberdeen University in 1863, joining the army soon after. He spent his first six years as Assistant-Surgeon to the 99th Regiment, which was posted to Natal at the time. Anxious for more foreign service, he volunteered to serve in India for four additional years before returning to Britain. He went on to serve as one of the very first instructors at the St John's Ambulance Association where he devised many of his innovative methods for first aid, including bandaging, pressure dressing, and wound and equipment sterilisation. Promoted to surgeon-major in 1876, he had recently written a small guidebook for the civilian populace on the treatment of minor injuries and illnesses; the first of its kind. He viewed his methods as simple common-sense, but they were to prove pioneering and particularly effective against disease and infection.

Doctors of the 24th
Surgeon-Major Peter Shepherd and Surgeon James Reynolds

Work details under the supervision of the battalion quartermasters as well as Commissary Dunne and his assistants, Assistant Commissary Dalton and Storekeeper Byrne, had toiled for weeks to consolidate the column's much-needed supplies. The storehouse was piled high with large bags of mealie, each weighing in excess of two hundred pounds, along with hundreds of biscuit boxes, and of course ammunition. Quartermaster Bloomfield and Quartermaster Pullen had a wagon designated for each company's resupply of ammunition, with B Company's own stock of over 20,000 rounds being kept in emergency reserve at Rorke's Drift.

A small room in the storehouse, scarcely bigger than a wardrobe, was currently being utilised as a makeshift office by Colour Sergeant Bourne of B Company. A square table cut from the lower half of a broken door sufficed as a desk.

Enlisted into the army on 18 December 1872, Frank Edward Bourne had just passed his six-year anniversary with the regiment. He was of average height, build, and completely unassuming in appearance. He had a keen knack for both strategy and tactics, as well as logistical understanding far beyond one of his experience. Because of this and his level of education and ambition to excel, he had defined the term 'Regimental High-Flier', since joining the ranks. He was promoted to corporal less than a year after enlisting, and sergeant a couple of years later. Now, at just twenty-four years of age, he was the youngest colour sergeant in the entire British Army.

As he sat going through some documents Lieutenant Bromhead has asked him to review, there was a knock on the door. Before he could answer, it was opened and in walked a face he had not seen in several years.

"Well, I'll be damned," he said. "Thomas Brown...*Colour Sergeant* Thomas Brown, I might add. I heard you were back with the regiment."

"Hello, Frank," Thomas said, removing his helmet and setting it atop his rifle, which he rested in the corner. "Only the second time we've seen each other since you were a baby-faced youth coming through The Depot."

"Yes, and you were the most diabolical corporal-instructor a lad could have," Frank replied with a grin, recalling his hellish days as a new recruit.

"I won't deny, it amazed me to see you wearing the same rank as me scarcely a year later. And if you think I was hellish then, you should have seen me when they brought me back as a sergeant-instructor!" The two men shared a laugh before Brown gave a nod towards the insignia Bourne wore on his right shoulder. "So do tell, when?"

"This past April," Frank answered. "And you?"

Thomas let out a sigh of resignation as he hung his head. "July." He reached across the desk and clasped his former pupil's hand. "Congratulations, old man."

"Thank you, Thomas. I suppose I've come a ways since you were beating me across the neck with your stick while calling me an *untrainable twat*."

Thomas shrugged nonchalantly at the memory. "If it makes you feel any better, I referred to every new recruit as such. It didn't matter if he passed every test the first time, which no one ever does, or was a model soldier from Day One. In my estimation, every last one of you was an *untrainable twat* until the day you passed out as a fully qualified soldier in Her Majesty's service. But now, it would seem you have become the master and I the pupil."

"Oh, I wouldn't say that. How about fellow peers among The Queen's distinguished corps of senior non-commissioned officers?"

"I will drink to that," Thomas said with an appreciative smile.

170

"That we will. And it will be on your bill, old friend. So tell me, since you will actually be crossing into Zululand, what are your thoughts on the upcoming invasion?"

"Provided all goes well, we should have the issue decided in a couple months," Thomas speculated.

"Yes, as long as all goes according to the GOC's plans," Frank remarked. "However, the column has a severe shortage of wagons and draught animals, meaning resupplies of food and ammunition will have to be forwarded in stages along the way to Ulundi. I cannot imagine the other two columns are having it any better than we are. Not exactly going according to the GOC's plans, now is it? I just hope his lordship knows that the Zulu are not like the Xhosa."

"I'm certain he does. The Zulus are cattle farmers, they cannot wage a protracted war like the Xhosa tried."

"Agreed," Frank concurred. "Still, I hear Chelmsford's greatest fear is they will avoid a fight altogether. Personally, I suspect they want to finish this with a single, decisive battle just as much as we do."

A knock at the door interrupted their conversation.

"Come!" Bourne called.

The door opened with an audible creak.

A private in shirtsleeves, carrying a wooden tray with a tea pot and a pair of cups entered. "Beg your pardon," the soldier, whose name was Henry Hook, said. "I've just finished making tea for some of the lads in the hospital and thought you might want some."

"Yes, thank you, Harry."

The private set the tray down, nodded to the two colour sergeants, and left.

"Sorry I don't have anything stronger to offer you."

"Pity," Brown replied. "Looks like I'll still owe you that drink."

"You can make it up to me when you get back. And none of that cheap piss that the canteen's been trying to get rid of for the past year!"

"Yes, of course. Still, tough break for you, old boy." Thomas then accepted a cup from Bourne. "Your lot will miss out on all the action."

Frank shrugged his shoulders and took a sip off his cup. "We each have our duty to perform. Yours is to hunt down the Zulus, mine is to make certain no one walks off with our stores."

171

"Alright," Allan said quietly. "I suppose I should thank you, Henry, and Joe for standing up for me."

"You can thank us by proving our confidence well-placed," Bourne emphasised. He dismissed the corporal, and told him to return to his section.

Barely a minute after Allan left, Henry Hook returned with a pair of despatches that Lieutenant Bromhead wanted Bourne to review for him before he gave them to Major Spalding.

"Did you hear any of that, Harry?" the colour sergeant asked.

"Not a word," Hook replied flatly, both men knowing it was a lie.

Bourne snickered quietly as he took the reports. "Be glad you're non-drinker, Harry. One less thing to complicate your life."

As he stood in the rolled up opening of his tent, Lord Chelmsford crossed his arms and watched the rain come down once more. In the past few weeks, there had been enough of a downpour to cause the uMzinyathi River to swell above its banks. Such would make the crossing for the artillery, cavalry, and NNC far trickier. Most of the regular infantry would be crossing via the ponts, so there was little concern there. However, something that did trouble the GOC was what the condition of the ground would be once they crossed into Zululand.

"The roads, if you can call them that, are little more than worn waggon ruts," he stated to the ever-present Crealock.

"One can only hope the rivers and dongas aren't all flooded," the colonel replied. "Otherwise, we may have to make our own road to Ulundi."

Their attention was soon diverted to a pair of men walking towards them in the rain. The sun was now blazing through the clouds in the west, an artistic contrast to the downpour. One of the approaching men was Lieutenant Melvill, the adjutant for 1/24th. The other was unknown to them. His face was partially hidden beneath a wide-brimmed slouch hat, and he wore a blue greatcoat with tan riding breaches and tall black boots.

"Good afternoon, my lord," Melvill said with a salute. "This is Mr Norris-Newman of *The Standard*. He's here to chronicle our little adventure into Zululand."

"My credentials, my lord," the journalist said.

Crealock snatched them from his hand.

A rather eccentric and somewhat mysterious young man in his mid-twenties, Charles Norris-Newman had already led an adventurous life filled with intrigue and much secrecy. Rumour was he'd been at the Siege of Paris during the Franco-Prussian War in 1870. Four years later, he married a wealthy woman twenty years his senior, ostensibly to acquire her vast fortune. The bitter divorce and bankruptcy that followed compelled him to take up work as a journalist, wherever there was a story to be found, and for whomever was willing to pay him for it.

"You have much experience in war, Mr Norris-Newman?" Crealock asked.

"Please, colonel, my friends call me 'Noggs'. And to answer your question, most recently I was with Don Carlos in Spain, as well as General Gordon in Egypt. On that particular expedition I was actually a volunteer officer. So yes, I have seen my share of warfare, sir. And I have been in Southern Africa for almost two years now."

"Good," Chelmsford said, even though something about this reporter troubled him. He decided he had best set the standard of expectations for any journalists accompanying his army immediately. "Be thorough in your observations, write everything you see, and write it well. You understand I cannot tolerate shoddy reporting, or any sort of unruly correspondence that would look poorly upon Her Majesty's soldiers."

"Rest assured, my lord, I shall be both thorough and accurate," Noggs replied. "I promise to stay clear of your men and not interfere in any way with their duties. But I will also be there with them, that the readers back home might get the most accurate and well-written account of what their armed forces are doing in Zululand." His expression denoted there were questions he wished to ask the GOC. He decided this was not the time for them. Instead, he took his leave and followed Lieutenant Melvill to where he could set up his tent.

"Hopefully Pearson and Wood will have little difficulties in making their crossings tomorrow," Crealock said, as they watched

"Tea," Richard said with a trace of irritation. "Though you could try smoking it, I suppose."

"Put it back," Brown ordered the sutler. "You made no mention of missing tea."

Stewart gruffly dropped the bag. It was futile. If they did find spirits and tobacco, there was no way to prove whether the soldiers purchased them or brought them from Fort Napier. Sergeant Major Gapp said as much to Degacher, who sent the sutler away.

"You didn't snatch any whiskey, did you?" Arthur asked quietly, as they closed their packs up.

"Of course I did," Richard replied deviously. "I gave a bottle to one of the engineers who's supposed to ferry us across. He's got the rest hidden in a sack in the river. That bastard's been charging us triple what we could purchase spirits for in the canteen, so I doubt a couple bottles is going to dent his profits much."

The transportation and logistics staff staged the wagons to be ready to move. The soldiers of the 24th found their rapt anticipation of crossing the river into Zululand tempered by utter boredom, as they stood around and waited.

"Damn it all, they could have let us sleep in a few more hours."

"Quit crying like a two-shilling whore," Sergeant Edwards chastised the grumbling private. He walked over to the men and said to Arthur, "Wilkie, all sharp-shooters will provide skirmishers to screen ahead of the column. Grab your kit and report to Corporal Bellhouse."

"See you on the other side," Arthur said to Richard, then slung his pack, donned his helmet, and grabbed his rifle.

"Don't be getting an assegai through the bollocks in the first five minutes," his friend replied.

The soft glow of the predawn gave just enough light to see by as Arthur found Bellhouse, Bill Johnson, and the rest of the company skirmishers. Every sharp-shooter section in the battalion was converging on the first pont where Colour Sergeant Wolfe of H Company waited.

"Can't see a damned thing, the air's thick as fucking soup," one of the skirmishers complained.

"Rumour has it Cetshwayo has promised to attack us, *'before the river water had dried on our feet'*," Johnson remarked.

"Where did you hear that?" Private Murphy asked.

"Over by Colonel Glyn's tent," Bill answered. "I think it was Chelmsford's ADC, Captain Parr. He sounded pretty convinced. I don't know if he believes such rumours or is just being dramatic."

"Well, it looks like we'll be the first to find out," Corporal Bellhouse said. "If I were Cetshwayo, I'd have every musket in the kingdom trained on the ponts, ready to blast us to pieces. Crammed shoulder-to-shoulder, unable to move…fuck it, even their marksmen couldn't miss."

"Thanks, John, that's real comforting," Bill said, then muttering under his breath, "Twat."

"Just for that, you get to be right up front," Bellhouse countered. "And I hope a Zulu cracks you on the knob before you even step off the pont."

The derisive banter between the corporal and lance corporal brought some much-needed humour to the nervous band of redcoats.

"As you can see," Colour Sergeant Wolfe spoke up, "the mist is insufferably thick this morning. We have no idea who or what may be waiting for us on the other side. When you step off the pont, do so quickly but carefully, forming a screen line. A Company skirmishers on the left, followed by C, H, and E. You'll be over before the sun comes up, so be sure to keep an eye out for your mates. And no fixing bayonets! You'll likely just end up sticking each other."

"Colour Sergeant, what happens if we do come into contact with the Zulus?"

"Shoot the bastards," Wolfe said, irritated by the absurd question. "You men will be the bayonet point of this invasion. Corporal Bellhouse, you and Corporal Miller of H Company will be in the centre. The entire formation will dress off you. Good luck, lads, and good hunting."

Behind them on a ridge overlooking the drift, N Battery unlimbered its six cannon in order to cover the crossing. Once the mist burned off, they would have an excellent field of fire. But for the first waves going across, there was very little the guns could do should they run into trouble. The fog clung to the men like a soggy blanket, and they could scarcely see the ponts. One soldier was grabbed from behind by the shoulder as he almost fell into the river.

The ponts themselves were flat-bottomed boats with rails along the sides, suspended by a pulley system that hung from a line of rope which spanned the river. Arthur shouldered his rifle and took a deep breath, sucking in the damp air that permeated off the water as he stepped aboard. The ever-clinging mist added to the gloom and seemed to swallow them completely. It felt as if the single pont bearing the first of Her Imperial Majesty's troops across the river was completely alone. The river at the Drift itself, swollen to chest height due to the recent rains, would be used by the mounted volunteers and the NNC. Chelmsford simply did not trust the surefootedness of the regular army redcoats, who were happy not to get soaked crossing into Zululand. Still, Corporal Bellhouse's morbid attempt at humour left every man nervous and alert. They strained their eyes for any sign of Zulus on the other side.

"Feels like bloody sardines," one soldier grumbled as they wedged in shoulder-to-shoulder, with each rank crammed against the next.

"Any fucker who breaks wind is getting a bayonet in the arse," Corporal Miller added.

Arthur leaned against the right hand rail near the front of the boat. He could only see a few feet in front of them. The only sounds came from the quiet chant of the NNC as they pulled on the ropes and the flowing of the river washing against the bottom of the pont. It was almost hypnotic, and his mind wandered. He knew he should be totally focused on the mission at hand, but his thoughts returned home. It was the middle of winter in England. Arthur wondered if they had snow during the holidays. He thought about his dearest Elisa and wondered if his pay stoppages had reached her. He envisioned her walking along the River Avon with frost clinging to the trees near the construction site of the new Shakespeare Theatre, before smiling as he realised that she may not be home at all. If his pay had reached her, with any luck she was bound for the Cape. As soon as this matter with the Zulus was sorted out, they would be together again…

He was startled when the pont suddenly ran aground on the far bank. He shook his head, his mind racing back to the present and the potentially dangerous task at hand.

I won't be seeing my dear Elisa again if complacency gets me killed, he thought to himself. He brought his rifle to port arms and leapt onto the sandy bar. The invasion of Zululand had commenced.

It would not be redcoats of the 24th who were first to land on the far bank, nor any imperial soldiers or auxiliaries for that matter. Downriver, near the spot where the Imperial Mounted Infantry and Volunteer Corps were set to wade their horses across, 'Noggs' Norris-Newman stood beneath a large palm, holding the bridle of his horse in one hand, his carbine cradled across the other. He was grateful for the mist. It shielded him from unfriendly eyes that would see a white man and skewer his guts, whether he was a soldier or not. It was a foolish act of pride, perhaps, but Noggs had seen his chance to write himself into the history books, and he took it.

He had crossed over an hour prior to the first sections of horsemen. It felt immeasurably longer. The tell-tale sounds of horses splashing in the river as they reached the bank brought relief to his face. He quickly mounted and rode towards the sound of men and horses. Captain Charlie Harford spotted him first, and the officer chuckled and shook his head.

Noggs removed his hat and waved it at him enthusiastically. "Mister Harford! Welcome to the Kingdom of the Zulus!"

Arthur and his companions knelt low in the short grass and sand near the ponts as the tried to see through the impenetrable fog. After ten minutes, when they saw no sign of the Zulus, the skirmishers advanced away from the beachhead. They soon linked up to the sharp-shooters from 2nd Battalion. The entire regiment's skirmishers formed a wide arc approximately two hundred yards from the Drift. As the line companies made their way over, along with the loud splashing and neighing of horses coming from the mounted troops, they pushed their skirmish line out further. Still no sign or sound of the Zulus. Arthur had little doubt they were there… somewhere. Perhaps nothing more than a few scouts watching their every move, but he was certain they were not alone. Soon the sun soon broke over the hills to the east, blinding them during that time of morning when an enemy would most likely launch an attack. And yet none came. Within a couple of hours the mist burned off and the sun glared down on them. Trepidation soon turned to boredom.

"Sounds like Cetshwayo's threats were exaggerated," Arthur grumbled to Lance Corporal Bill Johnson, hunkered behind a rock ten feet away.

"It's all bollocks," Bill muttered. "Perhaps the command staff thought they were being sneaky, crossing over in the middle of the night; never mind the amount of noise we all made. In the night mist none of us could see shit nor would the artillery be of any use. It's like Bellhouse said, if the Zulus were looking for a fight, they would have cut us to ribbons before we even got off the pont."

"Well they didn't, so lucky for you, you still have your knob."

"At least we're not stuck on labour details, lads," Corporal Bellhouse observed. He was one of the few who found a small shade tree to sit under.

Arthur looked back over his shoulder to the wagons being ferried across one at a time. It would prove to be a long and laborious process. The wagons could fit on the ponts, but only one at a time. The sixteen or more oxen required to pull them had to be swam across by the native voorloopers. This meant copious amounts of manpower to heave the wagons onto the ponts and then off again. There were a large number of NNC warriors, European volunteers, and imperial redcoats tasked with providing the muscle for this and other needed labour. For Arthur and his fellow sharp-shooters, boredom was the greatest adversary they faced this first day of the invasion.

The war had officially commenced. Thankfully no Zulu riflemen or skirmishers were waiting for them, though it was still proving to be a ponderously slow crossing. There was a massive backlog of logistics stores attempting to cross over and link up with the invasion force that now waited for them. The column transport officer, Captain Edward Essex, oversaw the off-loading and placement of the wagons, while Major Clery and the two battalion sergeant majors supervised the establishment of the camp.

"No chance of Harness getting his guns over today." William Degacher watched the chaos through his field glasses. Fortunately, the battalion's headquarters tent and equipment had been aboard one of the first wagons over. While Lieutenant Melvill kept the Queen's Colour safely enclosed in its protective case, there was still a lone Union flag flying next to Colonel Glyn's column headquarters.

"No matter." Melvill, too, watched the chaotic scene unfold. "The NNC battalions are across and covering the flanks. The mist is burning off so we can all see a little better." He turned his eyes to where Chelmsford and his staff were riding away to the north. "His lordship appears satisfied, as he now rides off to his meeting with Colonel Wood."

"Hmm." Degacher's attention was focused off to the right, where 2nd Battalion had crossed. "It appears my brother is not taking any chances; he's got his companies in 'receive cavalry' squares. We'd best do the same. Inform all company commanders, Mister Melvill."

"Sir." The adjutant saluted and rode off to inform his bugler to sound the order.

With most of his NNC troops scattered about on labour detail or picquets, there wasn't much for Charlie Harford to do at the moment. He happened upon Lord Chelmsford who, before departing to find the No. 4 Column, was discussing his thoughts on conducting a reconnaissance of the area with Major Dartnell of the Natal Mounted Police.

"I find the lack of knowledge about our enemy's whereabouts to be most troubling," Chelmsford said. "We have no eyes within Zululand. I have no way of gauging Cetshwayo's intentions or if he's even mustered his regiments. I need you to lead a patrol in the direction of Sihayo's kraal to the east."

"Very good, sir," the major replied.

"He is one of Cetshwayo's most senior *amakhosi*, and I suspect his lands to be well-fortified, regardless if the *impi* is assembling at Ulundi. See if you can find us some Zulus to fight, Major Dartnell. There's a good man."

The two exchanged salutes and the GOC rode off again. Dartnell spotted Harford, and his face broke into a grin. "Captain Harford, how would you fancy joining me on a little reconnaissance mission into Zululand?"

"Delighted, sir."

Within five minutes Harford was ready to ride. His carbine was kept close in its scabbard, where it could be easily accessed in an emergency. Twenty men from the Natal Mounted Police and a handful of volunteers from the Imperial Mounted Infantry accompanied the two officers.

Once beyond the picquets, the ground sloped downwards into the uMzinyathi Valley. Further on, it dipped down once more into the Batshe Valley, where the path curved to the left. Here it followed a stream towards the stronghold of Sihayo, known as kwaSogekle. The valley itself was mostly open farmland with large patches of mealie stalks growing in abundance. And yet, there were no farmers, herdsmen, or indeed any sort of people to be found.

Mounted police and infantrymen spread out and rode in echelons, covering as much ground as possible as they advanced cautiously towards kwaSogekle.

"Very strange," Dartnell said. "One would think there would be someone left here to tend their crops."

"I suspect there are, sir," Harford replied. "They likely saw us coming and have gone to ground. If the king summoned the *amabutho* to Ulundi, then Sihayo may only have a handful of warriors and caretakers to safeguard his lands."

They were now about eight miles from the crossing, and still no sign of their enemy. Then, in the distance, they heard chanting.

"It would seem the Zulus are here to welcome us after all," Harford mused. "His lordship asked us to find someone to fight, and I'd say they're just beyond that ridge, about two miles away."

It was early evening by the time Lord Chelmsford returned to Rorke's Drift. Colonel Wood's No. 4 Column crossed over into Zululand at Ncome, twenty-five miles to the north. Like the centre column, they found no sign of their adversaries. The GOC directed him to begin raiding all kraals and homesteads in the region, in an attempt to compel the northern barons to abandon their support of the king. Colonel Pearson's No. 1 Column was more than a hundred miles to the southeast, a few miles from the coast. The distance was too far for Chelmsford to observe him first-hand, but he'd directed the colonel to keep him well informed of his column's progress.

There were a few calamities throughout the day, with several NNC warriors falling into the river and sucked under by the current. Rupert Lonsdale suffered a terrible mishap when his horse became spooked by a snake and bucked him off. The commandant smashed the back of his head on a rock. His men rushed to aid him and at first thought he was dead. He was alive, but with a nasty head wound which Surgeon-Major Shepherd bandaged up for him. Despite the doctor's insistence that he be taken back to the hospital at Rorke's Drift, Lonsdale refused. He was compelled, however, to temporarily relinquish command of the 3rd NNC. Major Wilsone Black, one of the two battalion majors from 2/24th, was tasked by Colonel Glyn with assuming command of the NNC until such time as Commandant Lonsdale recovered.

Upon their return, Chelmsford and his staff officers retired to their tent, where his personal cook had some hot stew waiting for them. They were joined by Major Dartnell, who had just ridden in to camp to give his report.

"Ah, major," the GOC said as he sat down to his supper. "What news have you brought me?"

"We heard war chants and songs coming from above the Batshe Stream in the direction of kwaSokhexe, my lord," Dartnell reported. "They certainly know we're here. My guess is Sihayo intends to fight."

"I hope so, major," Chelmsford remarked. He then addressed the members of his staff. Crealock and his ADCs, along with Colonel Glyn, Major Clery, and all the battalion commanders were present. It was now known that Lieutenant Colonel Pulleine would be arriving within a week to assume command of 1/24th. In the meantime, Captain William Degacher continued to act in his stead.

"This inaction by the Zulus is troubling," Chelmsford observed. "Colonel Wood has seen no sign of them, and I suspect it will be a few days before I receive any reports from Colonel Pearson. The ferrying of our supply wagons across the river is proving to be as slow and laborious as we thought it might. I expect it will take several days before all our equipment and stores are over."

"And in the meantime," Colonel Glyn spoke up, "if Sihayo continues to elude us, what's to say he won't attack our outposts and supply convoy, once we decide to advance further into Zululand?"

Henry Degacher then added, "The Xhosa did it; quite effectively, too, I might add."

"But if he doesn't, a docile border chief does not help your political cause, my lord," Norris-Newman remarked. When the officers stared at him, he shrugged and smiled. "After all, the affair with Sihayo's sons and the boundary dispute are, to the best I can reckon, the *why* we have invaded their kingdom. Pretty hard to convince the folks in London the Zulus are a hostile threat when they don't come out to play after we've invaded their homeland."

Crealock took these remarks, coupled with the coy grin on the reporter's face, to be a grave insult to the GOC. He made ready to berate the man, when Chelmsford cut him off.

"You are quite right, Noggs." His genial smirk was a sharp contrast to Crealock's scowl. He looked to Major Dartnell. "Captain Harford accompanied you today, did he not?"

"He did, my lord. I asked him to join me since he speaks Zulu."

"And what of the chants and songs you heard? Did he say what their message was?"

Dartnell furrowed his brow. "We were still a couple miles away, and the sound was masked by the hills. All he could tell was it sounded defiant. He could not make out the exact words, yet he did say the tone was one of boldness, perhaps an attempt to goad us into attacking."

"Good," Chelmsford said. "Tomorrow we will take part of the column and render Sihayo's kraal a pile of ashes. Let he whose sons' aggression led to this war be the first to suffer the consequences."

As he finished speaking, there was an audible patter of raindrops on the roof of the tent. The general dismissed the officers to return to their own tents before the night rains worsened. He promised he would have fresh orders sent to each of them within the hour.

"Any thoughts, Crealock?" he asked his chief staff officer, after the others left.

"I think that damned reporter talks too much." His expression still showed his intense displeasure. "Excuse my language, sir, but he's a provocative shit who second-guesses every move we make. I sometimes think he wants us to fail or look foolish here. It would certainly give his readers back home a story worth devouring."

"Oh, come now," the GOC consoled. "Mr Norris-Newman is as slimy a weasel as I have ever met, but he is useful."

"Do you think that story is true? The one about him marrying that old girl for her money then going bankrupt during the rather messy divorce?"

"It would not surprise me. But it is also none of my concern. Noggs is a viper and an opportunist, but he is still and Englishman. He will report exactly what he sees, and once we give him his story about our first victory over the Zulus, the people back home will no longer question *why* we are here. They will only care that their boys are winning glory for the Empire by conquering a murderous savage. And who knows? Between your paintings and his stories, perhaps the two of you could collaborate on a book about our adventures in Zululand."

The GOC was chuckling at this last remark, and even the irritable Crealock grinned in appreciation. The one hobby that put his mind at ease was his passion for art. He had brought his sketchbooks and some water colour paints, so he could do landscapes of the country they passed through. Yet the idea of collaborating with 'Noggs' Norris-Newman made his stomach turn. With nothing left to discuss, he sat at his desk, while Chelmsford dictated the plan of attack for the morrow.

The rains were coming down harder, and Arthur clutched his blanket close. As insufferably hot as it was during the day, the nights when it rained brought cold discomfort in the form of incessant deluges. His fear on these nights was that the constant shifts in the weather, coupled with their long and exhausting days, would leave him ill with fever. He pitied the sick lads left at the Rorke's Drift hospital, and he had no intention of joining them. The poor bastards from the NNC didn't even have tents, only what they managed to scrounge together in the form of brush shelters with a soggy wool blanket to lay down on. He was further thankful not to be on picquet duty this night, as all any of them had was their greatcoats to keep the rain off.

The first day of the invasion of Zululand had begun all-too-early and ended far too late for him and his mates. Exhaustion now took hold of them. They had stayed up playing cards and smoking shag the previous night, and now the sounds of their combined snoring competed with that of the torrential rains hammering their tent. Arthur was fast asleep as soon as he closed his eyes.

Chapter XIV: Why have you come to the land of the Zulu?

kwaSogekle, Stronghold of Sihayo
12 January 1879

Natal Mounted Police (NMP)

The British army suspected most of Cetshwayo's warriors were now gathered at Ulundi, but Colonel Glyn was taking no chances when it came to assaulting the stronghold of one of the king's most loyal barons. Rather than risking his redcoats falling into an ambush, Glyn decided to allow 'Maori' Browne's 1/3rd NNC to spearhead the attack. C and H Companies from 1/24th would act in support. 2/3rd NNC, supported by four companies from 2/24th would come in from the north. Natal Mounted Police (NMP), carbineers, and other volunteer cavalry were set to swing around from the south. The remainder of their forces remained at Rorke's Drift as a ready reserve. Lord Chelmsford, Colonel Glyn, and their senior staff officers occupied a high ridge to the west. It would give them an excellent view of the coming battle.

It was now 8.00 in the morning, and Chelmsford was anxious to get the assault underway. "Mister Coghill, kindly tell Commandant Browne he may commence his attack."

"Yes, sir." Coghill snapped off a quick salute before turning his horse in the direction of Browne and 1/3rd NNC. He found them just a short ways behind the hill. Most of the NNC warriors were kneeling, eyes wide and faces full of fear. Only the iziGqoza, anxious to settle their decades-old score against their brethren Zulus, stood defiant and ready to do battle. Behind them were gathered the two companies from 1/24th. Coghill arrived just in time to hear a poignant conversation between 'Maori' Browne and Captains Younghusband and Wardell.

"Gentlemen, if I may ask a favour," Browne said. "I have three companies of iziGqoza, the only bastards of this lot worth a damn. The rest are cowardly jackals who will run when the first shot is fired. If you could keep your men in a line with bayonets fixed, they might decide facing an enemy to their front is preferable to getting spitted by friendlies from behind."

"Consider it done," Wardell replied.

Captain Younghusband added, "No one flees past the 24th."

"Much obliged, sirs." Browne turned to see Lieutenant Coghill waiting for him.

"Commandant Browne," the young officer said, "Lord Chelmsford's compliments. You may commence your attack."

"Very good, Mister Coghill." Though Browne maintained proper language, courtesies, and decorum when addressing his fellow British officers, his tone and demeanour changed immediately upon riding over to his battalion. With a few shouted orders laced with all manner of coarse profanity, the 1/3rd NNC hesitantly came to its feet. Fearing being shot in the back by his own careless men, 'Maori' had further prohibited his men from using their firearms this day.

Reginald Younghusband turned to address his company. "Designated marksmen will provide fire support from the ridge overlooking the objective. The rest will fix bayonets. If the NNC attempt to flee from battle without proper orders, you are ordered to stab them in the guts."

Kwanele had arrived at kwaSogekle a few days before, carrying just his sleeping roll and assegais. His shield and additional weapons had been left at his regimental barracks hut. As soon as the British began massing at Rorke's Drift, he returned with all haste to Ulundi to inform the king. He was now at kwaSogekle as the king's observer and, as such, was not expected to fight. Should the British attack, he was to immediately return to Ulundi and make his report directly to Cetshwayo.

Though he ordered the *amabutho* to Ulundi, he was still hoping to make a last-minute truce with the Natal government. And while the king had exempted those regiments nearest the border from rallying at the capital, Sihayo felt his duty was first to the king and took many of his warriors with him. Only a hundred or so locally mobilised volunteers now stood guard as caretakers of his stronghold. Leading them was one of Sihayo's sons, Mkhumbikazulu. A younger brother of Mehlokazulu, he was at first resentful he'd been denied the opportunity to attend the king's summons. Little did he know, he would soon have to fight for his nation and his home.

"You have over four hundred head of cattle," Kwanele observed. "Your father is placing great trust in you for their care and safety."

"My brothers all get to stand with the king," Mkhumbikazulu replied with a trace of scorn in his voice. "And I am worth no more than a mere herdsman to my father's cattle."

The two had risen early and stood atop a large rock outcropping. Volunteers were grazing the numerous cattle. Others milked the goats in their pens. There had been rains the night before and the ground was saturated, leaving many puddles. The legs of the two young warriors were wet from walking through the soaked grasses as they surveyed the scene below.

"What do you know of the British?" Mkhumbikazulu asked, knowing Kwanele had spent time on the other side of the river.

menace was made profoundly clear. Commandant Browne rode ahead of the battalion as they approached the first overwatch ridge, where Lord Chelmsford and his staff astride their mounts.

"Commandant Browne!" the GOC called to him.

'Maori' rode over and saluted sharply. "Ready to draw first blood, my lord."

"Very good, Maori. Round up any cattle you come across before assailing the heights. Under no circumstances are your riflemen to fire first. Nor are the women and children to be harmed in any way. We can't win the support of Cetshwayo's dissidents if we prove we're no better than he is."

"Very good, sir." Browne hesitated for a moment. "Understand, the iziGqoza are itching for a fight. I may not be able to stop them from going on a rampage. However, I will properly deal with any man who disobeys your lordship's orders."

It was a bit cowardly, perhaps, and could readily be taken as a slight against his own leadership abilities; yet for George Browne it was simply a matter of covering his backside should he lose control of his battalion. Brave and loyal as the iziGqoza may be, they were still cousins of the Zulus and just as prone to barbarism.

The advance continued, and soon they reached a high grass plane with the Ngedla heights clearly in view. Roaming cattle were quickly herded together. Some of the NNC warriors were all-too-eager to volunteer to lead them to the rear. The battalion continued on, eyes nervously watching every boulder, crevice, or anyplace the enemy might be hiding. A single shot rang out. The entire force halted and numerous warriors fell to their knees.

A single voice from somewhere on the heights shouted in English, *"Why have you come to the land of the Zulu?"*

Captain Duncombe took it upon himself to issue the official reply, which would echo down through history. *"We come by orders of the great white queen!"*

It was a lie, of course. No one in London, least of all Her Majesty Queen Victoria, knew their soldiers had invaded Zululand, much less sanctioned such actions. The captain, however, was completely unaware of this, and all felt his response was appropriate. Lord Chelmsford heard the exchange, and he beamed in approval.

The Zulus replied with a salvo of gunfire from the heights. Natives and Europeans alike dropped to the ground, seeking cover.

'Maori' Browne rode up on his horse, screaming in rage. "What in the bleeding fuck are you waiting for? Get on your feet and slaughter those bastards!"

The commandant then ordered the iziGqoza to press the frontal assault. The remaining companies flanked a large notch in the hillside where he suspected much of the fire was coming from. A band of Zulus soon rose up out the grass, banging their shields, with loud cries of, *"Usuthu!"* This brought the fury of their iziGqoza cousins. They viewed this as a taunting reminder of the terrible slaughter of their people more than twenty years before. Browne drew his pistol and fired a single shot at the Zulus as iziGqoza charged. Corporal Schiess, wielding a Martini-Henry rifle, urged his section on. His bayonet fixed, he too fired a single shot towards the mass of enemy warriors in the tall grass. Though not as proficient as the relentlessly trained redcoats, the burly Swiss corporal could more than hold his own when it came to bayonet fighting. He kept the long weapon protruding out front, electing not to chamber another round into the rifle for risk of shooting one of his own men in the back.

He allowed his enraged iziGqoza to take the lion's share of the fighting. Their shields clashed with the Zulu cousins, each side screaming epithets of *'imbuka...traitor!'* in their native tongues. Spears were thrust violently. Knobkerrie clubs battered against shields. The corporal thrust his bayonet into the shield of one Zulu, jerking hard and leaving the man exposed as one of the iziGqoza plunged his spear into his guts. The stricken warrior screamed in agony as Schiess wrenched his shield away. He stepped on the cowhide and pulled his bayonet free, as the frenzied brawl continued.

One of his officers, Lieutenant Purvis, continued to ride up and down the line, shouting and exalting his fighters. *"Keep pressing, lads! They're breaking!"*

"Damn it, man, they cannot understand a word you're saying," Schiess grumbled under his breath. Being one of the few who spoke any Zulu was a constant irritant to Ferdinand Schiess. There were plenty of settlers among his mates who had been in Natal far longer than he, yet few had made any effort to learn any of the local languages. Schiess, despite his lack of years, spoke fluent English, passable Dutch, and Zulu, in addition to his native Swiss-German.

After several minutes of relentless brawling, it became apparent that his lieutenant who was unable to speak to the natives was becoming the least of the corporal's worries. The battle ground to a stalemate with neither side able to break the other. With the thick undergrowth breaking up the formations on both sides, it was difficult for Schiess to see what was happening with the rest of the battalion. He glanced over his shoulder to see the companies of regular army soldiers still lurking behind them. With the NNC in the way, there was no way for them to effectively use their rifles in support of the attack. Their purpose was simply to prevent the more jittery Natal natives from running. Given the frenzy with which the iziGqoza pressed their attack, the redcoats' presence was completely wasted.

Sikhotha kaMpande

Major Wilsone Black, Lonsdale's temporary replacement, was riding back from where the 2/3rd NNC was making its advance from the south. He was accompanied by Lonsdale's staff officer, acting-Captain Charlie Harford. The lack of cohesion and discipline on the part of the Natal troops grated on Black, as did what he perceived as a lack of professionalism and competence from the European officers and NCOs. He had a passable rapport with Commandant George Browne, but Black found him wildly unpredictable, as well as a man whose stories bordered on fantasy. Because Wilsone had doubts as to Browne's tales from 'down under', he refused to call him by his nickname, 'Maori'. Only Harford, a regular army subaltern detached from the 99th Regiment, had any measure of what Black viewed as competent professionalism required of an officer.

"A far cry from leading your wing of a professional battalion," the young staff officer said, noting the exasperation on Black's face.

"A bunch of untrained natives led by amateurs who can't even speak their language," the major grumbled in his thick Scottish brogue. "What could possibly go wrong? I don't know how you deal with it, man."

They rode over to Colonel Glyn, who was now on foot and scanning the battle along with Major Clery. Lord Chelmsford was higher up on the ridge behind them, observing the advance of the two wings of the attack.

"Wilsone," Glyn said, as the major and Harford dismounted. "It would seem Commandant Browne's battalion is in a bit of a slog. See if you can sort them out."

"Aye, sir. Come on Charlie, let's have some fun!"

Black drew his pistol as he and Harford made their way past the two companies from 1/24th and into the tall grass and brush. 'Maori' was now off his horse, as was Lieutenant Purvis. The latter had been unhorsed by a flung assegai now embedded in his thigh. Purvis was lying with his back against a rock, tying a rag around his injured leg. The occasional crack of musketry from the far slope pierced the air.

"Major Black, sir." Browne quickly walked over to his acting commanding officer. His face was flushed and sweaty. "I'm trying to get some of my damned natives on the left to swing around and take the heights, but I need this bloody stalemate broken first."

"I'll take care of that, don't you worry laddie. You just keep pressing these bastards to your front." Black holstered his pistol and

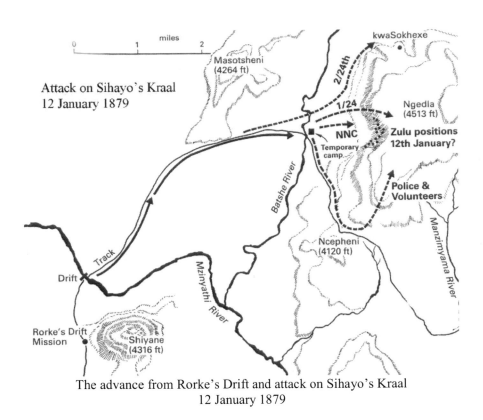

The advance from Rorke's Drift and attack on Sihayo's Kraal
12 January 1879

Chapter XV: First Blood to Us!

kwaSogekle
12 January 1879
***

As the two companies from 1/24th maintained their position barely a hundred yards behind the still-battling NNC, Captain Younghusband rode his horse up a tall slope on his left. He was quickly joined by George Wardell. Both men scanned the heights with their field glasses.

"It appears Sihayo has a lot of marksmen hiding among those rocks," Wardell said.

Reginald nodded and called down to his company. "Corporal Bellhouse! Bring up your sharp-shooters and provide cover for the NNC!"

"Sir!" The corporal turned to his gathered skirmishers. "Alright lads, you heard what the officer said. Get on my ass and follow me."

Arthur and the other skirmishers followed Bellhouse and Lance Corporal Johnson as they scrambled up the short, steep slope. Skirmishers from H Company were following suit, taking up positions to their far left.

"Controlled shots, corporal," the captain reminded him.

The NCO waved his men towards a nearby cluster of rocks. "Alright, fellas, spread out. Take up a good firing position."

Arthur's heart was racing, and not from the short sprint up the side of the hill. This was it. He was in the midst of his first battle! The targets he would be shooting at were not hanging bags of dirt, but flesh and blood men. He found a large, flat rock he hoped to establish a solid firing platform from, but when he laid his rifle across, the elevation was too high to be effective. He shifted over to a large 'V' in a lower set of boulders. "Much better," he whispered. He sat down, trying to make himself as comfortable as possible on the loose shale. Down below he could see the NNC brawling with what appeared to be no more than a few dozen Zulus, though the brush and tall grasses obscured much.

"Don't worry about what's going on down there, Wilkie." Bellhouse ran over and knelt beside him. The corporal was quickly checking each of his men, making certain they did not inadvertently fire down on their own troops. "Scan those boulders and that concave notch just across from us. Those are your left and right limits. And do not depress your weapon below the tops of those trees."

"Understood."

They could hear the sounds of gunfire, but it was impossible to see anything just yet. The smoke from the enemy's black powder muskets threatened to conceal any targets. It was early morning, and the sun shone in their faces, further impeding their vision. The far hillside was not only covered in large rocks, but tall grasses which allowed the enemy to remain mostly unseen. It was also nearly half a mile from where they sat. His assumptions were confirmed when Bellhouse gave his next order.

"Index eight hundred yards!" Arthur flipped up his rear sight and set the notched bar to the number *8* line. He then took a deep breath as the corporal shouted, *"Load!"*

The young private cleared his mind, allowing his training to take over. While loading and firing the Martini-Henry was a simple task, Arthur knew he had to keep as calm as possible, devoid of distractions, especially given the distance to their enemy and all the visual obstructions. He jerked the lever down on his weapon, opening the breach. He then took a single round out of his ready pouch and slid it into the chamber, closing the breach with a forceful slamming of the lever home.

"Three rounds, fire and adjust!"

As they were looking for individual targets, there would be no massed volleys from the sharp-shooters. In such situations, a limit was imposed to prevent rattled soldiers from wasting ammunition. The army was only a few years removed from using muzzle-loading muskets that could only fire roughly three rounds a minute. The Martini-Henry, on the other hand, could be fired as fast a soldier was able to work the breach handle. Twelve shots a minute was not unheard of. In the heat of battle, a nervous young redcoat could expend his basic load of seventy rounds in a matter of minutes.

Arthur pulled two more cartridges from his pouch and set them on a flat rock near where he rested his rifle. He took another deep breath as a smattering of shots echoed from his left. He then realized he was on the extreme right of the sections from C and H Companies.

He kept the buttstock tight in his shoulder, but he would not look down his sights until he found a target. It was maddening, hearing the sounds of enemy gunfire and not able to see them. The sun was making it particularly difficult. On this morning, he silently wished for cloud cover.

The battle below appeared to be coming to an abrupt end, with the Zulus scattering, though the sounds of musketry from the heights continued. He saw a European officer or NCO leading a group of men up the slope. There was a maze of boulders to navigate. Along one of the narrow paths Arthur spotted a Zulu marksman. The man, using an archaic black powder musket, was reloading. The young soldier could see his arm working the ramrod feverishly. Arthur kept his eyes locked on the man and brought his rifle up. Though his grip felt firm and steady, looking down his sights the front post looked as if it was wobbling badly. He tried to keep it steady on his target. He held his breath and squeezed the trigger.

The Martini-Henry erupted with a loud crack and kicked hard into his shoulder; his first shot fired against an actual enemy combatant. The smoke from the black powder was thick, though thankfully a gentle breeze quickly blew it away. It took a few seconds, but Arthur saw he had missed his target. The Zulu marksman, the European, and his NNC warriors were completely oblivious to him. He had not seen where the round struck, and had no way of knowing if it had gone short, long, or laterally off target. He cursed himself, and jerked the lever of his rifle, expending the smouldering case. Arthur reminded himself that hitting sacks hanging off a scaffold was far different than shooting at men who would not be sitting still and asking to be shot.

He chambered another round and looked down his sights. The Zulu had changed positions and was crawling on his belly, in an attempt to get a better position to fire on his assailants. They had yet to spot him as he leaned over a massive boulder. This exposed him more fully to the young soldier across the valley. Arthur took a calming breath and exhaled, his confidence returning. He paused and squeezed the trigger.

This time the wafts of smoke did not dissipate nearly as quickly. He strained his eyes and waved his hand furiously, trying to disperse the small, annoying cloud. When it did clear a few seconds later, he couldn't see the Zulu at all. The NNC troops were advancing up another side path off to the right. It looked as if the European leading them was hobbling about on one foot. Arthur panicked, wondering if he'd accidentally shot the man. It was absurd. The man wasn't even in his field of view when he'd fired. He then saw a figure slumping over backwards, his legs and lower torso wedged between the boulder and another rock. Arthur realized it was the Zulu marksman he'd been aiming for. He gasped, uncertain if he should be excited or horrified by what he had just done.

"Nice shot, Wilkie."

Focused on the task at hand, Arthur hadn't heard Sergeant Edwards walking up behind him. His section leader had a set of field glasses up to his eyes and was scanning the hillside, hoping to help the sharp-shooters find more targets. "Reload. Let's see if we can bag another one."

Arthur quickly chambered another round. The crack of a few more shots echoed from his left, but neither he nor Sergeant Edwards saw any more of the Zulus.

What Arthur would never know was that his second shot saved the European NCO, Corporal Schiess, from serious injury or death. Having routed the band of Zulus opposing them at the base of the hill, Commandant Browne had ordered the attack on the heights to continue. Schiess and his men were making their way slowly up one of the narrow paths, completely unaware of the Zulu sniper hiding among the rocks. Only when the Swiss corporal decided to take a path to the right did the hidden marksman become compelled to expose himself. Arthur's shot struck him between the neck and shoulder just as he made ready to fire. His musket discharged, the ball ricocheting off a smooth rock and smacking into the side of Schiess' foot as he raised it to climb over an outcropping.

"Hurensohn! Fick mich!" he shouted in his native tongue and stumbled about. He tripped and landed with his injured foot on a ledge of jagged rocks. Schiess swore some more. He used his rifle as a crutch for a few moments while he assessed the extent of his

injury. He had no idea of his good fortune, nor would he ever know the name of the redcoat who saved his life.

Mkhumbikazulu was finally getting his chance to prove his mettle to his father and to the king. He had dispatched half his warriors into the valley to deal with the iziGqoza. He knew the Natal warriors were cowards who would run as soon as the Zulus' treacherous cousins were dealt with. With such a small number of British redcoats supporting them, they would be trampled in the tide of their fleeing auxiliaries.

The *induna* had gone back to bring up the rest of his warriors who rallied from other nearby homesteads. Part of Sihayo's regiments, they were as duty bound as their lord's son to defend kwaSogekle. Kwanele accompanied him. When they reached the forming companies of warriors, Mkhumbikazulu turned and placed his hands on the young man's shoulders.

"This is not your battle, my friend," he said. "You must return to the king and to my father and warn them. Tell them, *'the land of the Zulu is red with soldiers'*."

Before Kwanele could respond, a series of loud cracks pierced the air as a salvo of carbines opened fire from atop a nearby ridgeline to the south. Mkhumbikazulu's body lurched as a heavy slug smashed into his back. The shot burst through his lower chest, spraying Kwanele with blood. The fatally wounded *induna's* eyes were clenched shut, his mouth wide in anguish, though he made not a sound. His twitching fists clutched at the young warrior for a few brief seconds before he collapsed to the ground.

The companies of warriors shouted in alarm and turned to face this latest threat. These assailants were all mounted on horseback. Many were in brown jackets and slouch hats, but those who fired on them wore blue frocks with spiked helmets. They were the Natal Mounted Police; not quite professional soldiers, but policemen and inspectors who happened to be able to ride. And they were proving to be better shots than the ill-disciplined settler cavalry. Only a few of the Zulus possessed firearms. As they began to return fire, half their weapons malfunctioned. The rest of their shots went wild.

There was only one thing he could do… Kwanele ran. He ran with every bit of energy he could muster and with much shame at leaving his fellow warriors to their fate. He consoled himself in that he still had a mission to perform; he had to warn to the king!

The enemy centre had fall and the right wing of the attack appeared to be underway. Colonel Glyn watched through his field glasses while the carbineers and other cavalry elements charged an unseen band of Zulus. The 2/3rd NNC and their support companies from 2/24th had yet to reach the kraal off to the north. Both battalions were bounding through the tall grass, keeping low, expecting to come into fierce contact at any moment.

"What in the bleeding piss are they waiting for?" Private Richard Lowe laughed to himself.

The rest of 1st Battalion watched with amusement as their brethren cautiously made their way towards the Kraal that, to the soldiers on the high ground, was clearly deserted.

Colour Sergeant Brown spotted another former student of his down below, Sergeant Henry Carse of 2nd Battalion's G Company. *"Carse, why the fuck are you hiding from a handful of old women?"*

A handful of equally colourful insults were hurled by soldiers looking down on what seemed to them a bit of a farce. Matters were not helped by the NNC's persistent state of panic making the redcoats think the kraal was heavily defended. Only the 2/24th's officers remained upright. While acceptable for soldiers in the ranks, ducking for cover was considered un-masculine and cowardly for officers holding the Queen's Commission. Better to risk being shot than be subjected to the endless shame that would come from the regimental mess.

Captain Younghusband called down to G Company's officer commanding, his old friend Lieutenant Pope. "Charlie, if they haven't shot you yet, you can get your men on their feet!"

William Degacher even had a few words of amusing scorn for his brother, who remained mounted on his horse, riding along the line behind his battalion. Feeling embarrassed, the men of 2/24th rose up and, with a great deal of prodding, compelled the 2/3rd NNC to storm the kraal. As expected, the huts were empty. Thus far, only a handful of women and children, unable or unwilling to flee, had been captured in one of the caves 'Maori' Browne's battalion assaulted. kwaSogekle was deserted.

It was not all laughs and larks. Charlie Harford and his NNC were now clearing out the caves where the Zulu marksmen lay hidden. At a large opening he saw several dead Zulus, their bodies shot to pieces; victims of the sharp-shooters from C and H Companies. Harford struggled to keep his pistol in hand as he and his fighters climbed over a series of large rocks. Accompanied by one of his European sergeants, he sent the rest of his men to clear out the remaining caves.

The sergeant offered his hands for Harford to step on. With a heave he reached the top of the large outcropping. He almost fell backwards into the valley below, startled by a Zulu rifleman seated behind a rock. His eyes were wide, and he was unmoving. It took the officer a moment to see the side of his head had been shot away.

"Usutu!" One of the man's companions leapt out of the cave, his musket pointed at Harford's head. The hammer fell and the percussion cap snapped, but the weapon failed to fire. Panicking, he threw the musket at Charlie before bounding back towards the cave.

Harford struggled to maintain his balance and fired his revolver at the fleeing man. The Zulu fell with a cry and crawled away from him.

Harford was highly embarrassed. He had emptied his revolver of its six shots, and only one struck his assailant, in the upper arm. He paused to reload. The action of his pistol stuck. No matter how hard he wrenched on it, he could not open the chamber. "Damn it all." He tossed the useless weapon aside.

He then crawled back to the edge, to have the European sergeant toss him a pistol. The man had panicked at seeing the Zulu. Hearing

Arthur laughed. He recalled the stash his friend had pilfered from the enraged sutler just a few days before. He was also glad he did not have sentry duty that night. Not only did his section wish to imbibe him with spirits, but Corporal Bellhouse and the sharp-shooters all came around to share a drink with their newest soldier to have spilled blood in the Queen's name. That night he slept fitfully; partially due to having partaken in too much drink, but also because he kept seeing the face of the slain Zulu. Part of him hoped that, should he have to kill again, it would become easier. At the same time the very thought terrified him. He then decided he would rather accept the pain, than become an emotionless shell of a man. He owed it to himself as well as Elisa.

In addition to the two wounded Zulus Chelmsford sent back to Rorke's Drift with their own casualties, they had captured a number of women and children. One of the women claimed to be a wife of Sihayo. Several huts had contained a large number of assegai and twenty or so muskets. These were in very poor condition, though there was a substantial amount of ammunition and powder. Most importantly, at least in terms of capturing Sihayo's wealth, were the four hundred cattle and numerous goats and other farm animals.

That evening at the officers' mess the GOC was feeling somewhat celebratory. He invited the battalion commanders who'd taken part in the fighting to dine with him. Rupert Lonsdale was still recovering from his head injury, so Wilsone Black appeared on his behalf. Though the mess was very austere by officer standards, Chelmsford brought several bottles of his best claret, and he decided this was the time to break open one of them. The officers filled their cups and stood as the GOC raised his in salute.

"Well done, gentlemen. A toast, 'First blood' to Her Majesty's finest!"

"A pity Sihayo was nowhere to be found," 'Maori' Browne grumbled. "I hear he is one of Cetshwayo's personal favourites. Not to mention his sons caused this war."

"Great work from your sharp-shooters today," Black said, raising his cup to William Degacher.

"Still have to admire their pluck," the usually snarky Crealock stated in a rare show of admiration towards their foe. "They fought with great courage; can't take that from them. Perhaps after this little scrap, Cetshwayo will feel a greater sense of urgency to press the issue with us in a more decisive engagement."

"One can only hope," Chelmsford remarked. "One can only hope."

Chapter XVI: Call to War

Ulundi, the Royal Kraal of Cetshwayo
13 January 1879

Prince Dabulamanzi kaMpande

Kwanele returned to Ulundi as fast as he was able. Though he had not stayed long after he saw Sihayo's son, Mkhumbikazulu, killed by an enemy mounted policeman, he knew the issue was never in doubt. The caretakers left at kwaSogekle amounted to not even half a regiment. They had been terribly outnumbered by the warriors from Natal and the iziGqoza, let alone the redcoats and their rapid-fire rifles. As much as Kwanele wished to fight, it had not been his duty this day. He and a score of other young men had been dispatched by the king to various strongholds and places of importance with the purpose of gathering intelligence about the invaders.

The young warrior ran all through the night and into the next day, stopping only briefly at various streams to quench his parched thirst. He had not eaten since the previous morning, yet his fierce sense of duty gave him the strength that hunger threatened to sap from him. By midmorning he arrived at the king's royal kraal, a vast complex consisting of over a thousand huts.

214

This was the home to thousands of Cetshwayo's relatives, servants, and retainers, along with tens-of-thousands of cattle and other livestock.

Since dawn there had been an ongoing meeting between king and court that was becoming extremely tense. There were calls for Mehlokazulu to be handed over to the British, whilst others demanded Cetshwayo condemn Sihayo for failing to control his loyal, albeit misguided sons. And still others, such as the king's younger and more hot-headed brother, Dabulamanzi, urged them instead to take the initiative and strike at the British first.

"The White Queen has betrayed us!" the prince stated emphatically. "Her soldiers will see our kingdom left in ruins and our people killed or destitute. We must drive them from our lands by the blades of our spears!"

Among the king's fiercest generals were the *amakhosi* Mnyamana kaNgqengele of the Buthelezi, and Ntshingwayo kaMahole. Both men had counselled prudence, as well as making preliminary preparations for war. Mnyamana, who served as the king's *induna 'nkulu*, or prime minister, remembered well the horrific losses their nation suffered during Dingane's war against the Boers nearly fifty years earlier. He was naturally anxious to avoid another such disaster.

At nearly seventy years of age, Ntshingwayo was the oldest member of the king's council, and arguably his most trusted advisor. Besides Mnyamana, who was of similar age, he was the only man at court who could remember the power, majesty, and at times sheer terror that came during the reign of the semi-divine Shaka. Ntshingwayo had served in Shaka's *amabutho* and was one of the few who witnessed the Zulu Kingdom's rise to power and its gradual decline. He had been an unwavering ally of Shaka's nephew, Cetshwayo, even during the bloody days of civil war between the sons of Mpande. And despite his many years and rotund belly, Ntshingwayo could still run with even the fleet-footed younger regiments. It was he who would lead the king's army should war with the British come.

"I fear, *Ndabazitha*, that no amount of placating will satisfy the British," the old councillor said slowly. "And while I believe the actions of Sihayo's sons were foolish and provocative, they were done out of love and loyalty towards their father. You have already offered much in cattle to compensate the British for the incursion. Whatever they may say, they care nothing for the unfaithful wives who were slain."

"You see, my brother," Dabulamanzi added, with more enthusiasm than the king cared for. "Even the wisest of our elders believes we should take the war to the British."

"Those were not my words, my prince," Ntshingwayo corrected gently. He addressed the king once more. "While I fear that war may be inevitable, *Ndabazitha*, we must make certain we are on the side of right."

"Agreed," Mnyamana spoke up. "If the white soldiers attack our kingdom, they must be driven from it 'by the points of our spears', as our prince so persuasively stated. But we must not cross the uMzinyathi River. Let the White Queen see that we only wish to protect that which is ours. Let her see we have no quarrel with her empire except that which they bring to our kingdom."

Dabulamanzi was clearly unimpressed by the generals' words of caution. For weeks he had been urging his brother to allow him to launch a raid into Natal to sack the white settlements and the trading post that had once belonged to their friend, Jim Rorke. The prince emphasised time and again that, since the coming of the white missionaries who wished to usurp the Zulu traditions with their own god, Rorke's old homestead had become a bastion of wickedness. Their own spies told them in recent days that the grounds around the drift were now covered in redcoats.

As he listened to his brother and his councillors, Cetshwayo contemplated how best to save his kingdom and people. Most of the dissidents who called for appeasement had returned to their homes during the previous two months, reluctantly accepting that war was becoming more probable, and they had to ready their regiments for the royal muster. Chief among these was Cetshwayo's erstwhile kinsman, Prince Hamu, who many rightly suspected was collaborating with the British.

The large force of redcoats and their Natal auxiliaries at Rorke's Drift were the most immediate threat. Scouts reported two more imperial columns; one in the north, and the other in the south. The northern column's intentions remained unclear, but it appeared the southern column was headed for Eshowe, a former kraal established

216

by Cetshwayo and now an abandoned mission station. Plans had to be made to delay these two elements, while the bulk of his warriors dealt with the main force at Rorke's Drift. If he could defeat them, it would drive a wedge between the British forces while destroying their arrogant sense of invincibility.

"We will make all preparations for war," the king said at last. "But we will not strike until the British give us no other option. The delay in receiving their ultimatum gave us little time. And as their terms are completely untenable, it is with a heavy heart that I must prepare our warriors to face our old friends in battle. But we cannot fight all the British forces at once. We simply do not have the warriors necessary, for their firepower is savage. It will take cunning, superior tactics, and far greater numbers to defeat them. We will send a few regiments to the north and south. These will harass their forces in those regions and prevent them from joining with their centre column. We will then destroy them, one by one."

The meeting was disrupted by a slew of anxious voices coming from the western gate to the royal kraal, announcing the return of one of the 'Eyes of the King'. Cetshwayo recognized the young warrior. His face was covered in sweat, and he was out of breath, having ran with almost no rest for more than a day.

"My king," Kwanele said, dropping to his knees, bowing his head low and holding his hands up towards his face in reverence. "I bring terrible news from kwaSogekle."

Sihayo's eyes widened. The other councillors shifted uneasily. Only Dabulamanzi and the king's other brothers remained standing.

"What news from the stronghold of our loyal friend?" Cetshwayo asked, with the emphasis on his undying support for his favourite courtier.

"Forgive me, *Ndabazitha*, but kwaSogekle burns," Kwanele answered.

"And what of my son?" the baron asked, fearing the worst.

The young man shook his head sadly. "I am sorry, but Mkhumbikazulu is dead, along with many of your warriors. They died bravely, *inkosi*, as true sons of Zulu."

Sihayo lowered his head and closed his eyes. His youngest son had yearned to fight for his king and nation. Now he was dead, having given his life in a futile effort to save his father's homestead.

The king leaned over and placed a consoling hand on his friends' shoulder.

"I grieve with you," Cetshwayo said quietly. He turned to his senior generals. "Assemble the *amabutho*."

For a society with no need for roads, where only a few of the wealthier nobles even had horses and messages were conveyed on foot, the Zulus were adept at disseminating the king's directives with astonishing speed. Signal horns and the shouts of men at the tops of hills relayed the general alarm that the nation was now at war. Runners with specific instructions from Cetshwayo made their way with all haste to the *amakhosi*.

It was, coincidentally, near the time of the *amakhosi* ceremonies that ushered in the harvest, when all regiments of the *amabutho* would assemble at the capital. This time, however, the king's regiments would be leaving all ceremonial dancing dress and regalia at home. Far from being a mustering of the younger, unmarried regiments who served the king during the harvest, this call-to-arms was sent to even those older, married men who were only summoned during times of extreme duress. Even the oldest regiments that made up the Undi Corps, men all in their forties and fifties, were ordered to assemble. Cetshwayo shared a knowing glance with Ntshingwayo. Each man silently acknowledged this was the gravest crisis ever faced by the Zulu people.

The rains had passed for the time being. Arthur sat on a camp stool, whose legs sank two inches into the mud, and continued to ceaselessly oil and wipe down his rifle, ever concerned about rust pitting.

"I'm glad to see you appreciate that your weapon is your life," Private Bray said as he joined him outside their tent.

The two had only spoken sporadically since crossing the uMzinyathi two days before, and the young soldier was glad for his company. Bray had become like an older brother to him; something Arthur missed since his own brother left for London eight years ago.

"It's not just for the officers' inspections," Arthur concurred, checking the breach action. He picked up his ammunition pouch and pulled out a battered and crimped bullet. "I am concerned about these rounds they issue us. This rolled foil is shit! If it gets too beat up or crimped it won't seat properly in the breach."

Bray took a slow drag off his pipe. "Doesn't exude confidence in their design, that the manufacturers felt the need to issue us with a musket-style ramrod so we can extract any cartridges that break inside the breach. Best you can do is take special care of your ammunition. Personally, I use a folded rag within my ready pouch and place the rounds on each layer. Keeps them from rattling about so much."

"Good idea. You know, at The Depot they let us shoot off a few machined cartridges that were much thicker and pretty solid. No issues with those, except Sergeant Edwards says the quartermasters tell him they are too expensive for the army to issue in mass quantities."

"Aye, always the benefit to the taxpayer," the older private said, a toothy grin clutching at his pipe. "At least they don't still issue us muzzle-loading Enfields, so at least we have a leg up on the Zulus there."

"Zulu marksmen are the least of my worries," Arthur told him. "I've seen their muskets; they're garbage. And they can't hit a damned thing either. Had those been even marginally trained soldiers with Martini-Henrys defending that kraal—even with these crappy cartridges—the NNC would have been shot to pieces."

"Then we'd best not let the Zulus get their hands on any Martini-Henrys," Bray responded.

Arthur finished function checking his rifle and leaned it against a nearby stump. He paused. "Bray, there is something I've been wanting to ask you, but I'm not sure if it's appropriate."

"You can ask me anything, Wilkie. What's on your mind?"

"What happened to her?" Arthur asked, his gaze fixed on the tarnished ring on Bray's left hand.

The old private continued to wipe down his rifle, only pausing for a half-second. His expression told Arthur this was not the type of question he was expecting.

"Forgive me. I...I should not have asked you that."

"No, it's alright. You've only been in country for four months now, but I consider you a friend; more like a little brother."

Arthur smiled at the shared assessment.

Bray stopped and took a few quick puffs off his pipe. Noting the tobacco was completely burned out, he set the pipe on his pack. "Typhus. Typhus took both Jennie and our little Jane. It's been eight years now, but it feels like only yesterday. Jane would have been a grown woman by now, and perhaps even made me a grandfather." His expression remained unchanged, though he spoke more slowly and softly. Behind the thick beard, Arthur could see the lines of a near-decade of anguish etched into Bray's face.

"Is that why you stayed with the army?"

"Part of it. I was nearing the end of my twelve year service enlistment. Jennie and I married not long after I joined the ranks, much like you and your lass. It seemed the entire battalion was a bunch of young bachelors back then, and so the colonel didn't mind giving the old regulations a slight overlooking. Most everyone I knew from those days is long gone. I know of one man, William Jones in B Company of 2nd Battalion, who's been in the ranks almost as long as me. Sergeant Edwards was a young lad then; hell he still is to me. He'd just gotten his corporal chevrons around the time I lost my family." He took a deep breath. "And now you know."

"I am sorry. I regret bringing back any painful memories."

"Not an hour passes that I don't think of my Jennie and little Jane. You've not brought back any memories. They have never left me. If you wonder why you don't see me shed any tears, it's because I have none left."

They sat in silence for some time before Arthur decided to take a walk down to the river. He always reckoned something must have happened to Mrs Bray, yet hearing his friend's story broke his heart. He remained stoic, though he could not help but wonder what would happen if he were to lose Elisa. Jason and Jennie Bray had been married for at least ten years, possibly more. And to lose his only child as well, Arthur could not begin to comprehend the magnitude of his loss. He wondered if Elisa coming to Natal was such a good idea after all.

The weeks aboard the HMS Tyne had been gruellingly tedious for Elisa Wilkinson and Eleanor Brown, contrasted sharply by their rather harrowing disembarkation at Durban. The seas were rough and a torrential downpour pummelled the young women with sheets of rain. Two sailors helped with their baggage, thankful that the ladies had travelled light. Before leaving Stratford, Eleanor had emphasised numerous times to Elisa to pack only the barest essentials and a few changes of clothes.

The wicker basket lowering them down to the lighter had been blown against the side of the ship repeatedly during its decent, and Elisa was certain her arms and bottom would soon be covered in bruises. They practically fell onto the floor of the barge and clung on to both the sides and to each other as it lurched towards the distant shore. As the lighter slammed against the side of the jetty, with the group of sailors helping them off, all they wanted was to find some shelter from the seemingly endless deluge. The jetty was slippery and Elisa fell hard onto her knees, biting the inside of her cheek as she stifled a yell. Eleanor helped her up and they walked with an arm around each other's shoulders as they sought the cover offered by the harbour master's office.

"Well my dear," Eleanor said, breaking into a fit of laughter, once they were out of the rain. "You did say you wanted to go on an adventure."

It was late afternoon on the 13th when a pair of wagons bearing the wounded and sick arrived at Rorke's Drift. Along with Corporal Schiess and another European NCO from 1/3rd NNC were two of 'Maori' Browne's wounded iziGqoza, and about a dozen soldiers from both battalions of the 24th who had come down with a terrible fever.

Surgeon Reynolds, his three orderlies, and a handful of soldiers from B Company came to assist the invalids into the hospital. Among them was Private Henry Hook.

At twenty-eight years of age, Hook was slightly older than many of the 'short service' soldiers in the company, despite having only joined two years prior. Before then, he had spent five years with the Monmouthshire Militia. A lay preacher and teetotaller, he was regarded as an excellent cook by his mates and was known for his sense of compassion.

"Private Hook." The soldier turned to see Major Spalding walking over to check on the patients being loaded onto stretchers.

"Sir?"

"Be a good man and brew these lads some tea," Spalding directed. "Also see about getting them something to eat. Most of them have not had a meal since yesterday."

"Very good, sir." Hook returned to his tent where he kept his personal kettle and stash of tea.

He was joined by his friend, Private John Williams. Just back from patrol, he was curious about the commotion near the hospital.

"I heard there was a bit of a scrap yesterday," the soldier remarked. "Lucky bastards."

Williams was seven years younger than Hook, though the two had known each other for a short time in the Monmouthshire Militia before transferring to active service with the 24th. Unlike his friend, who sported a thick moustache he was able to curl on the ends, Williams' face was smooth and unable, at the moment, to grow even a trace of a proper moustache. He was self-conscious about this, especially after being accused of secretly shaving each night.

"Don't be so anxious for battle, John." Hook knew that his friend, like many of the others, was terribly disappointed to have been left behind at Rorke's Drift. Though they had seen a bit of action at the end of the Xhosa War, the highlight of that expedition had been their captain getting accidentally shot in the back by one of their mates. "Remember, all of us have our duties to perform. And right now, yours is helping me make tea and scrounge a bit of supper for those poor lads at the hospital."

They returned an hour later with sausages and mealie porridge for those who were able to eat. One of the surgeon's orderlies, Second-Corporal Francis Atwood, informed Hook there was a lone patient at the end of the hallway whose fever was far worse than the others.

"A Sergeant from G Company," Atwood noted. He then shook his head. "Poor bastard's in a bad way."

The end room had belonged to Reverend and Mrs Witt and still contained their bed. Harry quietly opened the door and with the light from the cracked window was just able to see the pale young man who was fast asleep on the Witts' bed. His heart lumped up in his throat. "Bless me. It's Robert Maxfield."

"Who is Robert Maxfield?" Williams asked.

"A young lad I used to watch after. He's about your age."

"And a sergeant already." John held up the sleeve of Maxfield's tunic with its three gold chevrons. "A real 'high flyer', just like The Kid."

'The Kid' was a nickname the men in the ranks had for Colour Sergeant Bourne, though he was completely unaware of it. Hook gave Williams a stern look. He found the name to be disrespectful of Bourne's position as the company's senior NCO.

"Is that," Maxfield whispered, reaching up weakly with his right hand. "Is that Harry Hook?"

"It is." Hook forced a smile. "It's alright now. We've brought you some food. Can you eat?"

"No," the sergeant replied, shaking his head. "No food...water, I could use some water. So hot..."

Williams helped him sit upright, while Hook poured some water into a tin cup and helped Maxfield drink. He dampened a rag and wiped down the young NCO's forehead.

Maxfield closed his eyes and forced a tired smile. "Looks like old David and Harry are looking after young Robert again."

Hook replied appreciatively, "It looks like you are the one who's been looking out for the young lads, *Sergeant* Maxfield."

"Yes...don't worry about us, Mister Pope. We can handle anything the Zulus throw at us..." He continued to toss, muttering incoherent ramblings mixed with march orders and fire commands.

"He's in a bad spot," Williams said, sympathetically.

"I'll look after him," Hook asserted. "His brother, David, and I were mates back in school, and for a while in the militia before he joined the 99th Regiment. Robert used to follow us everywhere, annoying little shit that he was. All he ever wanted to do was live up to us. I pray this fever does not take him. He needs to know just how damned proud of him I am."

Chapter XVII: A Severe Rebuke and a Long Pause

Sandspruit, near Middle Drift
13 January 1879

Captain George Shepstone
Natal Native Horse (NNH)

The day following the razing of Sihayo's Kraal was one of rest for No. 3 Column. The wounded and sick, including Corporal Schiess, had departed by wagon for the hospital at Rorke's Drift. While the centre column took a day to catch its breath, for Lieutenant Colonel Anthony Durnford and the No. 2 Column the wait for definitive orders was maddening. Lord Chelmsford had changed his mind several times already as to what he wanted the column doing, which added to Durnford's frustration.

"We're on the wrong side of the river," he grumbled to one of his staff officers, Captain George Shepstone, as he gazed across the uMzinyathi with his field glasses.

A son of Sir Theophilus Shepstone, George had 'officially' been appointed as Durnford's Political Agent. And while the younger Shepstone had a strong rapport with his column commander, having stood by him during and after the disaster at Bushman's Pass, his father did not share the sentiment. Indeed, Sir Theophilus had complained vehemently to Sir Henry Bartle-Frere, stating he felt a posting to Lieutenant Colonel Durnford's staff was as good as a death sentence. His son, however, was loyal to his commanding officer, and the two had formed as much of a friendship as their differences in rank allowed. There were other officers within the column who had served with Anthony in the past and were also stalwartly loyal. Among these was Lieutenant Charlie Raw, a former carbineer who now commanded a troop within the renowned indigenous cavalry, *Zikhali's Horse*. His fellow troop commander, Lieutenant James Roberts, was another reliable officer Durnford could depend upon.

"The centre column has drawn first blood, sir," Captain Shepstone remarked offhandedly. Word spread quickly of the attack on Sihayo's kraal. Shepstone reckoned everyone in Natal and Zululand knew about the stronghold's destruction.

"A minor skirmish," Durnford countered. "Meanwhile, his lordship is advancing completely blind, while we sit here doing little more than watching the Zulu's habitat."

"Rider approaching, sir!" one of his pickets shouted from his far right.

Durnford turned his gaze. An African man dressed in a brown European frock and trousers, with a slouch hat atop his head, rode at great speed towards them. Anthony, with George following, quickly made his way down to meet this man. Several of his troopers had placed themselves on either side of the man, weapons ready, as he dismounted.

"Stand easy, men," Durnford told them. He recognized the rider as a member of the parish across the river belonging to Bishop Hans Schreuder.

"God greet you, colonel," the man said in heavily accented English.

"And to you," Durnford replied. "What news from our friend, the bishop?"

"He sends God's blessings and asked me to give you this urgent message." The rider produced a letter, which Durnford quickly tore open.

My dear Colonel,

It is with great urgency that I write to inform you that three Zulu amabutho have been spotted by my scouts approaching the Middle Drift. They intend to launch a raid, in reprisal for the recent attack by your forces on Sihayo's kraal.

Though recent developments have compelled me to withdraw back to Natal from my parish in Zululand, I still have a number of agents, foremost being Mr Eustace Fannin, whose acquaintance you may be aware of. He assures me that several thousand Zulus are waiting to attack across the Thukela. I urge you to act quickly to stop this.

Your loyal friend and brother in Christ,

Hans Schreuder

"An important piece of intelligence, sir," Shepstone noted when Durnford shared the letter with him.

"And yet our column is scattered across miles of open territory between here and d'Almaine," the colonel muttered.

"Can you trust this Bishop Schreuder, sir?"

"He has a vast knowledge of Zulu affairs. And his information makes sense, since our column has left Middle Drift only lightly defended." He scanned across the way once more with his field glasses. "The rains have flooded the riverbanks. I'm not certain if the drift is even passable for the Zulus. Still, best not take any chances."

"Agreed, sir," Shepstone concurred. "Shall I send word to the rest of the column?"

"Yes. All troops, including Major Russell and the rocket battery, are to rally at Middle Drift with all possible haste. We must act quickly, if we are going to prevent a Zulu counter-invasion."

The following night, with his scattered forces coming together, Lieutenant Colonel Durnford was anxious to get his column into the fight. Cavalry troops, as well as the NNC battalions and the rocket battery, had rushed as fast as they were able to Middle Drift. The rocket battery, being the slowest moving with their soldiers on foot and only mules to carry their equipment, were the last to arrive near sundown.

Durnford had heard no other reports regarding the movement of Zulu regiments towards Middle Drift; however, he was ready to find and pursue any elements that may be looking to raid Natal. Though the recent rains had caused the Thukela and uMzinyathi Rivers to swell, the drift was still fordable for both cavalry and infantry. And if his men could ford it, so too could the Zulus. This made the bishop's warning about a possible Zulu incursion seem all the more plausible.

At dusk his officers gathered under the glow of a handful of oil lamps.

"Gentlemen," Durnford said. "Ready your men. We advance into the Thukela Valley in one hour."

"Beg your pardon, sir, but there's a rider approaching," Captain Shepstone observed.

It was Lieutenant William Vereker, an NNC officer both Chelmsford and Durnford knew personally. He had ridden at great speed and his horse was completely spent as he jumped from the saddle. "Colonel Durnford, Thank heavens I found you on this side of the river."

"You're just in time, William," Durnford replied. "You can accompany my column across the river and report our successful crossing to his lordship."

"About that." His face was visibly grim, even in the pale lamp light. He handed a note to Anthony.

One of his staff officers, Captain Dymes, had the misfortune of standing next to the colonel and was able to read word-for-word the biting rebuke that came from the GOC:

Chapter XVIII: Warriors of the King

kwaNodwengo, near Ulundi
15 January 1879

Ntshingwayo kaMahole
Commander-in-Chief of the Zulu army

Due to the massive size of this kingdom-wide muster, Cetshwayo ordered his regiments to rally on a large plain called kwaNodwengo near Ulundi. Originally the site of the royal kraal of his father, Mpande, the king's predecessor was also buried there. Whatever differences had existed between father and son in life, surely the spirit of Mpande would not allow his great kingdom to fall to a foreign invader just to spite his son.

"The spirits of my father and ancestors weep," Cetshwayo said to an assembly of *amakhosi* and other Zulu elders. "My uncle, the great Shaka, was first among our people to befriend the whites. He called their King George, *brother*. My father and I have since referred to George's descendant, Queen Victoria, as *sister*. Yet the armies of my white sister have trampled our lands and murdered our people. And so it is here, on the plains enriched by the transcended spirit of my father, that our armies prepare for war."

Those regiments closest to the royal kraal had already arrived; thousands of men, running in step, spears and clubs beating a cadence against their shields. They chanted in time with their rapid footfalls or sang songs of victory and praise of their valiant ancestors. Kwanele's own regiment, the uNokhenke, was among the first to arrive. Their distinctive cowhide shields were white and black with occasional brown spots. These were young men who had only seen twenty harvests, and were among the most eager to bloody their spears in the bellies of the redcoats. Too young to have witnessed much of their king's prior friendship with the British, there was no remorse or sorrow to be felt, only pride…and aggression.

As soon as he had re-joined his company, Kwanele became something of a hero to his companions. He was the only one who had taken part in any sort of action thus far against the British. He had yet to bloody his spear, but his friends questioned him constantly about his exploits and what he had seen regarding the white soldiers in red jackets.

"Perhaps they will name you an *induna*," some of his friends said earnestly.

Regiments and their higher corps were all led by much older, experienced warriors appointed by the king and his councillors. The junior *induna* who led the companies of roughly a hundred men each were elected by their peers. Kwanele had never considered such a possibility before. It was a position of great pride and even greater responsibility.

One of their most senior *inkosi* was the venerable warrior, Mkhosana kaMvundlana. Both the uNokhenke and uKhandempemvu regiments fell under his command. A hardened warrior in his mid-forties, he was a magnificent specimen of fighting man. His muscles were large and limber, his stomach devoid of the common 'belly fat' seen amongst some of his peers. As an *inkosi*, he was one of few who wore more elaborate ceremonial garb than the individual warriors. On this particular day he had donned a leopard skin collar with long crane feathers tucked into his otter skin headband. He carried the white shield of his age *ibutho*, the iNdlondlo regiment. Such was his reputation, only Ntshingwayo and King Cetshwayo commanded more respect from the younger *amabutho*.

"That is exactly what I expect. And I suspect our reserves will be needed before the fighting is done. Do not forget, my brother, that your own *ibutho* is part of the Undi Corps. You are a prince of this kingdom, and I expect you to fight with the valour and honour worthy of our ancestors. But you will also be under the charge of Ntshingwayo, our nation's greatest general. And you will follow his orders as if they were mine."

It was normally not like Cetshwayo to publicly chastise his brother. However, he knew how erratic Dabulamanzi could be. He had been a wild youth, and usually among the first in his *ibutho* to create havoc with their rivals. Their father had hoped marriage and sufficient years would mature him, but the last years of Mpande's life were consumed by his rivalry with his co-ruler and heir apparent, Cetshwayo. He'd had little energy to focus on his younger sons. Dabulamanzi was fast approaching forty and still as unruly as he'd been in his youth. As brother of the king, he was entitled to serve at a high level of command, yet Cetshwayo knew he still needed a firm hand to guide him, and he could think of none better than his old mentor, Ntshingwayo.

Their chief adversary, Lord Chelmsford, was concerned that, like the Xhosa, the Zulus would avoid engaging him in open battle. He knew little about the Zulu culture of aggressively taking the fight to those who threatened their way of life. Conversely, Cetshwayo's spies kept him well informed as to the size and distribution of the British columns now desecrating his kingdom. However, he understood little of their logistical difficulties, only that their supply wagons caused them to advance at a very slow and measured pace.

He also knew nothing of the political troubles that threatened Chelmsford. For all Cetshwayo knew, his white sister, Victoria, had betrayed him and unleashed her armies to conquer his people. Even if he had known that a war of delay and manoeuvre could bring the war to a relatively bloodless end, with Chelmsford being sacked by his superiors in London, it was simply not feasible. Lengthy delays to the harvest would lead the people to starve, and his armies didn't have the logistical means to fight a protracted war. And if they had, the aggressive spirit of his warriors, honed to fearsome perfection by his uncle, Shaka, would never allow such cowardice in the face of an enemy who would destroy them. In the end, Cetshwayo and

Chelmsford both desired the same thing; a decisive victory and a quick end to the war.

On the morning of the 15th, Lord Chelmsford came to a decision as to how he should utilise Lieutenant Colonel Durnford and No. 2 Column. He was also feeling a touch of regret about his severe rebuking of Durnford. While he had instructed Crealock to have the staff send instructions to the commander of No. 2 Column, ordering him to cross the uMzinyathi River at Rorke's Drift, the GOC decided he had best send a personal message to Durnford. Rather than apologizing for his overreacting, Chelmsford offered Durnford a further set of instructions, stating the importance of his column in battling the local chiefs that thus far refused to abandon Cetshwayo. He reckoned giving Durnford an active role in this campaign and a sense of purpose would suffice for an apology. As usual, he kept his instructions vague, telling him to cross at Rorke's Drift and wait for additional orders. Either way, Anthony Durnford was at last getting into the fight.

When the message reached No. 2 Column, Lieutenant Colonel Durnford's glum demeanour quickly changed to one of high spirits. He knew Chelmsford well enough to understand that while he would likely never receive an actual apology from him, his message had implied as much, especially when the GOC stressed Durnford's personal importance to the war effort and his column. No. 3 Column was held up near Rorke's Drift, unable to advance much further than crossing the river; their raid upon Sihayo's stronghold notwithstanding. It seemed Chelmsford finally realised he would need Durnford, especially his large force of cavalry, as more than a border guard.

Two of his battalions from the NNC were to remain behind to guard the crossings into Natal, in case Cetshwayo did try to send some of his regiments across the river. On the morning of 16 January, Durnford prepared to depart with his strongest battalion from 1st NNC, all of his cavalry, the ever-loyal Basutos and Zikhali's Horse, along with Major Russell and the rocket battery.

For Private James Trainer and his mates, word that they would be crossing into Zululand in the next few days was the first bit of good news they'd had since before the invasion. For infantrymen who had trained for musketry and bayonet fighting, lugging around small iron troughs and bundles of Hale rockets was about as tedious an assignment as any could fathom. Even Bombardier Goff, the lone Royal Artillery NCO of the small detachment, found the rockets to be little more than a loud and cumbersome noisemaker. Only Brevet Major Francis Russell seemed to have any faith at all in the erratic and unpredictable rockets.

"Terrify the Zulus it will," he said repeatedly during drills. "This 'white magic' will bring them to their knees."

"The Zulus have faced our cannon," Bombardier Goff said later. "They will see these fireworks fly and laugh themselves silly. We're just as likely to spook the column's horses as we are the Zulus."

Goff had previously been a crewman on a seven-pounder cannon in N Battery when it was decided by the command staff that they would raise a battery of rockets. When Major Russel requested an NCO to assist him, Goff's name was volunteered. Theirs was a tiny detachment that could scarcely be called a battery. Besides the bombardier and Major Russell, were the eight 'volunteers' from 1/24th.

"I wonder how the rest of our boys are getting on," Trainer said that night as he and Harry Grant took their turn at sentry duty. "Think any of them got to see any action yet?"

"Even if they have, no one's bound to tell us shit," Grant remarked. "Those damned apes in the NNC were the ones to sack the enemy kraal, or so I hear. If our mates have fired any shots at the Zulu, then they are the fortunate ones."

"If we're lucky, perhaps we'll get to pot someone with our rifles once we set off all of Major Russell's rockets."

"You and I weren't exactly the best shots in the company. How else do you think we got 'volunteered' for this? I sure as bleeding hell didn't ask for it. Unless by some miracle our skills have improved since our last go at the range, we'll likely fare no better with our rifles than we will those damned rockets."

James did not like being reminded of his shortcomings. Every British soldier took great pride in his skills at musketry. He shot well enough during recruit training, yet for reasons he could not explain

238

he had struggled greatly during their qualification at the range near Fort Napier. From the standing position he'd had a devil of a time hitting even the two hundred yard target. While his skills with the bayonet were as good, if not better, than most of his mates, the intent was to not let the enemy, especially a shield and spear wielding Zulu, get that close.

"For the best, I suppose," he muttered. He gazed upon the moonlight dancing off the river below and shook his head. "Here's wish best of luck to our mates in the 24th. May they be Fortune's bastards, the lot of them!"

The return of the summer rains was making progress slow and nightmarish for the No. 3 Column. The blazing sun glared down on them throughout much of the day, but did little to dissipate the aftereffects of the constant downpours. It was now the sixth day since the invasion was launched into Zululand and the centre column had scarcely advanced any further than just across the river, still within full view of the garrison at Rorke's Drift.

"These storms are the devil," Crealock bickered as he, Chelmsford, and some of the other staff officers observed a stretch of the wagon track leading through the Batshe Valley. "It would save us a lot of bother if the Zulus would come down and attack us, take a good lashing, and then sue for peace."

The GOC dismounted and walked along a sodden stretch of track. The water was up to his ankles, and the ground squishy and soft. He could only guess how far their heavy wagons would sink when they tried to cross. The heat of summer and the rains made the air muggy, thick, and festering with flies. It was no wonder some of their men had come down with terrible fevers. Soldiers from the temperate climate of England, Wales, Scotland, and Ireland were simply not suited for the constant onslaught of heat and high humidity. Even those who'd been battling in the African bush the last few years were feeling the full misery of the sudden return of the summer rains.

"How goes our resupply efforts?" Chelmsford asked his staff, deciding to forgo the issue of the saturated landscape for the moment.

"It's seventy miles from the depot at Greytown to Rorke's Drift," Lieutenant Coghill answered. "As you know, my lord, we've been making preparations for weeks trying to store sufficient food, ammunition, and other supplies at Helpmekaar and Rorke's Drift. There just aren't enough wagons and oxen."

"And what of the No. 5 Field Company, Royal Engineers?" the GOC asked. "They are about the only reinforcements Whitehall has been willing to send. I would think they'd be here by now."

"They landed at Durban a week ago," Crealock answered. "But it would seem they, too, have been delayed by the inclement weather. The Thukela Valley is as much a mud-hole as this place."

"A week," Chelmsford said quietly, as he remounted his horse. "It will be at least another week until we can advance again. Colonel Crealock, send word to the No. 5 Field Company. I want an officer and half a dozen men detached here with all possible speed. Commandant Lonsdale's NNC will provide the labour force necessary to begin road repairs here to make them passable for our wagons. Colonel Glyn, detach as many volunteers as you can muster from the colonial units. Have them work the ponts and begin ferrying supplies across the river once they arrive at Rorke's Drift."

"Very good, sir," Glyn replied. "It will give them something to do. And for our regular infantry and artillery?"

"Nothing they can do at the moment except watch, wait, and hope like Colonel Crealock, that the Zulus decide to pay us a visit."

Once back at his tent, Lord Chelmsford penned a despatch to the High Commissioner, keeping him abreast of the column's issues. Reports received from Colonel Wood and Colonel Pearson said their columns were suffering the same issues with the weather, terrain, and logistics. Thus far, neither had seen any more of the Zulus than they had.

15 January 1879
My Dear Sir Henry,

The country is in a terrible state from the rain, and I do not know how we shall manage to get our wagons across the valley near Sihayo's Kraal. I do not see a chance of moving forward in under a week, as our supplies are not yet sufficient to warrant a forward movement, and we have not yet put our road in working order.

I am sending in an application for some colonial men skilled in pont work. We are at present working our pont and raft with handymen taken from amongst the Europeans of the Natal Native Contingent – these men, however, ought to go forward with the column as their services cannot be spared.

Chelmsford

With no engineers currently in the column, it fell upon the NNC to provide the labour force necessary to make the roads passable for the supply trains. 'Maori' Browne had to chastise his European officers and NCOs more than once for their constant bickering. All had complained, sometimes rather voraciously, that they came to fight the Zulus, not labour with spades in the mud under the hot sun and be assailed by swarms of flies.

"We draw first blood for the empire, and they reward us with a bunch of spades and manual labour."

Chapter XIX: Surrender of the Inkosi

The wagon track, east of Rorke's Drift
16 January 1879

Lieutenant Colonel John North Crealock

In addition to being tedious, miserable, and backbreaking work, it was hazardous for the NNC to be conducting road repairs away from the main camp. Lieutenant Colonel Degacher detached his other battalion major, William Dunbar, with four companies from 2/24th to provide security for the detail. Their safety concerns did not trouble the GOC. He had dispatched a cavalry contingent towards Siphezi Mountain, eighteen miles away. They reported the countryside and all the homesteads they had run across were deserted.

"And the road will not be made passable without considerable work," Lieutenant Colonel Crealock grumbled as he read over the report.

Rather than feeling greater irritation at this news, Chelmsford was in a somewhat contented mood this particular morning. He produced a report he had just received from the No. 4 Column, currently operating about twenty-five miles to the north and their left.

"No matter. Colonel Wood informs me they have been actively harassing the Zulu kraals and homesteads along the reaches of the Ncome River. And the Zulu *impi* still does nothing. If we have to advance in stages, compelling the local *amakhosi* to either surrender or face annihilation, then so be it."

Chelmsford then summoned the senior staff officers from the column to review his intentions. He had a rough map of the region acquired from a local trader a few months before. The senior cavalry officer, Lieutenant Colonel Russell, had made numerous sketches and notes based on what his detachment had spotted. Also present was the reporter from *The Standard*, 'Noggs' Norris-Newman.

"Gentlemen," the GOC said. "It would seem the terrain and weather are posing a greater threat to us than the Zulu. Though Colonel Pearson and the No. 1 Column to the south are having the same difficulties as us, Colonel Wood's No. 4 Column to the north has done a splendid job of harassing the enemy. Sadly, they have not taken the bait. It would seem they are waiting for us to come to them. Gather around, please." He ran his riding crop along a jagged line denoting the wagon track. "Our first stop shall be here at this hill...I cannot read the name, as the handwriting on here is terrible."

"It's called *Isandlwana*, my lord," Norris-Newman spoke up.

"*Isandlwana*," Colonel Glyn repeated, sounding the name out slowly.

"Yes, well," the GOC continued, "we shall first advance to Isandlwana, where there is plenty of forage for the horses and draught animals, as well as ample fresh water streams. After we establish a temporary staging point, we shall make our way east towards Siphezi Hill. From there we will reassess the next leg of our journey towards the king's kraal at Ulundi. Any *amakhosi* who wishes to surrender will be welcomed. Those who do not will have their cattle confiscated and their kraals razed to the ground. And now, gentlemen, if you will excuse me, I shall go check on the progress our natives are making on the road. I intend to be back in two hours' time with a healthy appetite for breakfast."

The GOC and a his select staff officers found the NNC labouring with shovel and pickaxe to level the road, fill in the flooded gaps, and make it passable for the column. Meanwhile, Major Dunbar and his four companies from 2/24th chopped away brush and established strongpoints to defend against possible attacks. One of the biggest men in the entire regiment, William Dunbar was both tall and thick in the chest, shoulders, and arms. A veteran of the Crimean War and Indian Mutiny, he had a reputation for being absolutely fearless in battle. With much attention, Lord Chelmsford listened when Major Dunbar expressed his consternation about the location of his camp.

"Your pardon, my lord," Dunbar said as he walked over to the GOC and his staff. "I request permission to move my companies. The terrain here is terrible. It's much too thick with brush, and we cannot establish any clear fields of fire. I ask that I be allowed to move back across the Batshe to where the ground is flat and more open."

Knowing Dunbar's fearless reputation, Chelmsford was troubled by his apprehension and turned to discuss the matter with his staff officers.

Crealock, who had designated the placement of the companies, sneered and spoke loudly and defiantly, *If Major Dunbar is afraid to stay here, we should find an officer who is not.*

Chelmsford grimaced.

The major stiffened and fought back the urge to issue a profanity-laced rebuke. Instead, he replied firmly, "If Lieutenant Colonel Crealock is volunteering to camp here, then he is welcome to the position. Now if you will excuse me, my lord, I have a camp to run. Please be advised you will have my resignation by nightfall."

The major clearly did not wish to discuss the issue further, so the GOC spurred his horse onward. He and his escorts soon left the forward camp behind. He glared at Crealock out of the corner of his eye. Despite being his favourite and most influential staff officer, this time he had gone too far. Chelmsford immensely disliked squabbles between his officers. He found it unbecoming of gentlemen who held the Queen's Commission.

The entourage continued on, and after nearly three hours of easy riding, they came upon a strangely shaped hill. Escort troopers rode ahead, conducting a thorough sweep of the hill and the large bowl that formed to the east, leading towards a series of ridges. The trail itself was difficult to see. It was little more than wagon ruts which were now overgrown with tall grasses.

"The area looks deserted, sir," the sergeant leading the escorts reported.

"Well then, how about breakfast?" Chelmsford asked. "I thought to feast when we returned to Rorke's Drift, but I am feeling a might peckish now."

The officers and their escorts finished their ride, sweeping around the southern face of the mountain. They then proceeded to have a humble breakfast, consisting mostly of canned bully beef and hard biscuits. The GOC's French chef accompanied the column, but Chelmsford's constantly being away from camp when it came time for breakfast or supper meant that Monsieur Lapara would see minimal use of his culinary skills during the expedition.

Chelmsford and his entourage sat near the nek of Isandlwana, the sun in their faces. With few trees about, there was very little shade to be had. What the position did offer was a commanding view of the valley and surrounding hills. Lieutenant Colonel Crealock thought to perhaps take out one of his sketch pads when he saw movement in the direction of a mountain known as Malakatha, several miles due south of Isandlwana. He took out his field glasses and scanned the landscape in the distance.

"Find something of interest, colonel?" Chelmsford asked, taking another small bite of bully beef.

"It looks like cattle." He continued to watch for a moment. "And people."

"Part of an enemy force?" Chelmsford stood up, his interest piqued.

"I don't think so."

"Looks to be a whole flock of migrants, sir," the sergeant from the Imperial Mounted Infantry remarked, handing the GOC his own field glasses.

"This land belongs to Sihayo's brother, Gamdana," the column's civilian interpreter, Mr Brickhill spoke up.

"They seem to be in a hurry," Chelmsford observed. "Finish up, and let's go say 'good morning' to this Gamdana."

Malakatha was nearly ten miles from Isandlwana. It was remarkable that Crealock had seen any sort of movement at all. There appeared to be about a hundred people and at least two score of cattle.

The ground between the two hills was extremely broken. It took Chelmsford and his entourage the better part of an hour to reach the party near the Ndaweni River. There were a number of military age

the army, not sitting on your backsides, hiding from an enemy who is still fifty miles from here."

Not wishing to discuss the matter further, Crealock kicked his horse into a gallop to catch up with the GOC.

Irritated, Browne turned to Captains Duncombe and Harford. "Bring in the iziGqoza and our Europeans. Have them establish defensive battle positions."

"What of the rest of the battalion?" Harford asked.

"Fuck them," Browne scoffed. "Cowardly shits will run as soon as trouble breaks, since they don't have the bayonets of the 24th sticking in their backs."

The following day, another detachment arrived at Rorke's Drift. Riding in a single engineer's wagon laden with equipment were five sappers and a driver. A single officer rode beside them on horseback. They arrived at the camp, where the tents of B Company, 2/24th and the thatched shelters of a single company from the NNC were spread out behind the hospital and commissariat storehouse. Alerted to the wagon's approach, Major Spalding went out to meet them with Lieutenant Bromhead. The wagon halted just short of the hospital, and the officer dismounted and saluted.

"Major Spalding?"

Henry nodded and returned the salute.

"Lieutenant John Chard, Royal Engineers," the officer continued. "Captain Jones' compliments, sir. The roads around Greytown are nearly impassable. When we received his lordship's directive, my light wagon was the only one that could get through the muck. At any rate, I am here to layout the fort that is to be manned by one of the companies coming up from Helpmekaar. I also hear you need work on the ponts."

"Yes, and we're glad to have you with us," Spalding replied. "This is Lieutenant Bromhead, commander of B Company. He and his men can help you and your sappers in whatever you need. If you require menial labour, we have a plethora of otherwise useless natives that we should get some work out of before they run off."

"One cannot even mention the word 'Zulu' around them without starting a panic," Bromhead added in his ever-loud voice. "Pathetic lot, these. It's no wonder they got left behind…" He stopped himself, suddenly red with embarrassment.

Spalding pretended not to notice, though Chard chuckled softly, catching Bromhead's unintended slighting of his own company, who were also left behind.

"With your permission, sir," Chard said to Spalding, "We'll set up our camp near the drift. No sense dragging our equipment through Mister Bromhead's camp every day."

"Carry on, then," Spalding said.

The two exchanged salutes and he left.

Bromhead called to one of his NCOs, "Corporal Allan! Kindly take Mister Chard and his sappers down to the drift. Show them a suitable place to set up their camp."

"Right away, sir."

While Chard's was not a glamourous job, yet one could easily argue that the Royal Engineers were as vital to the war effort as any number of infantry or cannon. Lord Chelmsford would certainly attest to that, given his column's inability to move beyond the far side of the uMzinyathi River.

Originally from Plymouth, John Chard was the middle of three sons and four daughters. His elder brother was also in the army, though the two had not seen each other in years. John had just celebrated his thirty-first birthday on 21 December and had held his commission for ten years. Unlike their counterparts in the infantry or cavalry, engineers went to specialist schools; in Chard's case, the Royal Military Academy at Woolwich. Because of their perceived superior education and skillset, they bypassed the rank of ensign / 2nd Lieutenant and were gazetted as full lieutenants upon passing out from of their schools.

Following his commissioning, Chard spent some time in Bermuda and Malta supervising the building of fortifications, though most of his tenure was spent in England. As part of the engineer reinforcements recently sent from Britain, he had been attached to No. 5 Field Company as an excess subaltern just prior to departure. Arriving in Durban on 5 January, they had now been in country for exactly two weeks. For John Chard, one assignment was as good as the next.

The infantry had a job to do, and he had his. And at that moment, his job was laying the groundwork for a new fort, while also conducting much needed repairs on the battered and worn ponts.

Lieutenant John Chard, Royal Engineers

Chapter XXI: Purified for War

kwaNodwengo near Ulundi
18 January 1879

Zulu Warriors

The *amabutho* had been arriving at the muster plain since around 8 January and was now fully assembled. Warriors from all over the Zulu Kingdom heeded Cetshwayo's call to fight for their people and their homes. These were not just ethnic Zulus, but an amalgamation of many different peoples who had served under the Zulu kings since even before Shaka. SiSwati, Mpungose, Buthelezi, Zungu, and Chube stood ready to do battle for King Cetshwayo. At least five thousand brush huts now lay clustered together, housing upwards of 30,000 fighting men. Simple shelters, they offered only scant protection from the incessant rains that pummelled both British and Zulu alike. The warriors of this growing army cared little about the discomforts of living in such a confined space, or the return of the long-dormant summer showers. At night, the landscape was lit up with thousands of campfires, which the warriors chanted and danced around.

Women were a frequent presence, even among the numerous camps of the unmarried regiments. Far from the blood-thirsty savages driven mad by enforced celibacy as the Europeans believed, the Zulu king and *amakhosi* allowed and even encouraged their

257

"*Sawubona kuwe, inkosi.*" Kwanele greeted the general.

"*Futhi wena qhawe induna,*" Mkhosana replied courteously. "Your first purging of the spirit ceremony?"

"Yes, *inkosi.* I hope the spirits of our ancestors will look upon us with favour, guide and protect us."

"We face a fearsome enemy. You are an *induna*; a hundred warriors look to you to lead them. Your mind and your courage are the best shields against the white soldiers in red coats. If you prove yourself wise and brave in equal measure, your men will follow you, and the ancestors will grant their blessings upon you."

They were profound words, and Kwanele took them to heart. He thanked the *inkosi* and returned to his hut. He had a substantial amount of time before the next phase of the ceremony and decided to lie down. He could not sleep. There was simply too much anxiety and anticipation flowing through him. He wished for his tortured guts to relax, yet as they did he became hungry. He then began to focus on the words of Mkhosana.

The way the *inkosi* spoke, telling the young *induna* to focus on his mind and courage, Kwanele wondered if he was expressing doubts as to the effectiveness of the *izinyanga's* medicines and charms. After all, even the most fanatical believers in the spiritual powers of the ancestors knew that no amount of diviner's charms could stop a bullet; least of all from those fearsome rapid-firing weapons the red-jacketed whites carried. Kwanele thought perhaps the spiritual blessing of the ancestors and purifying of the body and spirit were necessary for the *amabutho* to overcome such a fearsome adversary. Individual bravery was praised and expected, but it was more important that every regiment fight as one man. Their collective valour and fighting prowess would far exceed that of men fighting as individuals for personal glory.

Kwanele wasn't sure how long he laid on his sleeping mat. A number of his companions who shared the hut joined him when they finished the purging ceremony. All were ravenous with hunger, and they wished the rest of the *amabutho* would finish so they could move on to the next phase of the ritual.

As the early evening sun began to slowly fall into the west, the young *induna* emerged from his hut, his hand shielding his eyes from the sun. He saw that a few warriors were still making their way back from the Ntukwini stream. Viewed from the camp, it appeared

260

most had returned. He saw a gathering of the *amakhosi* were meeting with the lead *izinyanga*. Soon a low horn blast echoed across the plain, alerting the *amabutho* that the next phase of the ritual was about to commence. For the poor warriors who waited in the afternoon sun all day to perform the spiritual purging, there would be no time for rest or recovery.

Each regiment gathered around their *amakhosi* and were led to the cattle pens. The king's royal kraal was huge, allowing for the housing of thousands of people and tens-of-thousands of cattle. The youngest of the age-based regiments from each corps were called forward. They would prove their mettle by collectively killing a bull without the use of weapons. In his youth he had longed for the chance to prove himself against these beasts. This being a war ritual, Kwanele was glad his *ibutho* was not the youngest in his corps. It was one thing to be injured during the harvest ceremonies or the king's coronation, but to be trampled or gored during the purification ceremonies for war, thereby unable to march with one's regiment, was a shameful disgrace none wished to bear.

The bulls of the royal kraal were huge beasts with large horns and fearsome strength. The young men called forth were from an *ibutho* only raised the year before. These men were really little more than overgrown boys who had yet to see their twentieth harvest. The pure black sacrificial bull was led from the pens. Thirty of the young warriors circled it for a few moments before the shouts and berating of their companions compelled them to begin wrestling the animal to the ground. The bull, at first, seemed to find this an amusing sport, and he bucked and butted away his assailants. As several young men wrapped their arms around its neck, the beast seemed to realise this was no longer sport, but a fight for his life. It fiercely kicked backwards, its heavy hooves smashing one warrior in the chest, who fell to the ground, writhing in agony. The bull swung its head, the right horn goring another in the side, blood spilling onto the ground. Several others had their feet trampled. All the while the older warriors continued to shout and scold the young men for not finishing off the beast. Finally, after much struggle and two other lads kicked hard, exhaustion overcame the bull. He was wrestled to the ground, and after a few more minutes of choking by the battered young warriors, the beast was dead.

A loud ovation erupted from the assembled *amabutho*, and many of the older warriors came forward to carry the bull away. The beast was gutted and thrown on one of the large fires that circled the royal kraal. Kwanele turned his gaze to the centre where the king's hut stood. He could not see him, but he was certain Cetshwayo was watching and pleased with his regiments. The various beasts burned on the great fires, and the *izinyanga* cut off strips of meat which they rubbed with spices and special medicines intended to provide strength and spiritual protection during the coming battles.

The warriors were now chanting and stamping their feet, kicking up clouds of dust and dried cattle dung. They were ravenous with hunger, yet this was not meant to be a feast. Each strip of beef was flung by the *izinyanga* towards the starving warriors. They were to only bite off a small piece or suck some of the juices laced with the diviners' medicines. Once they took their bite, the warriors in the front tossed the strips over their heads, to be caught and consumed by their companions. If a piece landed in the dirt, its spiritual powers were considered lost. So great was their hunger and fatigue, many warriors picked up the soiled strips of meat and devoured them anyway.

Men shoved and jostled for better position. As an *induna*, Kwanele was fortunate enough to be in the first line of his *ibutho*. He caught one of the first strips and bit off a sizeable chunk. The meat was still fairly raw, and the medicinal herbs tasted terrible. He did not care. It was the only bit of food he'd eaten in the past two days, and it was all they would receive this night.

Contrary to the purging ceremony, which lasted almost the entire day, the consuming of the protective medicines lasted only a couple of hours. By the time the sun set behind the hills to the west, with only bonfires providing light on this cloudy night, all had ingested their humble portion of the protective herbs. The *amakhosi* dismissed their regiments to return to their shelters to rest and allow the medicines to take hold of their bodies and spirits. The charms were supposed to help against British bullets and bayonets, but they did little to protect against the rapacious pangs of hunger every last warrior at kwaNodwengo slept with that night. After about twenty minutes of stumbling around in the dark, Kwanele reached his hut. The first drops of rain began to fall. It would be a miserable night, especially for the hungry souls who had only their crude shelters to protect them from what looked to be a torrential downpour from the heavens.

"Perhaps the divines seek to clean the ground, as well as our spirits," he muttered philosophically as he allowed sleep to take him.

The sun was bright and hot the following day. It was the first time the famished warriors were allowed to have an actual meal. Porridge, freshly cooked bread, and strips of beef were brought forth and devoured in mass quantities. This was also the day the regiments would begin to parade before the king.

In the *amabutho*, regiments were often mustered in pairs, with intense and oftentimes savage rivalries resulting. After the harvest ceremonies ended in bloody brawls on numerous occasions, the *amabutho* were prohibited from coming before the king armed. Only their shields and ceremonial dancing sticks were allowed. On this day, it would be the iNgobamakhosi, the regiment which Sihayo's son—and Cetshwayo's favourite—Mehlokazulu belonged. The young *induna* was all too aware of the role he'd played in the manifestation of this war between Zulu and British. He knew his courage and tenacity would be expected to exceed that of any among their rivals the uKhandempemvu.

These particular warriors were a few years older and had been fierce rivals to their younger counterparts since their inception. Another *ibutho* had deliberately been allowed to marry themselves off to numerous young girlfriends of both regiments, yet instead of channelling their anger towards them, the two regiments instead blamed each other for the loss of their women, which in turn only intensified the hated rivalry.

Although Cetshwayo encouraged this, he now implored his warriors to unleash their pent up furies on the British rather than each other.

"*Warriors of the uKhandempemvu and iNgobamakhosi!*" he shouted with his hands and ceremonial staff held high. "You stand

of their weapons. In short, their firearms were of terrible quality when compared to the breach-loading rifles wielded by the British.

Still, knowing they possessed an overall greater quantity of firearms, Cetshwayo decided to let the *izinyanga* perform one last ceremony to aid the men and their musketry.

"Pass through once more," the lead diviner said. "We shall bless the barrels of your guns."

The riflemen did as instructed, running past the bubbling caldrons again; this time with the barrels pointed towards the pots. The pungent medicines were splattered on and inside the barrels. The *izinyanga* chanted prayers that their bullets would fly true and strike down the redcoats.

Ntshingwayo and Mnyamana sat on either side of the king, watching the proceedings. They looked at each other, nodding in approval. And though Mnyamana was commander-in-chief of the Zulu armies, he had expressed a desire to remain at Ulundi with his king. He asked his friend to lead the attack against the British forces massed at Rorke's Drift. Eight days after they began the ceremonies were complete. The Zulu *impi* was at last ready for war.

Chapter XXII: Shadow of the Sphynx

Isandlwana, ten miles east of Rorke's Drift
20 January 1879

Isandlwana

On the morning of 20 January, Arthur stretched his legs and yawned loudly as the bugler sounded reveille. He usually woke just as the predawn glow cast enough light to see by, but not yet subjecting one to the blinding rays of the morning sun. He would lay curled up on his bedroll; his thoughts varying between whether they would finally be on the move or would the Zulus bring the fight to them here. And as every day since he departed Stratford-upon-Avon, he was filled with a deep sense of longing for his dearest Elisa.

Soldiers emerged sleepily from their tents. Some stoked coals from the previous day's fires while they brewed coffee and cooked breakfast. Arthur and Richard stood gazing towards the river, gleaming in the early morning light. They heard a frenzy of activity to their right. Drivers and voorloopers were hitching up their oxen, shouting all the while at the difficult beasts.

"Something's happening," Arthur remarked.

"This might be it," his friend observed. "Perhaps we'll finally get this war underway."

267

Their theories were confirmed when Sergeant Edwards walked briskly over to them, his pocket notebook in hand. "Eat fast, lads. Then get your shit out of the tents and start rolling this bastard up. Captain Younghusband wants the company packed and ready to march in one hour."

Though officers and NCOs did not pull night-time guard shifts or other tedious details, they still got far less sleep than any of their soldiers. By the time reveille sounded, most had been awake and dressed for well over an hour. Orders for the day came down from the column staff and preparations were made at the battalion and company level. On this day, the orders were what every soldier in No. 3 Column had been waiting to hear.

"Today we begin the war in earnest," Captain Younghusband said to Lieutenant Hodson and Colour Sergeant Brown. Granted, the war actually began with the crossing of the uMzinyathi, and they had already fought one small action at Sihayo's stronghold. But there was little sense amongst the men that they were in the midst of a real war. After all, they'd seen no trace of the main *impi*, or of any other Zulus at all, for that matter. The only signs of war had been their skirmish, and word from Colonel Wood's No. 4 Column that they had laid waste to many of the Zulu homesteads in the north.

Both of Reginald's senior subordinates already donned their helmets. The captain rarely wore his, preferring the more comfortable forage cap. His mother's Spanish blood gave the captain a darker, olive pigment than his fellows, making his skin more tolerant of the sun.

"I hear it's ten miles to Isandlwana," Lieutenant Hodson remarked. "A good chance for the boys to stretch their legs a bit."

"And still no sign of the Zulus," Brown added. "They know we're here. I'm surprised they made no attempts at Major Dunbar's camp."

"They may walk around in animal skins with spears," the captain said, "but that doesn't mean they're reckless or stupid. I suspect they have their own preparation and logistical issues to sort out."

Thomas nodded towards where their soldiers were pulling down tents and packing up their kit. "The company will be ready to move as scheduled, sir."

"Very good," Reginald acknowledged. "Inform Sergeant Major Gapp as soon as our wagons are loaded and ready. Mister Hodson, F Company only just arrived yesterday. Coordinate with Captain Mostyn and let him know where to position his wagons behind ours."

"Very good, sir."

"And now, gentlemen, I need to meet with Colonel Pulleine and see what orders he may have for us once the column reaches Isandlwana."

A tin cup of piping hot coffee in his hand, Captain Reginald Younghusband made his way past the scores of men feverishly loading the wagons with tents, support poles, stakes, biscuit boxes, and mealie bags. He approached the area where the battalion headquarters tent had just been pulled down and happened upon his friend, William Degacher. Reverted back to his substantive rank of captain, he had remained as senior staff officer to Lieutenant Colonel Pulleine as promised.

"Morning, Reginald." He held up his mug in salute.

"And to you, William." He nodded to where Pulleine was having a hectic conversation with the battalion's quartermaster, James Pullen. "How's he managing?"

"I don't think he slept at all the past two nights. He means well, and it really isn't fair that he's being forced to learn his duties under such circumstances; however, he still needs to learn how to delegate. I think with the Frontier Regiments he was compelled to do almost everything himself. I'd bet you a case of claret Quartermaster Pullen and Sergeant Major Gapp are telling him, yet again, not to worry himself over their duties."

"To be fair, he can delegate authority but not responsibility," Reginald conjectured. "Everything that happens in this battalion is on his head."

"True. But you don't go around telling Colour Sergeant Brown and his non-comms how to do their jobs, do you?"

"No," Younghusband replied with a short laugh.

"You know Quartermaster Pullen came from the ranks. He was a sergeant major before they commissioned him. I think he's the last person Pulleine needs to worry about. Pullen told him yesterday, *'Sir, just tell me where you want my wagons, and I'll get them there'.*"

"He does trust Lieutenant Melvill well enough with personnel issues," Reginald noted.

"Yes, but they're old friends," Degacher countered. "Our colonel knows his adjutant well. And I do know he's under a huge amount of pressure both from Colonel Glyn and the GOC. I think he just needs to realise that he doesn't have to handle all of this alone. Before Pulleine arrived, I told Colonel Glyn to give us a week or two and we'll have him sorted out."

At that moment, Pulleine made his way briskly over to them. His eyes were bloodshot and his face pale. Reginald reckoned his friend was right. Their commanding officer had not slept in days.

"Ah, William," he said excitedly, before turning to address Reginald. "And a good morning to you, Captain Younghusband."

"And to you, sir. Looks to be a fine day." He held up his cup. "Can we offer you some coffee, sir?"

"No, no, thank you all the same. Mister Melvill force-fed me three cups already. He says I'm not getting nearly enough sleep at night."

"He's right, you know," William said candidly. "And I wouldn't stress too much over the placement of the camp once we arrive, sir. Major Clery is taking care of that. Just give us the orders to move out. If the Zulus decide they want to turn up and dance a bit, tell us where you want the companies deployed. We'll take care of the rest."

"Yes…thank you, William." Pulleine let out a sigh and donned his helmet. "And a good day to you, Captain Younghusband." He then abruptly left to find the orderly taking care of his horse.

"He'll be alright," Degacher said with a measure of confidence. "I think once we get 'stuck in' with the Zulus he'll see what kind of a battalion he has."

Reginald decided to find his own orderly and horse, as the company looked to be almost finished loading its tents and equipment. Section leaders were performing a final inspection of their men, and he could see Lieutenant Hodson coordinating with

Captain Mostyn of F Company. All in all, it was looking to be a chaotic but good morning to be a member of the 24th.

For the first time since first crossing the uMzinyathi nine days before, the No. 3 Column was finally on the march. Progress was slow as the supply wagons moved at a crawl along the rutted track. 'Maori' Browne's 1/3rd NNC provided the vanguard for the column, followed by 1/24th, whose companies acted as flank security for the supply train. N Battery with its six guns and numerous ammunition wagons followed, covered on their flanks by the volunteer companies of cavalry and carbineers. Providing the rear guard for the column were four companies from 2/24th under Major Wilsone Black. In all, the column stretched for five miles from end-to-end. It would be at least a couple of hours from the time the NNC battalions departed until the last of the professional infantry began their march.

The slopes of the surrounding hills were covered in lush green grasses, as a result of the otherwise torturous rains. When they reached the Batshe Valley the grasses turned to nasty thorns and thick stands of sticker brush. Soldiers on the flanks were compelled to remain on the track as they reached the rocky cliffs that marked the destroyed ruins of Sihayo's kraal. The old chief's stronghold was completely deserted except for the occasional jackal or other wild beast that continued to devour the remains of those unfortunate slain Zulus whose families had failed to find and bury them.

Private Arthur Wilkinson would not be roaming through the brush with the skirmishers this day. Lieutenant Porteous' A Company, as well as the recently-arrived F Company under Captain William Mostyn, provided flank security for the battalion. In truth, he was glad for the reprieve and being able to march in the column with his mates. He'd spent so much time with the company skirmishers lately he found himself missing the fellows from his section.

"At least it's not raining today," Richard Lowe mentioned, gazing at the puffy white clouds in the east.

With no other form of cover from the sun, this day would be a hot one. About two hours after they began, they spotted a strange shape jutting up in the far distance.

"What is that?" Arthur asked, squinting his eyes.

"Looks like a damned sphinx," Bray observed.

The men all noted the similarity in shape between the distant land mass and the insignia on their collars.

"Is that a good omen or not?" Richard asked.

Adding a bit of martial ambiance to the march, the regimental bands struck up. Each battalion within the army had its own band. During battle they became the stretcher bearers for the wounded. And contrary to incessant myths, there were no eleven or twelve-year old drummer boys marching with the 24th, though most of the bandsmen and drummers were quite young. The youngest, Joseph McEwen of 1/24th, was sixteen; practically a grown man by the standards of the day.

Band of the 1/24th

"Quite the distinctive landmark," Chelmsford observed, looking at the mountain through his field glasses. "What was its name, again?"

"The natives call it *Isandlwana*, my lord," Crealock answered. "Commandant Browne's iziGqoza informed us we will cross the Manzimyama Stream about a mile before the hill."

"Good," Colonel Glyn remarked. "At least we'll have a fresh water source. The grass is green and thick, too, plenty of fodder for our beasts of burden."

The GOC looked to Glyn's aide. "Major Clery, take representatives from each battalion and establish a proper layout for our camp."

"As you wish, my lord." The major saluted and then departed.

Colonel Glyn's face twitched. It continued to grind on him that Chelmsford was giving direct orders to Glyn's subordinates, bypassing him altogether. Though he was still technically the column commander, the GOC had essentially usurped all control from him. This left the colonel with little to do except menial tasking. He knew that it was Lord Chelmsford's right to accompany one of his columns; however, in most cases, a general officer commanding would defer the day-to-day running of the column to its commander and focus on the war at large. Chelmsford, however, was content to let Wood and Pearson manage their campaigns without interference or oversight, while he had wrested direct control of the centre column from Glyn.

With the Imperial Mounted Infantry providing escorts, Major Clery rounded up his advance party and made a mad gallop for Isandlwana. Rupert Lonsdale, despite still feeling the effects of his head injury, accompanied him on behalf of the NNC. Inspector Mansel of the Natal Mounted Police represented the mounted elements. Both Lieutenant Melvill and the adjutant for 2nd Battalion, Lieutenant Dyer, along with Sergeant Major Gapp and Quartermaster-Sergeant Leitch went on behalf of the 24th. Lieutenant Colonel Harness sent Lieutenant Curling and Farrier-Sergeant Whinham to represent N Battery.

The detachment rode up the eastern slope of the mountain, looking down into a large valley below. The top of Isandlwana was capped by a massive rocky outcropping that was completely vertical on all sides. It provided the sphynx-like shape the column could see in the distance. As the officers and NCOs surveyed the terrain and determined where best to lay out their various encampments, the soldiers of the IMI dismounted and provided security for the detachment.

Drawn from the regular army regiments, soldiers of the IMI were identical in uniform and appearance to their brethren redcoats with a few exceptions. Each carried the shorter barrelled Swinburne-Henry carbine and wore an ammunition bandoleer slung over the left shoulder.

After handing the reins of his horse to a designated horse-holder, a young IMI private named Sam Wassall took his carbine and walked a short ways down the slope. He was joined by his friend, Private David Westwood.

"Feel the damn ground here." Sam kicked at the hard shale. "I hope the officers don't expect us to entrench in this shit."

His friend knelt down and picked up a few pieces of broken rocks and tossed them down the slope. "It would take us weeks to dig in here."

"I wouldn't sweat it, lads," their lead NCO, Sergeant Naughton, said. "I doubt the column will be staying here for long. Just enough time to get all the supplies up from Rorke's Drift before we all bound along once more. Hopefully we can give the Zulus a damn good walloping before we get all the way to Ulundi."

"At the rate we're going, it's going to take months to reach Ulundi," Westwood grumbled as their sergeant wandered off to check on some of their mates.

"Well whether the Zulus come out to dance soon or not, I do hope we get at least some reprieve from the damnable rains." Sam let loose a loud cough in emphasis.

"Good Lord, man, are you alright?"

"I sure as bleeding hell hope so," Wassall answered. "Last thing I want is to end up like one of those poor sods left rotting away in the hospital at Rorke's Drift. I came here to fight the Zulus, not typhoid and dysentery."

Soldiers of the 1st Imperial Mounted Infantry (IMI)

Establishing camp with a vast force of thousands of men, wagons, and hundreds of draught animals was an arduous feat that required no shortage of organizational skill. The camp butted up against the eastern slope of Isandlwana, facing the valley and hills to the east and southeast. On the northernmost edge of the camp were the two battalions from Rupert Lonsdale's 3rd NNC Regiment. The only tents available to them were those of the European officers and NCOs; the indigenous levies would build traditional brush huts as was their custom.

Three companies from Lieutenant Colonel Degacher's 2/24th were next. As the remaining four were providing the column's rear guard, it fell upon their mates in the lead companies to establish where their tents would be placed. Those belonging to Colonel Glyn, the column staff, and Lord Chelmsford were erected a few dozen yards behind 2nd Battalion on higher ground. That gave the column commander and GOC a better view of the camp and valley.

The six-guns of N Battery took up as much space as any one of the battalions, owing to the vast number of horses needed to haul the guns and their ammunition wagons. Lieutenant Colonel Harness placed his guns and limbers in line in front of his camp, readily available in the event of an emergency. Ammunition carts were staged directly behind, with the horse and mule lines behind them. The tents for the gunners and drivers were placed on three sides

275

surrounding the horse lines. The troopers of the cavalry elements arranged themselves in similar fashion, with horses corralled in the centre. Tents for the volunteer cavalry, Imperial Mounted Infantry, and Natal Mounted Police encompassed the remaining three sides.

The five companies from 1/24th encamped on the far end of the line, south of the wagon track they had followed to Isandlwana. Each battalion's wagons were arrayed in a long line behind each camp. The pioneers, along with Surgeon-Major Shepherd and his hospital tents, were placed on the north side of the track about two hundred yards behind the IMI. A large wagon park was staged behind this where the unloaded wagons would be sent back to Rorke's Drift to bring up the next batch of rations and supplies. Keeping lines of communication open between the forward camp and the Drift would be crucial. The task of managing the continuous wagon runs fell to the column transportation officer, Captain Essex, and his assistant, Lieutenant Smith-Dorrien.

Around 5.00 in the evening, Major Black and the rear guard from 2/24th arrived in the growing camp. Most of the tents were erected, with one company from each battalion tasked by Colonel Glyn with providing pickets. The remainder began preparing their supper. A slew of cooking fires dotted the landscape. Meanwhile, cavalry troopers and artillerymen grazed and watered their horses.

Commandant Rupert Lonsdale emerged from his tent to admire the display of British military might that extended nearly a mile from end-to-end. Despite its splendour, there was something unsettling about it all. George 'Maori' Browne walked up to Lonsdale's tent with Captain Duncombe, expressing in more vulgar terms the same sense of trepidation.

"My God, Maori, what do you make of the camp?" Lonsdale asked.

"The staff have lost their fucking minds, Rupert," he stated bluntly. "Look how spread out we are. Someone at the top has gone completely mad."

Captain Duncombe added with equal candour, "Do the staff think we are going to face an army of schoolboys? Why in God's name do we not laager? We're completely exposed in the bloody open here."

"Yes, this is concerning," Lonsdale concurred. Still feeling the nagging after-effects of his head injury, he cursed himself for not realising sooner what his subordinates were now making plain to him. "I shall go speak with the GOC at once."

"I'll come with you," Browne insisted.

As a gentle breeze blew over the escarpment, the two officers walked the half mile to where the column and overall army commanders had established their tents. Lord Chelmsford, content with the layout of the camp, was sitting down to his supper. He'd insisted Glyn and Clery join him, though he pretended to ignore the incessant hostilities that existed between Clery and Crealock. In truth, Crealock was one of the most unpopular staff officers in the column. Colonel Glyn's orderly, a very young private named Williams, was bringing a bottle of claret for them to share as the two NNC officers arrived.

"Ah, Commandant Lonsdale," Chelmsford said with a smile of approbation. "I am glad to see you returned to us. I trust you are well?"

"Some lingering issues, headaches and occasional dizziness. Nothing that will keep me from performing my duties, my lord."

"Splendid. Please, come join us. You always have a place at my table. Oh, and you are welcome to join us this evening as well, Commandant Browne."

"Kindly, my lord, but we came to discuss a rather urgent matter with you," Browne responded.

"Really? What could possibly be of greater urgency than satisfying one's hunger after a rather vigorous day?"

"It's the camp's defences, sir," Lonsdale answered. "Your own *Regulations for Field Forces in South Africa* stresses the need for each camp to be partially entrenched on all sides."

"We should also circle the wagons in a laager, my lord," Browne quickly added. "The Boers have learned some rather painful lessons over the years that many never lived long enough to profit from."

Colonel Glyn stared hard at both men. Neither could have guessed that he'd had this very conversation with the GOC mere hours before. Chelmsford, rather than becoming irritated at the repeated questioning, explained himself in a calm, if somewhat pandering tone to the two NNC officers.

"Have you not seen the ground here, gentlemen?" he asked. "It is rock and shale; not exactly conducive for digging with shovels and pickaxes. And look at the size of this camp. It would take two days of trying to get those frightful beasts to pull the wagons into any sort of defensive position. And what would we use to bring supplies up from Rorke's Drift, if we hid behind our wagons, which I don't need to remind you we are critically short of? And in case you did not know, I do not plan to remain here for long." He paused and took a few bites of his supper, while downing half a glass of claret.

"Firepower, gentlemen, is our defensive stronghold here," Chelmsford continued. "No need to go through the backbreaking, and at this point futile, attempts at laagering, when a wall of lead will stop any Zulu attack in its tracks…that is, provided Cetshwayo is bold enough to fight us in the open. We have six cannon and over fifteen hundred professional infantrymen available, not to mention the cavalry and your own NNC battalions. We have numerous pickets posted. If they give the warning, we can form a wall of musketry in a matter of minutes that will make it impossible for any primitive army to get within three hundred yards. Rest easy, gentlemen. As long as our firepower remains concentrated, Cetshwayo would be a fool to try and face us here."

It was not the answer either man wanted to hear, but the tone in Chelmsford voice was firm. They knew this was the end of the discussion. Both Lonsdale and Browne understood the GOC's point regarding laagering. If they had a full complement of wagons and draught animals, it would have been a practical measure. As it was, most of the wagons would be continuously running back and forth between Isandlwana and Rorke's Drift, until they made the next move towards Siphezi or Mangeni, where the process would start over. 'Maori' wished to express his concern that they should concentrate their camp into a more manageable and close-knit square; however, the looks from Colonel Glyn and Commandant Lonsdale, as well as the finality in Chelmsford's tone, put an end to the issue.

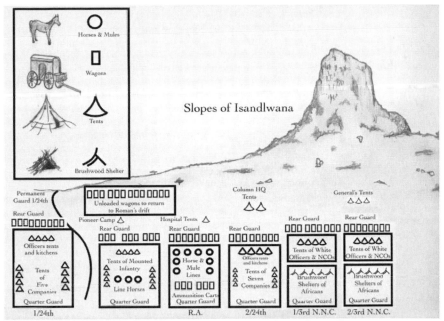

The various camps along the eastern face of Isandlwana

Chapter XXIII: A Deserted Land

No. 3 Column camp, Isandlwana
20 January 1879

A Zulu kraal

C Company was not on picket duty, so the men were able to lounge, play cards, and relax for a spell with what remained of the day. After the long march and establishing their camp near the slopes of the sphynx-like mountain, they were glad for the reprieve. They were on the extreme right of 1/24th's camp, south of the wagon track near the base of the stony koppie immediately south of Isandlwana.

"I don't get it, this land appears to be completely deserted," Richard Lowe remarked.

He was playing cards with a few of the men underneath the shade offered by the entrance of their tent.

"I thought there were hundreds-of-thousands populating the Zulu kingdom," another soldier added.

"Oh, they're out there," Bray remarked, playing his next card. "The Zulus may not wear proper clothes or be what we would think of as 'civilised', but do not mistake that for having no brains. They're a clever lot. How else do you explain their rapid acquisition of an empire that rivalled Napoleon's in just a few short years?"

"I always took one black savage to be the same as the next," Richard replied, though his voice lacked conviction.

"If you believe that you are the one who is a fool," Bray said candidly. "The Zulu *amakhosi* are wise men. They know the capabilities of our soldiers and firepower. They're not stupid enough to walk into our guns so we can slaughter them like sheep. Nor do I think they will try to conduct a long-term guerrilla war against us either."

"Why is that?" Arthur sat upright. He'd been lying inside the tent penning another letter to his wife; one which he hoped to deliver to her in person when she arrived in Natal.

"Because they are farmers, and their harvest looms," Sergeant Edwards spoke up as he knelt down next to the tent entrance and removed his forage cap. He quickly changed the subject. "Bray, Lowe, Wilkie, I need you three for a detail in the morning. Half the company is taking part in a patrol to the north to scout possible enemy avenues of approach."

"I thought his lordship dismissed the notion of the Zulus coming at us from the north," Lowe remarked. "That's all mountainous terrain. Surely they wouldn't try to negotiate that."

"If you were the Zulu *inkosi* would you march right through the valley, exposed and in the open, to be slaughtered by our Martini-Henrys?" the sergeant countered. "Or would you take your army around more difficult terrain that would allow you to flank your enemy? At any rate, that was Captain Younghusband's assessment, not his lordship's. We do not know which direction the Zulus will come from, but he is not one to take chances. Colonel Degacher agrees. With little else for us to do at the moment, I doubt Colonel Glyn or the GOC will object to us taking a bit of initiative."

Lowe scrunched his brow. "If half the company is going on the patrol but not us, what exactly is our tasking for tomorrow?"

"Range markers," Edwards stood and donned his cap. "Enjoy the reprieve this evening, lads. I want to make an early start tomorrow before the sun cooks us in our uniforms."

It was now late in the morning, and the staff breakfasted together before conducting their reconnaissance to the southeast. Chelmsford not only wished to find out what happened to all of the Zulus, but how passable the terrain was between Isandlwana and where he wished to establish the next camp. The ever-present Lieutenant Colonel Crealock accompanied him, as did Majors Clery and Dartnell, Captain Gosset, Lieutenant Milne of the Royal Navy, and Lieutenants Melvill and Coghill. Mr Fynn, the local magistrate, accompanied the party as an interpreter.

The IMI were again tasked with providing escorts for the staff, which suited Private Sam Wassall just fine.

"Far better than sitting around camp waiting for a bored officer to find menial labour for us," he said to his friend, David Westwood, as they saddled their mounts and made ready to ride.

The GOC and his entourage made their way southeast at a leisurely pace, while still noting the region was devoid of any signs of life. About twelve miles from Isandlwana they spotted a magnificent place known as Mangeni Falls, where a splendid waterfall cascaded down into the river below. The scene was breathtaking.

Mangeni Falls

While Chelmsford and the staff rested for a spell, various reconnaissance patrols were sent out from the falls to scout the surrounding region. One of these was led by Lieutenant Neville Coghill and Chelmsford's Royal Navy liaison, Lieutenant Berkeley Milne. The staff officers were accompanied by twenty men from the Natal Mounted Police led by Sub-Inspector Phillips. A few miles from Mangeni they happened upon an abandoned kraal. The cattle and goats were gone, but Coghill noticed a few chickens scattered about.

"Here we are!" He excitedly jumped down from his horse.

"It's just chickens, sir," Phillips remarked, confused as he was by the officer's enthusiasm.

"Yes, and his lordship was just saying yesterday that he has had a craving for some roast chicken."

"So why don't you just shoot one?" the inspector asked.

The young officer was crouched low, arms out front. "That gets messy. Best to snap their little necks, then you don't have to worry about picking bits of bullet and shattered bones out."

"Here, Neville, I'll give you a hand," Milne said as he dismounted and handed the reins to one of the policemen.

The two men chased the terrified bird around the gated kraal for some minutes. When they finally thought they had it cornered, Coghill tried to lunge for the chicken, only to have his toe catch on a buried rock. He pitched forward, catching the side of his knee on another rock buried under a thin layer of dirt. He cried out in surprise and pain.

"Bugger me with a sodding leak!" He rolled onto his backside, clutching his injured knee.

"Good heavens, Neville, are you alright?" Milne asked, rushing over to him.

"I appear to have dislocated my bloody knee," Coghill said through gritted teeth as Milne helped him stand. "Dash it all, this is the same leg I hurt a year ago during a camp spear-throwing competition."

"What happened?" Milne asked.

"Somebody struck me with a bloody spear."

It took Milne and two policemen to help Coghill back onto his horse. His face was pale and covered in sweat. He took slow deep breaths, fighting the pain in his throbbing knee. The loud crack of a pistol shot echoed from inside the kraal.

"I got your bird." Inspector Phillips held aloft the bloody chicken.

Coghill's injury, which wounded his pride as much as his leg, was the only real highlight of their excursion towards Mangeni. Lord Chelmsford knew the region belonged to a Zulu chieftain named Matshana, though there had been no sign of him or any of his followers. There was much uncertainty as to whether he would defect like Gamdana; or was he a loyalist to his king and a potential hostile? Henry Fynn, who was familiar with the region, warned the GOC that the Zulus could readily make their way down the Mangeni valley using the thick forests as cover. If they then moved up the uMzinyathi, they would catch his army from behind.

"Or they could avoid your army altogether, my lord, and make straight for Rorke's Drift," he added.

Chelmsford then decided the region needed a thorough reconnaissance, a mission suitable for the fleet-footed NNC. Once again he tasked Rupert Lonsdale and 'Maori' Browne with conducting the scouting mission of the region. The GOC was now convinced Mangeni was the most likely approach route for the Zulu *impi*. If the Zulus did attempt to strike south across the uMzinyathi and into Natal, Lonsdale's men would be in a better position to discover and delay such actions until the redcoats and artillery could arrive.

That evening, Neville Coghill retired to the tent he shared with one of Chelmsford's ADCs, Captain Parr, with feelings of physical pain and no small amount of embarrassment.

"Damn it all, I must be the most accident-prone man in the entire army." He hobbled over to his camp bed and laid down, propping his leg up on his pack.

"You do kind of bring it on yourself," Parr remarked. "Wasn't it you who tried jumping your horse over a table in the officers' mess in Brecon?"

Neville laughed out loud. "Yes, that was me."

"And how exactly did that work out in the end? Those who were supposedly there will neither confirm nor deny anything."

"Suffice it to say my horse made the jump fair enough." Neville paused. A sheepish grin crossed his face.

Parr knew there was more to the story.

"I, on the other hand, was knocked silly when I fell over backwards and cracked my head on the end of the table. And now I do this to my knee, thinking I might win a bit of favour with his lordship by snatching up a chicken for his supper."

"You'll likely be off that for a few days," Parr observed. "Let's hope you don't miss out on all the fun should, the Zulus decide to come out and play."

The morning of the 21st came thankfully devoid of rains. And though it would be the NNC making up the core of the expedition, Chelmsford decided to attach some of the carbineers, mounted police, and colonial volunteers. Major Dartnell of the Natal Mounted Police, highly respected by both the colonials as well as the regulars, was placed in overall command. Much to the chagrin of Colonel Glyn and Major Clery, Chelmsford issued the orders to Major Dartnell and Commandant Lonsdale without bothering to pass it by Glyn. It was just another example of Glyn's authority being taken away due to the GOC's habit of dictating everything himself. This left the entire column staff at a loss, and they felt unable to function effectively.

Acting-Captain Charlie Harford had spent his supper the previous evening with his friend, Charlie Pope from G Company, 2/24th. Pope's company was slated to go on picquet duty for the next twenty-four hours while Harford accompanied the NNC with Major Dartnell. The two had achieved a splendid rapport following the previous excursion that led them to Sihayo's kraal at kwaSokhexe.

"Good hunting, Charlie," Pope had said to him. "Just don't go and slaughter all the Zulus before my lads come off picquet duty."

The following morning, Harford joined his battalion on its mission to find the enemy for Lord Chelmsford. Major Dartnell essentially had four elements making up his reconnaissance force. He personally led an element of forty-six Natal Mounted Policemen. The rest of his cavalry troops were led by George Shepstone's

"We know the camp is going to be attacked," he protested. "Every cock fights best in his own yard. When the general hears our news he will order the camp to be laagered. We can put up a fight there against the whole Zulu nation. Here, we shall be stamped flat in a minute."

None of them knew that two of Browne's lieutenants had already snuck away and headed back to the perceived safety of Isandlwana. Lonsdale was beginning to explain to Browne that it was Major Dartnell who was in command of the detachment when an outpost alerted them to the sound of horses. It was Lieutenant Walsh and his pack horses. In addition to food, he brought what blankets he had managed to scrounge.

"Well done, Mister Walsh," Dartnell said, walking over to the tired officer. "I am amazed you made it here without hassle."

"The ground is relatively flat and open," the officer explained, recalling that the expedition had made its way over the much harsher terrain south of the Ndaweni River rather than follow the wagon track from Isandlwana. He relayed his orders from the GOC; they were to hold in place and, if the opportunity arose, attack the Zulus.

Few would get any sleep this night. The lights of thousands of campfires across the valley unnerved every last man in the bivouac. The occasional shot was fired from terrified men on the outposts who mistook dancing shadows for enemy warriors. Charlie Harford had later gone to check the guard posts only to find some of them completely deserted. He let the offenders know in no uncertain terms that the next man found having abandoned his post would be shot. And one particular scare during the night had roused the entire camp. Norris-Newman was nearly trampled by a panicked mass of NNC warriors. 'Maori' Browne cursed his own men as 'curs' and 'filthy cowards' as he attempted to restore order.

Harford, feeling they were very much exposed, said as much to Major Dartnell, after order was restored. The numerous fires alone told of a very large enemy force within just a few miles, possibly the main Zulu *impi*. Dartnell therefore tasked Lieutenant Walsh with riding back to Lord Chelmsford and informing him of the situation.

"Tell his lordship we need redcoats and artillery at once!"

It was now 1.30 in the morning, though to be roused in the middle of the night was never unexpected for an commanding officer. Therefore, it was with excitement rather than irritation that Lord Chelmsford found himself awoken by Major Clery.

"Beg your pardon, my lord, but a message has just come in from the picquets. Colonel Glyn said I should find you at once."

The GOC was immediately alert and sitting upright. "Who is the message from?"

"Lieutenant Walsh of the Imperial Mounted Infantry." Clery handed Chelmsford the scrap of paper with its hastily-written pencil notes.

"He made his way back here, fifteen miles in the dark," the GOC surmised. "Impressive. His message must be important."

"Yes, sir." Clery turned up the flame on his oil lamp so the despatch could be read easier. "He says the Zulus are operating in force. It would not be prudent for the NNC to attack them without the support of our regulars."

"This may prove fortuitous." Chelmsford squinted his eyes, trying to read the message for himself. "It would seem the enemy wishes to dance after all. Unfortunately, we cannot uproot the entire column and leave our supplies unprotected. Send Colonels Glyn, Degacher, Harness, and Pullcine to me at once."

"Right away, my lord."

His mind already racing, the GOC pulled on his boots and began to formulate his plan of action. He disliked the idea of dividing his forces, but if Major Dartnell had indeed found the main Zulu *impi*, then he'd have little choice but to do so. If he ordered Dartnell to withdraw, the enemy would simply slip away and regain the initiative. As long as his forces kept the Zulus within their sights, they retained the advantage. Within minutes his senior commanders gathered in the general's tent. The commotion awoke Crealock in the next tent over. His presence had not been requested, so he listened intently and politely waited to be called upon.

"Gentlemen," Chelmsford began. "It would seem the NNC have found the Zulu *impi*. But we cannot take all of our men and leave our supply lines exposed. Colonel Degacher, your battalion has seven full companies, whereas Pulleine only has five. 2nd Battalion will therefore lead this mission."

"Very good, my lord." Degacher's excitement was evident. "Just be advised, sir, my G Company is on picquet duty and will not be coming off until morning. They will have been awake for twenty-four hours at that point."

"Yes, well, you can spare one company. Inform Lieutenant Pope his company will have a day of rest once they come off the picquets. A pity for them. They will miss out on the hunt." Chelmsford then turned to Lieutenant Colonel Harness. "Colonel, I want four of your guns limbered and made ready."

"I'll take them myself and leave Lieutenant Curling's section here."

Chelmsford then spoke to Pulleine who was somewhat disappointed it was not his battalion being sent to engage the Zulus. Degacher was far more experienced as a battalion commander. And even with Lieutenant Pope's company being stood down and Bromhead's left at Rorke's Drift, he still had nearly a hundred more riflemen than his counterpart.

"Colonel Pulleine, you will be left in charge of the camp's defences. However, I do not wish to leave you understrength in case the Zulus try some form of trickery to raid our supply and communication lines. We will bring up Colonel Durnford's column of cavalry to support you. But they must be ready to advance, should we have need of them."

"Beg your pardon, my lord," Crealock called through the tent wall. "But do you wish Major Clery to issue the order to Durnford?"

"No, you go ahead," Chelmsford replied. He then addressed his commanders once more. "Understand, gentlemen, we do not know for certain the strength of the Zulu force under observation by the NNC. However, every piece of intelligence that we've been able to collect together indicates what we've suspected all along; the *impi* has left Ulundi and is approaching from the east through the Mangeni Valley. The sightings of enemy warriors further to the north are likely either scouts or small raiding parties. I cannot imagine the Zulus sending 25,000 men over mountaintops when they have an easy access corridor to reach us."

"Sir, what if we pull the NNC back and consolidate our forces here?" Colonel Glyn asked. "Cetshwayo wants a fight. We should do so with all of our firepower and from a position of strength."

"We are not entirely certain he intends to fight us," Chelmsford countered. "As our friend, Mr Fynn, suspects, Cetshwayo may be attempting to slip away in the night and get behind us. If he is allowed to cross the uMzinyathi at Rorke's Drift, our supplies and communication lines will be severed and the whole of Natal subjected to invasion. *That* is something we simply cannot allow. The Zulus may or may not be looking for a battle, but I, sir, *am* looking for one. Therefore, 2nd Battalion of the 24th and four guns from N Battery will make ready to depart immediately and reinforce the NNC. With any luck, by evening we should have caught the Zulus and routed them in a decisive battle of our choosing."

The officers were then dismissed. There was much to do besides rousing the men of 2/24th and having them ready to march in the middle of the night. After dispatching his adjutant to alert the companies, Lieutenant Colonel Henry Degacher made his way over to Quartermaster Bloomfield's tent.

"Ah, colonel." The bleary-eyed quartermaster roused himself and wiped his eyes.

"Edward, I need you to have your ammunition wagons made ready," Degacher directed him. While each man carried his allotment of 70 rounds of ammunition, the battalion quartermasters controlled the companies' wagons of reserve cartridges. Every company was assigned a wagon, either military issued general purpose or requisitioned colonial variant, bearing thirty-four boxes of 600 rounds each. If the Zulus were massing in the east near the NNC as suspected, 2/24th would need their reserve ammunition ready to move at a moment's notice.

"Very good, sir. Will you be taking the colours with you?"

"No." Henry shook his head. "We could end up in a scrap in the bush or scaling rocky slopes. Taking the colours would be impractical."

"Well no worries on your ammunition, sir. I'll have it ready to send forward should you need it. And if not, it'll still be here waiting for you when it's over."

Quartermasters of the 24th Regiment
Edward Bloomfield and James Pullen

In addition to ordering his ammunition made ready to deploy forward, Henry Degacher sought out the band sergeant from his battalion. The chances of men being injured were high, and he needed his bandsmen on-hand to act as stretcher-bearers. Two empty ambulance wagons were also ordered ready. Surgeon-Major Shepherd was roused and directed to make ready to receive casualties. His 'hospital' was really more of a first aid station, consisting of a pair of tents where the lightly wounded could be tended, and the more serious stabilised before being sent back to the column's field hospital at Rorke's Drift. Shepherd had thought to send word back to his counterpart, Surgeon Reynolds, at the drift and advise him of the situation. However, there was simply no one to send. He then reckoned that Reynolds would receive word once the first of the seriously wounded were brought to him.

Making matters difficult for the column was the GOC's order forbidding the use of bugle calls. Alerting the camp would have been a simple matter of having the buglers sound reveille. However, Chelmsford was concerned Zulu scouts may be roaming the hills. The last thing he wanted was for word to reach the enemy that the column was coming to support the NNC.

It seemed the entire matter of stirring the companies and passing on all viable information, not just to the expeditionary force but to the camp at large, fell to Colonel Glyn's ADC, Major Clery. As soon as he'd finished speaking with Lieutenant Colonel Degacher, Clery realised that neither Glyn nor the GOC had left any specific instructions as to the defence of the camp. The major was reluctant to ask the colonel, who'd given up on issuing any sort of orders and would have told him to speak with Lord Chelmsford. The GOC was already dressed, mounted, and anxious to be underway. And so, Major Clery took it upon himself to scribble directions to Lieutenant Colonel Pulleine, orders he knew were in keeping with Chelmsford's intent.

Lt Col Pulleine,

You will be in command of the camp in the absence of Colonel Glyn. Draw in your infantry outpost line in conformity. Keep your cavalry vedettes well to the front. Act strictly on the defensive. Keep wagons loaded with ammunition ready to start should the general's force be in need of it. Lt Col Durnford has been ordered up from Rorke's Drift to reinforce the camp.

He gave this to his orderly and watched the man entered Pulleine's tent. He then sought out his horse and kit and made ready to depart. The two spoke briefly before Clery rode out to meet the GOC and Colonel Glyn. While Pulleine was Clery's superior in terms of rank, it was understood that the directive was implied to be Lord Chelmsford's intent. This was confirmed when the major rode out to where the command staff was watching the companies from 2/24th parade themselves as the artillery guns were being wheeled into position.

"Beg your pardon, my lord," Clery said. "But I left written instructions with Colonel Pulleine, stressing your intent that he act strictly on the defensive."

"I cannot tell you what a relief it is for me to hear this." This was the GOC's own way confessing he'd neglected to leave detailed instructions with Pulleine, and he was grateful for Clery's initiative. Neither man suspected that the camp would be in any danger. Every viable sighting of the Zulus came from the east, where they were now headed. However, decorum and military protocols still needed to be followed.

Chapter XXV: Skirmish in the Valley

Isandlwana
22 January 1879
6.30 a.m.

Lieutenant Colonel Henry Degacher
Commanding Officer, 2/24th Regiment

Like the rest of his mates, Arthur Wilkinson woke with excitement during the night-time alert; however, once word was passed that they would not be departing with the assault force, he immediately went back to sleep. Some of his mates stayed up, grumbling about their misfortune. Arthur reckoned he could wait until morning to complain about 2nd Battalion getting to take the fight to the Zulus.

He slept deeply, having a cacophony of strange and sometimes disturbing dreams. In one so vivid it seemed real to him, he was standing on the grass outside the church in Stratford-upon-Avon where he and Elisa were married. It was a sunny summer afternoon, and the two stood near the river. Elisa rested her head on his shoulder. He was filled with profound feelings of joy at being home with his beloved. This quickly morphed into the next dream which was very strange indeed. He was running, but he was not in his own body. Instead, he was with a swarm of black-skinned warriors carrying shields and spears and chanting in a language he did not understand.

Suddenly, he found himself standing near the rocks of the cliff-face near Sihayo's kraal. He was staring at the face of the Zulu marksman he had killed. Only now the man's eyes were open and filled with life despite the horrific wound and the pale colour of his skin. The man did not speak, but his eyes pierced into Arthur accusingly. The young soldier's physical body jolted as his dreams shifted once more. He was now in a field of tall grass, the sky was grey with thick clouds, and he could not tell if this was England or Natal. What he saw was a woman on her knees, her hands over her face. She was weeping uncontrollably. He could not see her face, but he knew it was his dearest Elisa. He went to kneel beside her, so he could take her in his arms and comfort her, yet could not move. He was frozen in place and could only watch as his beloved's sobs wrenched his heart. This last dream consumed his subconscious as the bugler sounded reveille.

Arthur jolted awake, his body trembling and his face covered in sweat. It was the first time since crossing the uMzinyathi that he'd been woken by the morning bugle call. He was breathing heavy, and his heart pounded in his chest. He pulled on his boots and grabbed all of his kit for morning parade, quietly saying, 'It was just a dream…'

Ten miles away at Rorke's Drift, the day was beginning much like any other. Lieutenant Bromhead and Colour Sergeant Bourne paraded their men, while Lieutenant Chard held a much smaller formation with his own detachment. Work on the ponts had gone well, and he assured Major Spalding the wagons and men could cross without fear of the barges or their support ropes failing. The major was relieved to hear it. Empty wagons from Isandlwana were due back that day. Plus, he was expecting reinforcements from Helpmekaar, two companies from 1/24th, to arrive at the drift at any time.

"Mister Harford, Commandant Lonsdale has ordered 2nd Battalion to join the attack on Phindo Hill. My lads are to continue their sweep across the summits."

"Very good," Charlie replied. Though he was not the senior officer from 2/3rd NNC, he was the most senior ranking present aside from Commandant Browne, who was riding off to rally his own battalion. Harford, with Norris-Newman following close behind, rode down to where the jumbled masses of NNC infantry were making their way tentatively towards caves that dotted the far hill. There was no sign of the regular army redcoats from 2/24th just yet, and Harford could only assume they were somewhere off to his far left, hidden from view by the terrain.

The caves offered an excellent field of fire for the Zulus hidden within. Despite the archaic quality of their firearms, they had managed to strike down thirteen NNC warriors who lay sprawled in the grass. Five were dead, the rest writhing in agony as they clutched at their shattered arms, legs, or splayed open guts. Despite their losses, Harford was impressed by the tenacity being shown by the NNC this day. Far from being the 'cowardly blacks' that 'Maori' Browne berated them as, they were showing great pluck and stalwart courage. Their own riflemen had taken cover behind the rocks and were returning fire.

In what seemed like déjà vu, Charlie Harford found himself assaulting caves, attempting to capture or kill any enemy fighters within. Accompanied by a handful of his more resolute warriors, with Norris-Newman documenting the entire ordeal in his notebook, the young officer shouted for the Zulus in the first cave to surrender. His men were simultaneously attacking the other caves. Trying to get the enemy to surrender would be far less costly than battling them, but his fighters were incensed by the losses they had suffered and were anxious for revenge. Some even brought up thatch, which they attempted to set alight in the mouth of one of the caves before Harford stopped them. And while the fighting was rather harrying at times, this was little more than a skirmish with a few renegade bands of Zulus. The main *impi* itself was nowhere to be found.

As he sat astride his horse on the Magogo Hill, Chelmsford could see the ongoing fight between the Zulus and the NNC. He had ordered the cannon and two companies from 2/24th to follow him up the hill. Progress proved slow, especially for the artillery. Scores of infantrymen were needed to help the gunners lift the heavy limbers over rocks and through crevices.

At the narrow nek between the hills, the GOC called for a halt and scanned the terrain to the east towards Siphezi Hill. "If Major Dartnell is correct, then this is the direction the enemy went."

Colonel Glyn and the remainder of the staff caught up with him. Lieutenant Colonel Degacher was still with the remaining four companies of his battalion on the wagon path below.

"What the hell are they playing at?" Crealock asked. He then spotted several small bands of Zulus lurking in the tall grass near Siphezi in the distance. To their far left they could see Lieutenant Colonel John Russell's Imperial Mounted Infantry in pursuit of about fifty Zulus, who were fleeing across the valley leading from Silutshane Mountain to the perceived safety of Siphezi. A couple were shot down by the redcoats on horseback. Russell halted his men well before the far hill, fearing they might be lured into a trap.

"Is this their rear-guard?" Chelmsford asked aloud, speaking to himself. "And if so, where is the main *impi*? Why don't they attack?"

The valley was about four miles long, covered in tall grass that masked crevices and dongas. Tall rocks abounded that could trip up man and horse alike. With only sporadic firing and so few signs of the enemy, it appeared the Zulus had retired for the moment. Russell and the IMI soon reached the safety of the Silutshane Mountain, dismounted, and rested their men and horses. In contrast to the stormy days they had endured off and on over the past weeks, the skies on this morning were completely cloudless. The midmorning sun promising a very hot day.

"Well, gentlemen," Chelmsford said to his staff. "How about breakfast?"

Breakfast would be an austere affair, especially by the standards usually enjoyed by the gentry officer class. The GOC's French cook, Monsieur Lapara, had remained at Isandlwana. There was no call for a world-class chef to risk his neck while the heart of the column went about chasing Zulus. There was no silver or bottles of claret, nor was there even a folding table. All any of them had was a mess tin with its accompanying knife and fork for their biscuits and tins of bully beef. The heat was now beating down on them. Chelmsford removed his helmet and ran his fingers through his sweat-soaked hair.

The staff was soon joined by Lieutenant Colonels Russell and Degacher, as well as Major Dartnell and Commandant Browne. Rupert Lonsdale and Charlie Harford had remained with their men to finish clearing out the caves that were still swarming with hostiles.

"Major Dartnell," Chelmsford said, calling the officer over to him. "It would seem the enemy force you saw last night has given us the slip."

"For the moment, my lord. However, I do think our action this morning has given some credence to Mr Fynn's assessment that the Zulus may be looking to exploit our right flank. They may still attempt to get behind us and block the crossing at Rorke's Drift."

"We are of one mind, major." The GOC sat with his back against the side of the hill. An overhanging outcropping of bushes provided some shade from the sun.

"Sir, we may wish to veer to the southwest and make certain Matshana is properly pacified," Degacher added.

"Yes, good point, colonel," Chelmsford concurred. "Since we do not know where the main *impi* is, only that they are somewhere between here and Ulundi, I see no point in returning to Isandlwana only to risk having our flanks exposed when we return."

"Are you proposing we re-establish our main camp here?" Colonel Glyn asked.

"Precisely, though not exactly here. The basin just above Mangeni Gorge will do nicely. I never planned to stay at Isandlwana for long. This way we've got the terrain working to our advantage. I think we can safely say Cetshwayo's army is somewhere to the east. No sense letting him slip away."

"Beg your pardon, my lord," Degacher said, his brow furrowed. "It's nearly fifteen miles from here to Isandlwana. Even for a rider on horseback, it will take roughly an hour to send a message back to Pulleine. With over half the column already here, there will be a severe shortage of labour to pack up all the tents, rations, and other equipment. It'll be almost nightfall before they are on the move."

312

"A trifle that is easily remedied," Chelmsford reassured him. He turned his attention to 'Maori' Browne who was already dreading the GOC's next directive. "Commandant Browne, once you've eaten, take your battalion back to Isandlwana and provide Colonel Pulleine with the necessary labour force to get the camp packed and ready to move to Mangeni Gorge."

'Maori' was nearly beside himself at this order. He was the only man still standing, while the other officers picnicked. He gazed around at the haphazard sights surrounding the small encampment. Nearby, the four guns Harness brought with him were unlimbered and pointing in the direction of Siphezi. The IMI were looting an abandoned kraal, where a dozen men were emerging with sacks of grain to feed their horses. The various companies from 2/24th were scattered about, mostly in 'receive cavalry' squares with lookouts posted, while the men ate some of the hard biscuits they'd brought with them. Some were already beginning to suspect they were in for a much longer day than originally anticipated.

Chelmsford sensed Browne's strain. He reckoned it was due to lack of sleep or hunger from having been denied his breakfast.

The GOC stood and offered his tin to the commandant. "Have you eaten yet, Maori?"

"No, my lord. And neither have my men…nor did any have a proper supper last night." Known as a scourge in the NNC, who decried all but the iziGqoza as 'useless niggers', Commandant Browne was showing a surprising amount of concern about the welfare of his men. Perhaps it was because his own hunger made him sympathise with them.

"Ah, yes. Well I can understand, as commandant, it would be poor for morale if you ate now in front of your fasting men."

Browne's expression remained unchanged. He asked Chelmsford incredulously, "Sir, do you realise I was still in contact with the enemy when you summoned me? Even as we speak, Commandant Lonsdale is engaged with the black devils that refuse to come out of those cursed caves."

"No," Chelmsford replied nonchalantly. Whatever trouble the locals created, it was little cause for alarm. He turned to his chief-of-staff. "Crealock, Browne tells me he was engaged when he received the order to come here."

Lieutenant Colonel Crealock, who had issued the order for Commandant Browne to come to the general's breakfast, was in a foul temper at having his judgement questioned. "Commandant Browne, I want you to return to the camp at once and assist Colonel Pulleine in striking camp and bringing the rest of the column here. Are we clear?"

Knowing it was useless to argue, 'Maori' snapped off a sharp salute with no attempt to mask his exasperation. "And if I should come across the enemy?"

"Brush them aside and go on," Crealock replied.

This type of nonchalance irked Browne to no end. Chelmsford used Crealock as his 'wasp' to issue the more unpleasant orders, making him the villain. All knew that an order from Crealock was as good as one from his lordship. 'Maori' was in a particularly bitter mood due to exhaustion, hunger, and the state of his battered battalion, rather than fear of any possible threat. After all, many troops, including almost all of 2/24th and most of the artillery, had crossed the Isandlwana valley both during the daytime and at night and had come under no harassment from the enemy. If the Zulus were threatening their rear, they would have known about it. Surely Cetshwayo's army would not have missed the opportunity to ambush an entire battalion of redcoats and four guns of artillery. But for Commandant Browne and 1/3rd NNC, their seemingly endless day was showing no end in sight.

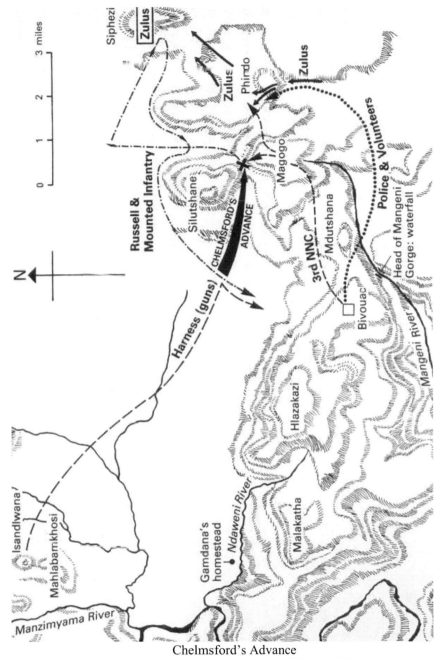

Chelmsford's Advance
The NNC had advanced the previous day via Ndaweni Valley between
Malakatha and Hlazakazi

Chapter XXVI: Durnford's Return

Rorke's Drift
22 January 1879
6.30 a.m.

Lieutenant Horace Smith-Dorrien
Assistant Transportation Officer, No. 3 Column

It had been a hard night's ride for Lieutenant Colonel Durnford's No. 2 Column. With most of their African infantry left to defend the other crossings into Natal, they had just two companies of NNC to act as escorts to the rocket battery. The majority of their troops were mounted auxiliaries, 315 in all, divided among five troops. Durnford's ever-loyal Basutos and the venerable Zikhali Horse made up the core of this fighting force. The column also had a number of wagons bearing ammunition, tents, rations, and grain for the horses. They found the river low enough to ford their horses across, saving the ponts for the supply wagons. They had ridden past B Company's small camp at the mission station, approximately half a mile from the actual drift. Durnford had quickly briefed Major Spalding on what was transpiring and was then on his way.

The column had paraded around 3.00 a.m., anticipating coming into contact with marauding bands of Zulus. As the pre-dawn glow lit the ground, it became apparent there were no enemy forces between Durnford's cavalry and Isandlwana. And since Chelmsford's orders only stated to come to Rorke's Drift, Durnford ordered his column to stand down while he rode into Helpmekaar.

"I'm concerned about the condition of our wagons," he explained to Captain George Shepstone. "The axles are weak on some. Others look as if their bottoms will fall out once we hit a difficult patch."

Shepstone knew it would be futile to try to convince any of the settlers to hand over more wagons, even at the outrageous rates they had already charged the government. Still, he knew it was pointless to debate this with his colonel. Durnford left about an hour before dawn, crossing back over the river and riding towards Helpmekaar, about fifteen miles from the drift. Within twenty minutes of his departure, sentries alerted Shepstone to a rider approaching from the east. In the faint light, it wasn't until the man dismounted and made his way over that George recognized him as Lieutenant Horace Smith-Dorrien.

The youngest officer in the entire No. 3 Column, Horace Smith-Dorrien was twenty years old; his fellow classmate at the Royal Military College, Sandhurst, 2nd Lieutenant Edwards Dyson of E Company, 1/24th being five months older. The son of a colonel and a graduate of Sandhurst two years earlier, he had served previously with the venerable 95th Rifles before volunteering to serve as a 'special service' officer in South Africa. Though his duties as a transportation officer were anything but glamorous, offering little chance of action, he relished the independence and empowerment that was not enjoyed by his fellow subalterns within the line companies.

"Captain, sir," he said with a salute. "Despatch from Lord Chelmsford for Lieutenant Colonel Durnford."

"The colonel just left for Helpmekaar," Shepstone explained, taking the despatch.

He dug through his ammunition pouch and pulled out eleven loose rounds, which he handed to the young transportation officer.

"Much obliged, this does make me feel a little better."

"Coffee's ready, gentlemen!" Dalton called from over by the fire.

Lieutenant Colonel Anthony Durnford was filled with unbridled excitement as he splashed his horse across the river and linked up with his column. Captain Shepstone already had the cavalry troops paraded and ready to ride. The NNC companies and rocket battery were standing to as well. Tents had been expediently loaded onto the wagons, and the column was ready to ride. The combatant elements would immediately make for Isandlwana, while it fell to Lieutenant Cochrane to oversee the safe transportation of their wagons and supplies. He rode over and saluted his colonel.

"Your pardon, sir," Cochrane said, somewhat self-consciously. "I know my duties as your transportation officer are tend to the wagons and supply trains. But it is a pretty straightforward journey from here to Isandlwana, and…well, this may be my one chance to see any real action, sir."

"I admire your dash, Mister Cochrane," Durnford replied. "You can ride as one of my ADCs this day."

"Honoured, sir." The lieutenant saluted and rode over to the lead conductor, giving him hasty orders to halt their wagons just short of Isandlwana and await instructions. He reckoned if there was a battle to be fought, parking his supply wagons could wait. Besides, it would take the slow-moving beasts at least four hours or more to reach the camp.

Perhaps the only soldiers within No. 2 Column who were less-than-enthusiastic about this journey to Isandlwana were the eight recoats from 1/24th assigned to the rocket battery, for they would have to make the ten mile journey on foot. Their indigenous Natal escorts were used to running, and all of the other white soldiers had horses. The best they could manage was to hold onto the mules that carried the cases of rockets and their troughs. The pack animals were surprisingly fast. Bombardier Goff had shown them they could hold onto the cargo straps and bound along beside them. It was awkward at best, yet the small band of 'volunteers' knew they had to make the best of it.

Though still early morning, it was now fully light out. Having been dismissed by Lieutenant Colonel Pulleine, John Chard made ready to leave Isandlwana. As he mounted his horse, he heard a commotion from the north end of the camp. He rode over to see several soldiers from C Company, 1/24th watching the far hills to the north. "See something of interest, colour sergeant?"

Thomas Brown was scanning the Nyoni ridge, approximately two miles to the north, with his field glasses.

Having never seen Lieutenant Chard before, Brown gave him a puzzled look. "Yes, sir. Looks to be a handful of Zulus on the ridge."

"May I borrow your glasses?" Chard asked. "Mine are scratched and damned near useless."

Thomas handed his up to the officer. From atop his horse the engineer lieutenant could see at least a hundred Zulus in the distance. They did not look to be massing for an attack. Instead, they were advancing off to the left, as if they were trying to avoid Isandlwana altogether.

"What do you make of it, sir?" the colour sergeant asked.

"Too few to be the main *impi*," Chard surmised. "And if Lord Chelmsford has gone out to meet them, then they are still miles to the east."

"A raiding party?"

"Perhaps." Chard's face suddenly twisted in an expression of alarm. "They could be making a dash for the ponts."

He handed Brown's field glasses back to him and turned his horse about. He then reassured himself; if they did try to assault the ponts, the Zulus would run straight into Durnford's column, who could more than handle them. Even if the Zulus had friends lurking behind the ridges, Chard was comfortable in the knowledge that the hundreds of riflemen at the camp, their auxiliaries, twin artillery

"Well, it's a matter of protocol. I mean, we are both lieutenant colonels; however, your rank is substantive. Mine is only a brevet. That makes you the senior officer here."

Neither man knew that Anthony Durnford had also been breveted to full colonel, effective six weeks earlier. The orders carrying this brevet promotion were still aboard a steamship that had yet to reach South Africa. Regardless, it was understood that Durnford was substantively senior to Pulleine. However, the last thing he wanted was to be left in command of a static camp. He was anxious to get his men to where Chelmsford needed them, but since his orders had only said to come to Isandlwana, there was no way of knowing exactly what the GOC had in mind for his cavalry.

"While I understand your concern, colonel," Durnford replied. "I am waiting for follow-up orders from Lord Chelmsford. I can say with a fair amount of certainty that it does not involve my mobile column remaining here for very long. Rest assured, the camp is yours. I will not interfere in any decisions you make regarding its defence."

This was not an answer the Lieutenant Colonel Pulleine wished to hear, but he knew it would be pointless to argue. He simply accepted it. While the daily running of the camp was still his responsibility, if an unforeseen emergency were to arise, he was not in the position to give Durnford orders. He hoped Chelmsford would send word back for the No. 2 Column to join him and relieve him of any potentially embarrassing chain-of-command confusion.

"Beg your pardon, sirs." Lieutenant Coghill hobbled over to the men. He had a long stick that he was using as a makeshift crutch.

"Mister Coghill, I trust you are not badly injured?" Durnford asked.

"Just a minor mishap involving a chicken, sir," the lieutenant replied, somewhat embarrassed. He then addressed Pulleine. "I've penned my message to Major Clery. Per Quartermaster Bloomfield, the companies' ammunition wagons are ready to be dispatched as needed; however, that last donga near the kraal is near impassable."

"Thank you, Mister Coghill," Pulleine replied. "I have a work detail under Lieutenant Anstey tasked with making the road passable."

"I passed Lieutenant Chard's sapper detachment," Durnford added. "They should be here within the next twenty minutes or so."

"Thank you, colonel," Henry acknowledged. "I'll send them with Mister Anstey. Hopefully they can make the necessary improvements to the road. Mister Coghill, see Mister Melvill. I have a brief despatch to be sent to his lordship. He may be in contact with the main Zulu *impi*, but he needs to be kept abreast of what we've seen here."

"Very good, sir." Coghill was clearly in great discomfort, as he limped back to his chair. Feeling a bit unwell from the painful swelling in his leg, he handed his message to a passing soldier, repeating the orders from Lieutenant Colonel Pulleine.

The two colonels decided to go for a walk along the gradual slope that gave them a commanding view of the camp and the open valley.

"Tell me, Henry." Durnford called Pulleine by his given name, perhaps to assuage him of any doubts or misgivings. "How many men do you have in the camp?"

"Not nearly enough. My own battalion is terribly understrength. That's why Chelmsford took Degacher's boys with him. Even with the arrival of Captain Mostyn's F Company, that only leaves me with five total. D and G Companies have made it as far as Helpmekaar, or so I've heard, and I'll feel much better once they've arrived. As it stands, I have sixteen officers and a little over four hundred other ranks. Lieutenant Pope's G Company from 2nd Battalion was on piquet duty all night. They are here now catching some rest. Degacher left a number of his soldier-servants, unattached men, and a few sick who aren't too ill to move to Rorke's Drift. So that brings the 2nd Battalion's detachment to..."

"One hundred and seventy three," Lieutenant Melvill said, joining the men. "Beg your pardon, sir, I did not mean to interrupt. I was just saying that that is the number of men from 2nd Battalion in the camp, including Charlie Pope's company."

"I see you have a pair of seven-pounders as well." Durnford nodded towards the pair of guns and the numerous horses being fed by their gunners.

"We also have thirty men from the IMI as a rear detachment, sir," Melvill continued. As adjutant, even if only for 1/24th, he had a firm grasp on the personnel situation in the camp. Pulleine was only too happy to let him continue explaining. "Plus we have a hundred and fifteen horsemen, consisting of Captain Bradstreet's Newcastle Mounted Rifles and Natal Mounted Police. And finally, we have four companies from the NNC currently on piquet duty, sir."

"An impressive force," Durnford commended. "That gives you a thousand men total?"

"Closer to twelve hundred, sir," Melvill corrected.

"And what of the movement of Zulus to the north? Lieutenant Chard made me abreast of their presence shortly before my arrival?"

"I think we may get an answer to that shortly," Melvill answered.

A lone rider was making his way in from the cavalry vedettes to the northeast.

The three officers went down to the NNC officers' tents. There they found Lieutenant Higginson and the battalion's sergeant major talking with a frantic European officer, Lieutenant Gert Adendorff.

"Alright, Mister Adendorff," Higginson was saying, "We'll come have a look for ourselves."

The nervous European adjusted his hat and walked quickly back to his horse, muttering to himself incoherently.

"Something amiss, Mister Higginson?" Pulleine asked.

"Hard to say, sir. That damned German is a nightmare to understand. I know he speaks Zulu, but that doesn't help us when his English is atrocious. Something about the Zulus in the north."

"Yes, we saw them, too," Pulleine remarked.

"We haven't heard any firing yet," the sergeant major said. "All the same, we should go see what is happening. Captain Barry and Lieutenant Vereker are out there now, sir."

"Keep me informed," the colonel stressed. "I cannot imagine the Zulus have gotten all the way around to the north."

"There are many warriors and kraals in this land, not just the main *impi*, sir," Melvill said as the cavalry officer and sergeant major departed. "For all we know, these could be men fleeing from Colonel Wood's column. We know he's been giving the Zulus a damn good thrashing to the north."

"I'll keep my men ready to ride should the need arise," Durnford noted. He then took his leave of Pulleine before returning to his column, which was still arriving a few troopers at a time.

"What do you make of it, Mister Melvill?" Pulleine asked when Durnford was out of earshot. Having not taken part in the previous war, the colonel had no way of knowing whether or not the Zulus spotted to the north posed any sort of threat

"I spoke with Henry Curling, and he is of the same mind-set as I am," Melvill replied, referring to the lieutenant in command of the two cannon left at Isandlwana.

"And that is?"

"We've seen this before. Thousands of Xhosa would be lurking in the bush or behind ridgelines, yet getting them to actually fight was damn near impossible. I keep hearing that that is not how the Zulus fight; however, I don't think they have ever faced the onslaught the Martini-Henry before. It wouldn't surprise me if they are being a little tentative in engaging us."

"All the same, I don't want to take any unnecessary risks," Pulleine remarked. "Order 'stand to'."

"Right away, sir." Melvill saluted and jogged back to the battalion's headquarters tent. He ordered the young bugler to sound the order.

The bugle notes echoed along the length of the large camp. Swarms of soldiers spilled out of their tents, grabbing their stacked arms and helmets as they did so. Lieutenant Colonel Pulleine then sought out the column's civilian interpreter, Mr Brickhill. A weathered, heavily-bearded man in his mid-forties, James Brickhill had been employed as an interpreter for the Natal government for almost nineteen years.

"Mr Brickhill!" Pulleine spotted him cooking his breakfast near Lieutenant Smith-Dorrien's empty wagons that were to be sent back to Rorke's Drift later that morning.

"Ah, colonel, I hear your bugles blowing. Nothing too alarming, I hope."

"Just a few wild bands of Zulus. But in case the situation becomes a little hectic, I need you to order our wagon drivers and voorloopers to round up any cattle wandering the camp. Tie the oxen into their yokes as well. Can't have hundreds of scared beasts rampaging through the camp in a panic, should my lads have to do a bit of shooting."

"Of course, we must take precautions." Mr Brickhill had lived in Natal most of his life and was very familiar with the Zulus. That he did not seem terribly alarmed at the moment helped put Pulleine's mind at ease.

As the interpreter shouted orders in the Natal warriors' tongue to start rounding up cattle and yoking oxen, they noticed a handful of mounted troops coming up the road from the direction of Rorke's Drift. Pulleine recognised Captain Bradstreet of the Newcastle Mounted Rifles among them. They were part of the observation post that had been placed behind the camp, near the Manzimnyama stream.

"Did you hear that, colonel?" Bradstreet asked, as he rode over to Pulleine. The men stood silently and listened closely. Soon Pulleine heard it. A muffled popping sound like a series of gunshots in the far distance.

"Sounds like our good general has found the Zulus," the colonel remarked.

"Could be, though it sounds like it's coming further from the north," Bradstreet observed. "Perhaps Colonel Wood has come up and is engaging the enemy?"

"That is a possibility as well," Pulleine said uncertainly. He knew that Wood's column had its own axis of advance towards Ulundi, so it would not be operating so closely to the centre column without good reason. He then remarked, "It would explain those swarms of Zulus we spotted earlier."

This was soon followed by shouting voices coming from down below, where Lieutenant Porteous' A Company stood in a long firing line. There was a small band of Zulus approaching, eight in all. They appeared to be extremely nervous and had their hands in the air.

"Friends of yours?" Durnford asked, re-joining the men along with Lieutenant Melvill and Captain George Shepstone.

"That would be *inkosi* Gamdana," Pulleine explained. "Lord Chelmsford spoke with him just yesterday, negotiating the terms of his surrender. It seems he has come to honour his part of the bargain. Mr Brickhill, kindly bring Gamdana and his followers to us."

The *inkosi's* followers carried a stack of old muskets between them, offered up as part of the arrangement made with the GOC. The weapons were taken by soldiers from A Company. A dozen others, accompanied by Lieutenant Porteous, escorted the men to the two colonels.

"Usuku oluhle," Gamdana said, holding his hands near his face and bowing slightly.

"Usuku oluhle," Mr Brickhill echoed, offering the same gesture of greeting.

The *inkosi* spoke at length, gesturing back towards the ridge behind them and then waving his hand to the southeast.

"He says he has come to honour the terms of friendship with Lord Chelmsford," Brickhill translated. "But he is fearful, due to the numbers of Zulus lurking in the north."

"Inform him that Lord Chelmsford is not in the camp," Pulleine instructed.

Mr Brickhill did as he was told. Gamdana's face betrayed his disappointment as he spoke in reply.

"He is sad to see his lordship is not here. He also asks that he and his followers be allowed to leave the camp. Their cattle are grazing near Hlazakazi, a few miles to the southeast. He does not wish for the Zulus to take his property or the British to mistake his cattle for those belonging to the enemy."

Pulleine looked to Durnford. While Anthony had no desire to assume command of the camp, he understood that as the senior officer present, it was his decision to make. He felt it wise to hear the thoughts of the interpreter.

"Do you accept his word in good faith, Mr Brickhill?"

"Well, his men have turned in their guns," James replied. "All they have to protect themselves is their assegai. And I doubt they're spies. There is nothing in this camp that the Zulus lurking to the north haven't already seen."

"He's kept his end of the bargain," Pulleine added. "If they were any threat to us, they certainly would not have handed over their firearms."

"Very well," Durnford agreed. "Send them on their way. But let him know, he is to send a runner back to us immediately if he comes into contact with the Zulus."

As Mr Brickhill translated, the officers present noticed an air of impatience surrounding the commanding officer of No. 2 Column.

They then heard more of the distant popping. However, it was impossible to tell if it was coming from the north, like it sounded.

331

That would mean Colonel Wood was operating within ten miles of them. Another possibility, one that seemed more likely, given the circumstances, was that they were the sounds of gunfire coming from Chelmsford's attack force in the east, and the noise was ricocheting off the hills. Either way, Lieutenant Colonel Durnford felt useless standing around waiting for orders. He shifted his disabled arm; his hand pinned inside his jacket.

Chapter XXVII: Nothing Will Happen

Ngwebeni River Basin, nine miles northeast of Isandlwana
22 January 1879
8.30 a.m.

Brevet Major Henry Spalding
Officer Commanding, Helpmekaar and Rorke's Drift

It can be described as nothing short of remarkable that both Chelmsford's advance force from No. 3 Column and the Zulu *impi* of 25,000 warriors completely missed each other. While the NNC, as well as Chelmsford himself, had been led to believe the scattered forces along the Magogo and Siphezi hills were elements from the main Zulu army, Ntshingwayo had no knowledge that Chelmsford had left Isandlwana. For the Zulus, this was still a war of manoeuver. With their uncertainty as to Matshana's loyalty, and not wishing to risk a head-on engagement with the British, the *inkosi* had little choice but to take his *amabutho* on a long and arduous trek across a range of mountaintops to the north.

Despite his seventy years of age and protruding belly, Ntshingwayo was still able to keep pace with his warriors on foot. It helped that they were following the king's directive to run at a far more measured stride, lest they wear themselves out before coming into contact with the redcoats. Prince Dabulamanzi, Sihayo, and a few of the other *amakhosi* continued to ride on horseback, despite being shamed by the elderly warrior who still ran with his men. For Ntshingwayo, the rhythmic cadence of his men helped clear his mind, for he was troubled by many questions.

He knew the British had marched towards Isandlwana. However, he knew not if they were passing through or intended to make a more permanent camp, complete with stone ramparts and wagon laager. He had no idea how their camp was arranged, where their cannon were positioned, how many cannon they had, their cavalry vedettes, picquets, placement of their firing lines. In truth, he was as blind to his enemy as they were to him. All of these concerns raced through his mind during the early morning of 22 January, as his forces reached Ngwebeni River, nine miles northeast of Isandlwana.

The *inkosi's* intent was to rest his army this day while beginning a slow and deliberate reconnaissance towards Isandlwana. He had to get as many sets of eyes on the British camp as possible, provided it was still even there! Knowing and respecting their firepower, Ntshingwayo knew he had to get his huge army as close as possible without being spotted. Stealth and manoeuver were the keys to this next phase of the battle plan. He had already designated which of the *amabutho* would make up the 'chest' and 'horns' of the attack. He had a rough idea as to the layout of the land, and thought it possible to get the right horn completely around the backside of Isandlwana before unleashing the chest and left horn. There were plenty of dongas his regiments could use for cover, particularly under the cover of night. And yet, he knew that no matter how long he managed to keep his army concealed or how close they got to the camp, there would still be that last rush over a large expanse of open ground before they could close with the redcoats and their Natal allies. Even under perfect conditions, Ntshingwayo knew many of his young warriors would die.

By the time Lieutenant John Chard returned to Rorke's Drift, he expected to see the number of redcoats at the garrison doubled, or even tripled. Major Upcher and Captain Rainforth were supposed to have already arrived with D and G Companies, 1/24th. Yet the only men currently guarding the ponts were warriors of the NNC, who were nothing more than excess levies Chelmsford left under the command of a local captain named Stevenson. As these men milled about, the only other men on the ponts were a lone sergeant from The Buffs, who was tasked with running the ponts, along with six riflemen and a lone corporal from B Company. Chard recognized the NCO as William Allan, who had kindly helped him and his sappers establish their little camp at the drift.

"Mister Chard, sir," the corporal said, coming to attention and saluting.

"Corporal Allan," Chard replied, returning the courtesy. "I need to see Major Spalding at once."

"Of course, sir. He should be in his tent. Something amiss?"

"Keep your eyes open. There might be trouble afoot," the engineer officer stated.

He found Major Spalding sitting on a camp stool outside his tent, reading a local newspaper whose headlines proclaimed the war against the Zulus in bold letters. A pipe was clenched between his teeth, his morning coffee brewing in a kettle over a small fire.

"Mister Chard," he said. "I guess they didn't need you up at the column after all. Any news?"

"Lord Chelmsford thinks the NNC may have found lead elements of the main Zulu *impi*." Chard took a seat across from the major. "He's taken over half the column on a hunting expedition to find them, at least that's what Colonel Pulleine said."

"So I heard from Lieutenant Smith-Dorrien." Spalding took a drag off his pipe and letting the smoke waft out his nostrils. "Hopefully his lordship gets the matter sorted soon enough."

"About that, sir. I spotted a large force of Zulus before I left the camp. They were well north of Isandlwana and moving west. I informed Colonel Durnford, who I met coming up the road, but I fear they might be a raiding party. Are we not supposed to have another company here guarding the ponts?"

"We are," Spalding acknowledged. "Rainforth is well overdue, as is Major Upcher, who is expected to join the main column. You said so yourself, the roads are a soggy mess; however, his men should still be able to walk here in due time."

"I'm no tactician, sir, I build bridges for the army," Chard remarked with a self-deprecating grin. "But I do not trust Stevenson's natives, nor him for that matter. He strikes me as a rather shifty fellow. And no seven men, even Her Majesty's finest sharp-shooters, can hold the drift for long."

"Yes, this is a bit distressing, isn't it?" Spalding's tone was nonchalant, in stark contrast to his words. Though as he folded his paper and stood, Chard could see he was a bit unnerved at the prospect of Zulu raiders. "If Colonel Durnford views them as a threat, I'm sure he'll disperse them with his cavalry. Still, I'd like to know what is keeping Rainforth and Upcher. I think I shall take a ride to Helpmekaar and see what the delay is."

While he had little doubt about what Chard had seen, Major Spalding was clearly not as concerned as the engineer lieutenant. However, his overdue reinforcements had caused him a bit of stress, especially after the column had departed for Isandlwana. The garrisons at Helpmekaar and Rorke's Drift were both his responsibility, as was the transportation of supplies and men between the two stations. The last thing he wished was to be held responsible for the incessant delays.

The major's horse was tethered nearby. He packed a tin of bully beef and some biscuits into the saddlebags, along with a bag of tobacco. He then looked over his shoulder to the engineer officer and asked, "Who is senior, you or Bromhead?"

"I don't know, sir," Chard replied.

"Hmm." Always one for formalities and propriety, Spalding went back into his tent and found a copy of the Army List for the column. He scanned it until he found both of their names. "I see you are senior, so you will be in charge until I return. Nothing will happen, of course, and I shall be back this evening. Until then Rorke's Drift is yours, Mister Chard."

336

It was now 9.30 in the morning. Twenty-five miles away, near Mangeni Gorge, the decisive battle Lord Chelmsford longed for had failed to materialise. Whether it was the heat or the Zulus playing like the Xhosa and refusing to fight, Lord Chelmsford's mood was darkening. No sooner had 'Maori' Browne left to rally his battalion for its return to Isandlwana than a cryptic note was delivered to Major Clery from a Natal Mounted Policeman. The man had just come from the camp and seemed to be in a hurry. He said nothing, but simply handed the short note to the major. It read:

Staff Officer,

Report just came in that the Zulus are advancing in Force from the left front of the Camp.

8.50 a.m.

H.B. Pulleine, Lt Col

Clery was troubled by this, but what bothered him even more was the complete lack of detail given by Pulleine. Were the Zulus attacking? How many were there? *'In Force'* was such a generic term. It gave no meaning whatsoever to how much trouble the camp may or may not have be in. The GOC was seated nearby, so Clery decided it was best to show it to him.

"What is to be done about this report, sir?"

Chelmsford scanned the message and gave a dismissive shrug. "Nothing is to be done about it. If Pulleine were in trouble he would have said as much. If a few Zulus wander into his midst, a couple of volleys from the Martini-Henry will deal with them properly."

"Beg your pardon, my lord." It was Captain Mainwaring of A Company, 2/24th whose men were taking a rest up the road. He'd spoken with the mounted policeman beforehand. "It sounds to us like there might be more than what is in the message. The camp may indeed be surrounded and under attack."

Chelmsford forced himself to refrain from rolling his eyes as he stood and scanned with his field telescope towards the camp. Nearly fifteen miles away, he could still make out the white smudge that marked the lines of tents.

337

"Mister Milne," he said to his Naval ADC, Archibald Berkeley Milne of the HMS Active. "Kindly take your telescope to a high point and see if you can spot any unusual activity in the direction of Isandlwana."

"Right away, my lord." Milne hefted the large case carrying his naval telescope and began the climb up the side of Magogo Mountain.

Chelmsford then addressed Mainwaring. "Captain, do tell your men to calm themselves. The nervous ramblings of a jittery police orderly are nothing for them to get worked up over. I've already dispatched Commandant Browne's NNC battalion to return to Isandlwana. Perhaps he and Colonel Pulleine will get lucky and bag a few more Zulus than we've been able to."

It was unusual for Chelmsford to allow subordinates to see his frustration. As their expedition to Mangeni was looking more and more like a complete bust, the GOC was losing his earlier enthusiasm.

No one at Mangeni, not even the ever cautious Colonel Glyn, had any suspicions the camp might be in danger. Glyn, however, shared Clery's frustration that Pulleine had not been more specific in his despatch. If he had stated how many there were, what they were doing, and from which terrain features, they might have had a better idea what was transpiring. Instead, all they knew was that anywhere from a hundred to a thousand wandering Zulus were lurking in the vicinity of Isandlwana. Regardless, it was nothing Pulleine and 1/24th couldn't manage.

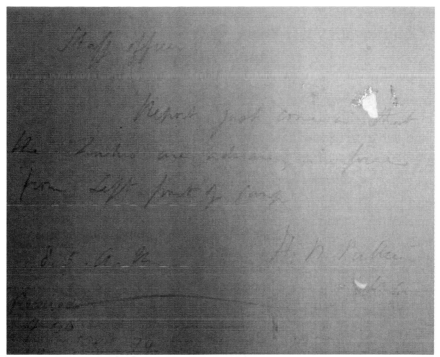

Lieutenant Colonel Pulleine's despatch
Received by Major Clery at 9.30 a.m.

When he returned to the headquarters tent, Melvill found Pulleine scanning the northern ridgelines with his field glasses. Whatever awkwardness had passed between them was apparently forgotten.

"There." He pointed towards the hill of Mkwene about a mile-and-a-half distant, where an NNC piquet was manned. "To the left is the blind spot. Damn it all, I should have seen it before."

"I don't see anything, sir," Melvill said, scanning with his own glasses.

"Precisely," the colonel replied. "Something's been troubling me ever since that engineer fellow, Lieutenant Chard, mentioned the Zulus possibly making a go for the ponts. We haven't had any word back from the direction of Rorke's Drift; however, I think the enemy is out there, and they might be manoeuvring past us towards the west."

For being completely new to battalion command, and having spent almost his entire career as a staff officer, Henry Pulleine was showing a surprising amount of tactical insight, which impressed Melvill greatly. Pulleine knew he had a large camp to protect, with less than half the manpower assets necessary. A Zulu force of one to three thousand warriors could cause a great deal of trouble if not promptly checked. Intelligence would be key, and the NNC picquets were simply not sufficient.

"There's a valley just to the left of that hill," Pulleine continued. "Dispatch Lieutenant Cavaye and E Company. They should have eyes on both the eastern dongas, as well as the Manzimnyama stream behind us."

"Very good, sir. What of the rest of the battalion?"

"Order the stand-down," Pulleine answered. "They can return to their tents, cool themselves a bit, and finish their breakfasts. However, I want every last man ready to move to the firing line at a moment's notice."

In that moment, Pulleine was feeling rather pleased with himself. On the surface, his mission of defending the camp was not one that required supreme tactical skill and manoeuvre. However, he felt he had made the necessary precautions, in case the unknown Zulu force should decide to make a return. If Melvill was correct and the Zulus spotted were refugees fleeing Colonel Wood's column, then they had likely scattered to the winds. In which case he could rest easy.

Still, he wished Colonel Wood would send a rider to inform them of the situation. Chelmsford had undoubtedly told him the centre column would be establishing itself for the time being at Isandlwana. One would think Wood would inform them if he was operating in the vicinity. No word at all from No. 4 Column cast doubts about this assessment.

Arthur removed his helmet and ammunition belt. He slumped onto his sleeping mat. The hours spent on parade in the growing heat of the sun had been, in his mind, a needless misery. His legs were stiff and his feet sore from standing in place for so long.

"I think my papa was right," he said as he lay on his back, tunic opened, arms and legs splayed out. "I should have stayed in Stratford and taken a respectable profession, like a farrier."

"What?" Richard protested. "And miss out on all this fun? What kind of stories does a farrier have to tell his grandchildren? You, my friend, have already seen more over the past few months than any of our mates back home ever will. Imagine how many more stories you'll have in six years…or twelve, if you prove mad enough to stay in the army."

"At least we're not with them," Bray said, nodding out the entrance to their tent. E Company was marching past, their soldiers having spent just as much time on parade, yet were being denied so much as a few minutes of reprieve in the shade.

"It must suck to be them," Arthur said, lifting his head up for a moment before letting it flop onto his bed roll. In that moment, he did not care if Lord Chelmsford finished off the Zulus this day. He had already seen action on this campaign, even if it amounted to little more than a prolonged skirmish. He'd only fired two rounds at the enemy, but one of those had killed a man. The face of the Zulu he'd slain would haunt him for the rest of his days. That should be enough to satisfy his sense of duty to both the Queen and the Empire.

While most of the column headed due east with Durnford, one troop from Zikhali Horse was headed back down the trail towards Rorke's Drift to escort in their baggage and ammunition wagons. Two others, under the commands of Lieutenants Charlie Raw and William Roberts, had been ordered to head northeast around the escarpment. They would first veer north around the hill of Mabaso and drive any stray bands of Zulus into Durnford's main column, which by that time would be sweeping in from the west. Unfortunately for Major Russell and the rocket battery, Durnford had neglected to mention where he wanted them. His forces broke into a gallop of excitement and neither the artillery officer nor any of his men knew where they were supposed to link up.

Chapter XIX: By God, We've Found Them

Natal Native Horsemen

The two officers leading Zikhali Horse rode together out of the camp. Their troopers acted as a single entity, at least until they got as far north as Mkwene Hill. Durnford had informed Charlie Raw that a company of NNC were on picquet duty at the hill and he was to round them up and take them with him if needed. Captain George Shepstone accompanied Raw, though for the time being deferred all tactical decisions to the troop's commander.

It was a basic, yet tactically sound plan Durnford had briefed his officers on. Raw and Roberts would head due north and skirt across the ridgelines until they reached Mabaso. Durnford would take the remaining two troops in an arc veering east and then northeast. Any Zulus would be caught between them, and the column commander hoped to capture a few and gather what intelligence he could about the main *impi*. As the directive from Chelmsford, requiring the camp be moved to Mangeni Gorge, had yet to reach Isandlwana, no one from either Durnford's or Pulleine's command had any knowledge of how the fight in the east was progressing.

"The enemy is retiring, and I intend to follow them up," the colonel had told his men.

About three miles from the camp, well past the first conical koppie and beyond another hill called Itusi, they spotted several small bands of Zulus who immediately fled at the sight of the mounted troopers.

"If they are going towards the General, we must stop them at all hazards!" Durnford stressed to his men who took off in pursuit.

As Charlie Raw's troop reached Mkwene Hill, he came upon the NNC picquet. To his left he saw the redcoats of E Company, 1/24th, scattered among the rocks on high ground. Raw relayed Durnford's order to the NNC commander, informing him that they were to join him and provide support. Without question, partly due to the relief of a bit of action rather than the continued tedium of picquet duty, the NNC warriors quickly complied.

Lieutenant Roberts' troop pressed further north before veering east, keeping along a ridge which looked down on the Ngwebeni River to the north. As they advanced east, towards Mabaso Hill, both officers deployed their troops into echelons. The NNC followed not far behind Raw. The terrain was extremely rugged, only allowing for their horses to run at a modest canter. The ground rose and fell, broken up by the occasional donga; however, the troops were separated by less than a mile, and their officers made certain they stayed on line with each other. Neither had any sort of visual contact with Colonel Durnford, who was two to three miles to the south of them, hidden by a series of ridges and hilltops. Fortunately, the Mabaso Hill stood out starkly against the skyline, dominating the landscape. For Lieutenant Roberts, it was simply a matter of following the Ngwebeni River, which wrapped around the north side of the hill. At the same time, Charlie Raw led his troop straight towards the mountain's pinnacle.

There were small bands of Zulus, no more than four or five in each group, roaming about. These men were foragers, bringing food back in the way of mealie and stray cattle for their friends. Raw, like Durnford, understood the value of gathering intelligence from enemy combatants, and these were the first Zulu men of fighting age they had seen since the attack on Sihayo's kraal.

"*Emva kwabo!*" he shouted, ordering his men to chase after the Zulus.

Their quarry abandoned the cattle and were sprinting across the rough terrain, skirting the north side of the mountain. The numerous crevices and rocks prevented the Zikhali horses from overtaking them. Raw veered his troop back to the right, once he realised that Roberts and his men were about to run straight into them. Leading his men from the front, he managed to sprint his horse the remaining distance, keeping just to the right of the Mabaso peak. He reached a long ridge that extended about a mile from end-to-end, and with eyes wide he reined his horse to an abrupt halt. Below the ridge, reaching back to the Ngwebeni River, was a massive bowl. What lay within filled him with alarm and dread.

"Oh, fuck," he whispered, his voice suddenly hoarse.

The entire ground from the base of the ridge all the way back to the river was black with the massed horde of Zulu warriors. At least twenty thousand men lay encamped along the slopes and down by the river. As Captain Shepstone, Lieutenant Roberts, and the lead elements of their troops reached the ridge, Charlie Raw had an overwhelming and terrifying realisation. Lord Chelmsford had been chasing shadows this whole time. The main Zulu *impi* was not east of Mangeni but here, nine miles northeast of Isandlwana.

"By God," Raw said. "We've *found* them."

For Ntshingwayo and the main Zulu army, their day of rest was proving to be filled with misfortune. The phases of the moon were not right just yet, and to go into battle this day was an ill omen that would undoubtedly offend the divines. He was determined to attack on the morrow, when the omens were more favourable, and after

351

they had a better understanding as to their enemy's strength and disposition.

All morning they heard gunfire echoing, and like the British at Isandlwana, they struggled to ascertain where it was coming from. Like Pulleine and Melvill, the Zulu *inkosi* thought perhaps it was coming from the British forces to the north. He later ascertained that it was in fact coming from the east. He then realised, with much guilt, that Matshana must have proven loyal, and he was now being savaged by a raiding party from the enemy column.

From the minute they made camp near the Ngwebeni River, the Zulu general knew, though he did not intend to fight on this ill-omened day, he needed to conduct a thorough reconnaissance of the ground in and leading up to the enemy camp at Isandlwana. Unfortunately, neither he nor any of his men had ever purchased field glasses from the white traders. Even from the top of Mabaso, they could not see any details of the British encampment, just the white splotch where some of their tents lay.

Ntshingwayo knew coordinating such a massive army would be a gargantuan undertaking, and he had thought to get at least some of the *amabutho* in position. Given the alarm caused at the enemy camp, he was now having doubts as to the wisdom in sending the regiments of the 'Right Horn' west in an effort to get behind Isandlwana. He knew it was a practical move, but one riddled with risk. Even under Mkhosana's venerable leadership, the younger warriors were still prone to errors. Foremost was advancing along the tops of the ridgelines, exposing themselves to the enemy's picquets. Unbeknownst to Colonel Pulleine and the camp's defenders, the warriors they spotted were not a lost band of raiders nor refugees fleeing from Colonel Wood's column. They were, in fact, the 'Right Horn' of the Zulu *impi*.

There had been much excitement since the return of the advance elements of the uNokhenke and uKhandempemvu regiments. Word spread rapidly, and the blood-lusted warriors were anxious to attack the camp, ill omens be damned! Ntshingwayo was having none of it, for he did not wish to offend the spirits of those protecting them. By late morning he called an immediate council with the senior *amakhosi*. The regimental *izinduna* were tasked with calming their men and not allowing passion to overtake them.

It was proving especially difficult for Kwanele to curtail his warriors' enthusiasm. They had taken part in the excursion to the west, before being ordered back to their bivouac. He was thankful his fighters hadn't inadvertently exposed themselves to the whites at Isandlwana, like some of those fools from the uKhandempemvu. However, there was now a growing sense of anxiousness. During the past few days, they had made the journey of more than sixty miles, including a rather arduous trek across the mountaintops to the northeast of Isandlwana. The last thing they wanted now was to wait to attack the enemy, when they were so close.

"We saw them," one man said in disbelief. "We actually *saw* them!"

"My blade thirsts for their blood," another snarled, hefting his broad stabbing spear.

"I will feed my club with the brains of our enemies," another chanted, brandishing his knobkerrie.

"Easy, my brothers." Kwanele tried to calm them, despite feeling the same growing sense of wrath as his warriors. "Soon our weapons will feast on the corpses they have made, but we do not strike until the great *inkosi* tells us to…"

His words were cut short. One of his men stood, shouting and pointing his spear towards the southern slope of the bowl. They and most of the uNokhenke were resting barely two hundred yards from where a long line of horsemen emerged. They were mostly black Africans. They were dressed like the whites and led by white officers. Within seconds the valley echoed with the sound of a hundred carbines firing. A man not thirty feet from Kwanele screamed as the heavy slug smashed into his upper chest near the shoulder. Blood sprayed his friends and he fell to the earth, clutching at the terrible wound, with bits of splintered bone protruding through the bloodied skin. Several others had fallen nearby. Kwanele saw the top of one poor young warrior's head explode. The bullet entered just in front of his temple, then burst out the top of his head, disgorging a horrific spray of bone and brain.

The *induna's* heart sank. These men were his brothers. Together they had taken part in the eight day ritual that purified the mind and spirit. Their bodies and minds were supposedly shielded by the magic of the *izinyanga* and the spirits of their ancestors. Yet now, with every salvo from the troopers atop the ridge, these brave men

Quickly recovering from the horror of his initial shock, Lieutenant Raw knew the camp must be warned immediately. The quickest way to sound the alarm was to take the fight to the Zulus, here and now. He drew his pistol and, having taught fire commands to his Zikhali Horse in English, gave a loud shout, *"Volley...fire!"*

His troopers had no time to adjust their sights; however, the closest Zulus were but two hundred yards away. As thick as they were, his men could simply sling bullets at the black mass and have a reasonable chance of scoring a hit.

"Reload! Volley...fire!"

The Zulus were now on their feet and charging en masse, and it was impossible to see in the swarm how many were felled by his troopers' bullets. Their horses whinnied and reared up in fear, and Raw knew they could not stay on the ridge much longer. One of his black troopers cried out. Struck by an enemy musket shot, he fell from his horse. He was bleeding profusely from the shoulder, gritting his teeth in pain and terror. Three of his mates dismounted and heaved the man back onto the saddle of his startled horse. They turned his mount around and slapped it on the rump. With his arm disabled, the trooper was out of the fight. Now it would be a matter of whether or not he could escape with his life.

Raw quickly ordered one last volley. By that time, the Zulus were almost upon them. He fired his pistol three times in rapid succession, catching one man twice in the chest. So great the force of his onslaught, the stricken warrior lurched forward to within a few feet of Raw's horse before falling in a twitching, dying heap.

There was no need to sound the order to retreat. Troopers had already turned their mounts and were galloping with all speed away from the black storm of death that pursued them. Charlie Raw found himself at the very back of the troop. Knowing the speed of a furious Zulu sprinter, he prayed that his horse was faster.

For Ntshingwayo and the *amakhosi*, the sudden arrival of the white-led cavalry was deeply unsettling. Not only was the day one of hapless portents, but there were additional rituals each warrior was to be subjected to before plunging headlong into battle. These were to compensate for any loss of potency from the medicines and rituals of the *izinyanga* during the purification rites at Ulundi. Before any engagement, the army was supposed to be drawn together into the sacred circle of their people, the *umkhumbi*, from where they would be splattered with the last-minute medicines and protective charms. And then the *amakhosi* would implore them with grand speeches, goading each regiment to fight harder than their brothers, earning heroic glory in defence of their people and in the name of their majestic king, Cetshwayo. On this day there would be none of that. By a mere stroke of misfortune, the sons of Zulu would rush into battle unprotected and fully exposed, both physically and spiritually, to the savagery of the British firepower.

"Return to your regiments!" Ntshingwayo shouted to the *amakhosi*. "The gods test us this day, let us not allow misfortune to be compounded by undisciplined recklessness."

Even with the frenzy of bloodlust brought on by the unexpected onslaught of their mounted foes, the Zulu army was still a highly organised and surprisingly disciplined fighting force. At least a score of their companions had been slain, with perhaps three times as many badly wounded or maimed by the destructive power of the white men's carbines.

While Mkhosana and the *amakhosi* of the main regiments chased after their men, the younger *izinduna* attempted to reform them into company lines. Ntshingwayo managed to halt the attempted frenzy of the most senior regiments which made up Prince Dabulamanzi's Undi Corps. These men were much older, the youngest in their early forties, and the oldest around fifty. Grey-haired, with many a grandfather among their ranks, they were the elders of the Zulu warrior nation. Ntshingwayo was determined that as the reserve corps this day, they would set the example of pride and dignity expected of the king's *amabutho*.

The *inkosi* held aloft his shield and shouted, *"Sons of Senzangakhona and Shaka, brothers of our majestic king, Cetshwayo! This is the love charm of our people! You ask why this person is loved so much. It is caused by the love charm of our people. You are sons of Zulu! There is no going home!"*

Scrambling his way to the top of Mabaso, Ntshingwayo was relieved to see that, even in their frenzy, the *amabutho* appeared to be in their correct formations. Just under half his force, roughly 10,000 men, were pursuing the fleeing horsemen who he surmised would head straight for Isandlwana. The uNokhenke and uKhandempemvu of the 'Right Horn' were following generally the same route. They were headed due east towards the north side of Mkwene Hill, five miles away. Many of the warriors of the 'Chest' were angling towards the long Nyoni Ridge, a two-mile stretch between Mkwene and Itusi Hill to the southwest. Most of Dabulamanzi's Undi Corps, about 4,000 men, followed the north side of the Ngwebeni River, keeping parallel with the 'Right Horn'. Another thousand from the Undi Corps were detached to the extreme left, providing rear and flank support to the regiments of the much younger uVe Corps who made up the 'Left Horn'.

There was still much apprehension within the old *inkosi*. Despite the legendary speed a Zulu warrior could run into battle, the shortest approach to Isandlwana was at least nine miles. Without a doubt, the whites at the camp had heard the sounds of gunfire. They would now have ample time to prepare their defences. Ntshingwayo lamented that they had not been able to conduct a proper reconnaissance of the camp. He still had no knowledge of its layout or their total strength. The clumsy *ibutho* who allowed themselves to be seen earlier had failed to properly scout their enemy. And while he could conjecture that a British force had attacked Matshana to the east, he did not know how many there were, let alone what was left at the camp. In short, he had no better knowledge of his enemy than he had when they first arrived at the Ngwebeni River. He feared his warriors would pay a terrible price for this lack of knowledge.

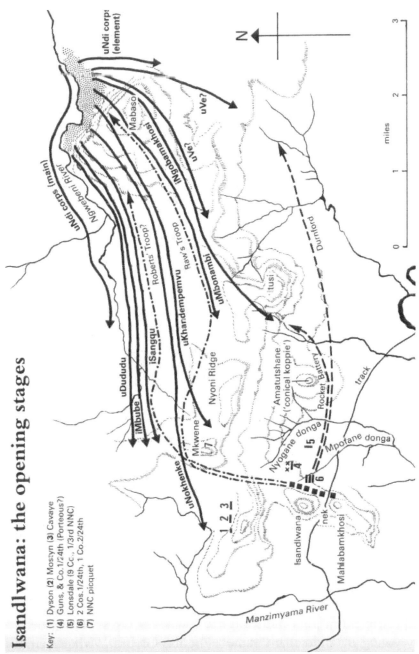

Isandlwana: the opening stages

Key: (1) Dyson (2) Mostyn (3) Cavaye
(4) Guns, & Co. 1/24th (Porteous?)
(5) Lonsdale (9 Cc., 1/3rd NNC)
(6) 2 Cos.1/24th, 1 Co.2/24th
(7) NNC picquet

The initial Zulu advance, which opened the Battle of Isandlwana
No. 1, 2, and 3 denote the disposition of E Company, 1/24th

"If you want to have some fun, go to the top of the hill," his companion said. His mouth twisted in a macabre smirk. "They are thick up there."

"We'll head that way," Major Russell nodded to Captain Nourse.

"Suit yourselves, sir. If you follow the donga and skirt the stream you should make it. It'll be a hard slog, but you might get to the top in time to say 'hello' to the Zulus."

Major Russell intended to berate the man for his impertinence, but he was now in a rush. Besides, the carbineers were racing back towards the picquet at the conical koppie. He and Captain Nourse remained mounted while the NNC and rocket battery crews climbed their way along the broken terrain, struggling to help the heavily-laden mules over the rocks and up the steep slope. The small band of redcoats had heard the entire conversation and were filled with apprehension. Were they walking straight into the enemy? The NNC warriors couldn't understand English and were completely oblivious to the pending danger. These were Natal Africans, and not iziGqoza. Captain Nourse was deeply concerned they would bolt as soon as the enemy showed themselves.

After much grunting, climbing, slipping, and cursing, they eventually reached a long spur that extended the rest of the way up the hill.

Anxious to see the situation for himself, Major Russell kicked his horse into a gallop and rode to the top of the hill. He halted, mouth agape as he scanned the horizon that was now swarming with Zulus. They were no longer moving at a maddened sprint but had found their discipline. The *amabutho* were now advancing in company lines, with most were veering towards Isandlwana. There was, however, a very large force directly to Russell's front. He turned his mount and shouted, *"Action front!"*

"Oh, bugger all," Private Johnson muttered, as the 1/24th soldiers quickly unpacked the v-shaped rocket troughs and hastily made ready to fire their Hales rockets.

The troughs were simple enough to set up with fold-out legs that formed a supporting tripod. The privates set up the troughs, while Bombardier Goff and Private Trainer began breaking open the first box of rockets.

They laid the first into Grant and Johnson's trough, while
Captain Nourse shouted orders to his NNC to make ready for battle.
His riflemen, though armed with Martini-Henrys, only had five
rounds apiece.

"We should save these for next Guy Fawkes Night," James
Trainer muttered with morbid sarcasm. He extended the lanyard
which he handed to Goff.

"I'll save one just for you, James," the bombardier replied.

The severity of their predicament became apparent when a mass
of Zulus appeared on the ridge scarcely two hundred yards from
where they stood. Rather than charging, they held in place, chanting
'Usuthu!' over and over again, banging their weapons on their
shields. Large numbers of skirmishers bearing old muskets were
deploying along the ridge in front of their companions.

Major Russell swallowed hard before issuing his next order.
"Fire!"

It was Mehlokazulu and the iNgobamakhosi who happened upon
the rocket battery with Nourse's pitiful escort. A large regiment,
consisting of over 3,000 men, they were a fearsome force in their
own right. Forming the innermost echelon of the 'Left Horn', their
intent was to skirt east of the conical koppie with the uVe on their
left and the thousand-man element from the Undi Corps in reserve.
They would follow the wagon trail two miles west and assault the
eastern face of Isandlwana. The regiments of the 'Chest',
approximately 10,000 warriors, would attack from the north over the
Nyoni Ridge. The 'Right Horn' was making the far more arduous
trek to get behind Isandlwana and attack from the west. But for the
moment, the iNgobamakhosi had some flies they needed to swat
away.

Their *inkosi* ordered their riflemen and skirmishers to deal with
any minor threats, allowing the main body of warriors to save their
energy for the final assault on the redcoat lines. Maintaining the

and sobbing that he didn't want to die. Even if they got him slung across a mule, he was in desperate need of a surgeon.

Meanwhile, James Trainer continued to fight his own one-man fight against the Zulu hordes. He thought he saw an enemy warrior fall after his fifth shot, though he could not be certain. He then noticed the NNC riflemen had ceased firing. Two of them had the extraction levers half-open with cartridges clearly stuck in the breaches. James stumbled over to them as bullets continued to kick up rock chips and dirt around them.

"Here, you need to use the damn ramrod to clear that!" he shouted.

The warriors could not understand him and were beginning to panic. He tried to take a rifle from one man to show him how to clear the jam. The warrior was having none of it. He shouted a few berating words in his indigenous tongue. Having expended their ammunition or with weapons jammed, the riflemen fled.

James then saw Johnson guiding the major's horse towards them when another enemy salvo unleashed. Blood misted off Major Russell's back and neck. His head snapped back, eyes closed and mouth open. A trickle of blood ran from his lips. His body went limp, and he was mercifully dead before he hit the ground. His horse simultaneously panicked and sprinted away.

"Damn it all," Johnson said. "There goes our way out of this shitty mess."

Bombardier Goff was trying to drag the badly injured soldier away when several bullets struck the poor man in the stomach and chest.

A ricochet grazed Goff's upper arm. "Fuck!" he shouted.

Captain Nourse and a small number of stalwart NNC warriors were still making a stand, though they could not hold for much longer. Goff then waved for the remaining members of the rocket battery to follow him.

"Come on! If we stay here, we die!"

Trainer and Johnson, both having lost their helmets at some point, scampered down the slope, slipping and falling on the loose shale. They soon came upon Harry Grant, who'd managed to retrieve one of the terrified pack animals.

"Where's Major Russell?" he asked. "And what about the rest of our mates?"

"They're dead," Goff said plainly.

They continued to run southwest, back from where they had come. What had taken them thirty minutes to climb, they tumbled down in less than ten. The utter exhaustion they'd felt after trekking ten miles to Isandlwana, and another three since leaving the camp, was completely forgotten. Their hearts pounded in their chests with the overwhelming yearning to survive.

"Where the hell do we go now?" Johnson asked in exasperation.

"Not west, that's for certain," Goff remarked. "The Zulus are likely already between us and the camp."

They then spotted Lieutenant Colonel Durnford riding towards them from the east. His column was clearly in serious trouble. Having only two troops of horsemen, he knew he needed to reconsolidate his forces quickly.

"You there!" he shouted, recognising Goff's blue artillery tunic. "You men are with the rocket battery, yes?"

"We are, sir…what's left of it."

"Where is Major Russell?" Durnford asked, looking around in confusion.

"He's been shot, sir," Trainer answered bluntly.

"Then you'd best go fetch him," the colonel directed.

"He's fucking dead, sir," the private retorted. At that moment, he didn't care if Durnford court-martialled him for insubordination; the Zulus were far more terrifying than any officer. "There's at least a thousand Zulus between us and him. And those damned NNC cowards have all hoofed it."

"Come with me," the colonel said sternly. He turned his mount and continued on his way. Nearly two hundred Basuto cavalrymen followed close behind. Trainer wondered if Durnford was going to have him shot for insubordination, once they were clear of the Zulus.

"Son of a bitch!" Johnson saw several rider-less horses in the throng. Within moments, the Basutos were gone, leaving the remnants of the rocket battery alone in a cloud of dust. He turned to Goff. "What now?"

"We follow them," the bombardier replied. "Hopefully we can find your friends somewhere in this shit."

Their already long day had turned into an unholy nightmare. Major Russell and five of their mates were dead; Colonel Durnford had essentially abandoned them; and with 25,000 Zulus converging on Isandlwana, they knew not what would happen to Lord Chelmsford's force or their friends left at the camp.

Chapter XXXI: First Contact for the 24th

Zulus advancing in company lines
Induna in the foreground

The latest bugle call was sounded with urgency. Arthur sat upright, having fallen into a light doze. Though he could not explain why, his instincts told him the situation had become grave. To what degree he could not begin to fathom. He buttoned his tunic, buckled his waist belt, and donned his helmet, squinting his eyes as he stepped out into the midday sun. Soldiers were grabbing their rifles and following the calls of their officers and NCOs. This was no mere 'stand to' in front of their tents. Officers on horseback were leading their men north and northeast of the camp, establishing themselves into a very long firing line. C Company was ordered to take the extreme left, near the northern spur of Isandlwana. It was a full mile from their camp, and the soldiers were moving urgently at a quick jog.

The sound of the growing battle was much easier to hear, though. They settled in to watch and wait, not knowing the next few hours would change their lives forever.

At the hospital, Private Harry Hook was bringing some freshly brewed tea to the patients. Acclaimed as one of the best cooks in B Company, he had awoken well before dawn to cook them breakfast. He was particularly worried about Sergeant Robert Maxfield. His delusions and fever had only worsened over the last few days. As he approached the hospital, he saw Corporal Ferdinand Schiess sitting on a camp stool just outside one of the side doors, his injured foot propped up on an empty biscuit box.

"Some tea, corporal?" Hook asked.

"Very kind of you." The Swiss corporal accepted a tin cup from him. He looked down at his bandaged foot and shook his head. "Can you hear it? Those popping sounds in the distance?"

Harry cocked his head to the east. "Seems the column won't have to go all the way to Ulundi to find the Zulus."

"I should be there with them," Schiess said, unable to hide his frustration in his accented voice. He thought he would be back with his battalion in just a few days, but had fallen over in pain when trying to stand, a week after the attack on Sihayo's kraal. The injury was worse than originally thought, when Surgeon Reynolds discovered a hairline fracture.

"I would say you've done your bit already," Harry reasoned. He then walked through the hospital, his tin mugs clattering as he offered tea to the patients who were lucid.

It took him half an hour to navigate his way in and around the various rooms in the rather eccentrically laid out house. Finally, having done his duty, he took a deep breath and opened the door that led into the Witts' bedchamber. Poor Robert Maxfield slept fitfully. He fidgeted about, muttering gibberish under his breath. His mind was elsewhere, possibly reliving a battle from the Xhosa War, when he harshly whispered, *'Stand firm, 24th!'*

Knowing there was little else he could do, Harry knelt beside the bed and prayed for his childhood friend.

Alarmed by the reports he had just received, Henry Pulleine outwardly managed to keep his composure. His orders to 'defend the camp' suddenly took on a very real and harrowing significance. His first issue was manpower. The camp was spread thin, and now Pulleine found himself needing to defend the vast open space with less than half the men in the column. He donned his helmet, climbed onto his horse, and sought out Melvill. The adjutant had ridden over to Surgeon-Major Shepherd's hospital tent, informing him to make ready to receive casualties.

"The surgeon and orderlies are ready, sir," he reported. "Sergeant Major Gapp is organizing the band into stretcher details."

"Very good," the colonel acknowledged, glad to have officers he could rely on. He was beginning to see what Captain Degacher meant when he said Pulleine did not have to do all the work himself.

"If only we had our D and G Companies," he lamented. The two companies, around 180 men in all, were en route from southern Natal, and last he knew, still about two days' march from Isandlwana. They may as well have been in England at this point!

With E and F Companies on the ridge, Pulleine ordered Captain Younghusband's C Company to cover the extreme left, anchoring off the steep face of Isandlwana, to prevent the camp from being flanked. The rising ground on the near side of the dongas running across the foot of the escarpment was the most logical place to position the remainder of his companies. This was being overseen by William Degacher. Stuart Smith had anchored the artillery just to the left of George Wardell's H Company, with Porteous' A Company left of him. Charlie Pope and the 2/24th detachments covered from Wardell's right to the western slopes of the conical koppie.

A loud boom startled Pulleine. Smith's two guns had come into action. The seven-pounder RML fired a much smaller shell than the standard nine or twelve-pounders; due to its low muzzle velocity, many within the Royal Artillery questioned their effectiveness at ranges beyond 1,000 yards. At the moment, there was no time nor any point in arguing the capabilities of the weapon. Raw and Roberts' troops of Zikhali Horse were on the run from an unknown, yet certainly massive, force of Zulus. The cannon were set to max elevation, launching the anti-personnel projectiles, known as 'common shot', at their maximum range of 3,000 yards. Smith could see traces of the Zulus through his field glasses, and he thought he knew where Raw's troop was. Of Roberts, he had no knowledge. No one from Durnford's column had informed him or Pulleine that there were two troops of horse past the Nyoni Ridge. He could only assume the mounted troopers he was able to see were all the friendly forces north of the firing line. The second cannon fired, and the crew of the first began to swab out the barrel, with gunners calling for the next charge and shot to be brought forward. None would ever know the tragic consequences of their blind shooting.

It was a frantic flight for survival for the two troops of horsemen that first came upon the Zulu *impi*. The NNC infantry from the Mkwene picquet had taken one look at the mass of enemy warriors and fled. Rather than making their way back towards the camp at Isandlwana, every last one sprinted either north or west, away from where the battle would soon take place. No amount of threats or berating from their officers could stop them. Lieutenant Roberts cursed them for their cowardice, though in truth he could not blame the men for wanting to remain alive.

Like his peer, Charlie Raw, Roberts was galloping his horse for all it was worth in a desperate attempt to outrun the Zulu hordes. The ground was extremely broken and rocky, greatly slowing the pace of their mounts. Roberts had heard stories about how fast the Zulus could run, that they could cover twenty miles across such terrain in just a couple of hours and rush straight into battle afterwards.

There a loud bang a few dozen yards behind him, and he chanced a quick glance over his left shoulder. There was a burst in the air, and the lieutenant knew the artillery was trying to cover their escape. However, their sights were clearly off. The Zulus were still about a quarter mile behind him, and that first shot had burst close to a section of his Zikhali troopers.

"Shoot straight, you bastards!" Roberts shouted.

The 'common shot' consisted of a shell projectile filled with explosives and steel balls. The intent was to send both shell splinters and balls into the enemy ranks. But because of their slow velocity, they were largely ineffective at such range. Unfortunately for Roberts, the next round fired flew in front of the cavalry officer and burst not ten feet from him. Shards ripped into his face and neck, blinding him. Roberts shrieked. His horse bucked and threw him off, sending him crashing onto the rocks. The blow to his head rendered him senseless, while his life's blood gushed from the horrific tear in his neck.

A Zikhali sergeant cried out, "God have mercy!" his horse rearing up as he pulled hard on the reins. The African Christian leapt from his mount and cradled his officer's head in his lap.

It was clear that James Roberts was dying. With the Zulus in close pursuit, it was simply not possible for the sergeant to heave his body onto the horse and still be able to escape. He made a quick 'sign of the cross' before remounting and riding away. Within moments the Zulus came upon the body. One of them sliced open his guts, for they believed this would release the slain man's spirit. Tragically, the first British soldier slain at Isandlwana was killed by their own cannon.

The sounds of men shouting and horses galloping in the distance forewarned Lieutenant Charles Cavaye and E Company.

"Look alive, lads!"

If there were friendly cavalry rushing towards them at such speed, then the Zulus could not be far behind. Cavaye waved his helmet at the horsemen who turned and galloped frantically towards his position.

"Get ready, boys, they're not far behind us!" Charlie Raw shouted, as he rode past the company on their far left.

Cavaye kept the bulk of his men over-watching the ground to the north. However he'd earlier detached a section under his lone subaltern, 2nd Lieutenant Edwards Dyson, about five hundred yards to his left to protect his flank. They, like everyone else, heard the shooting coming from Raw's troop, yet were still oblivious to just how large of a Zulu force they now faced. Cavaye had arranged his men in extended order, with six feet between each man. They readied themselves for the coming fight.

"Over there, sir," his colour sergeant said, nodding towards Mkwene Hill, seven hundred yards northeast.

Both men scanned with their field glasses. They saw at first a handful, then growing numbers of Zulu warriors.

"What the devil are they doing?" Cavaye asked.

The Zulus were crouching low and moving laterally rather than towards them.

"Doesn't matter," the colour sergeant said matter-of-factly. "Shall we announce ourselves, sir?"

The officer commanding nodded and called out, *"Contact front! At 700 yards...volley by sections!"*

Knowing his company was too spread out to effectively manage alone, he had briefed his sergeants and corporals that, should they come into contact, each section leader would take control of their firing. He had further stressed the need for fire discipline. Each man had only seventy rounds, and Quartermaster Pullen's ammunition stockpile was nearly two miles away.

Seven hundred yards was an astounding distance to try and hit a stationary target from, let alone nimble, fleet-footed Zulus moving with much speed and purpose. Still, Cavaye could not sit idly and watch them, not when they were technically within range of the Martini-Henry Rifle. Shots rang out from his various sections. He watched through his glasses and could see the puffs of dust and breaking rocks from his men's bullets. Occasionally a Zulu would fall. One warrior was smashed in the hip, the force of the bullet's impact kicking his legs out from under him.

"Mister Cavaye!" a voice called from behind him. It was Captain Edward Essex, the senior transportation officer for the column. He was mounted on a horse and appeared very excited.

"Captain," Cavaye replied calmly.

"Compliments of Colonel Pulleine. It would seem we are dealing with the entire Zulu *impi*, and not some renegade *ibutho*."

"That would explain their bizarre movements," the colour sergeant said, watching the long line of Zulus manoeuvring gradually southwest. They were now within four hundred yards, and section leaders were shouting at their men to adjust their sights.

378

Captain Essex observed the bounding mass of enemy warriors and gave a nod of understanding. "That means these men are one of the horns." He then grimaced. "By God, the way they are formed up they even look like a bloody horn! Captain Mostyn's F Company is coming up to support you. He was on foot, but sent me ahead to inform you. They should be on the field in just a few minutes."

"Good to know, sir." Cavaye's demeanour was unchanged, yet his stomach turned. His men were facing an enveloping horn of the main Zulu army! If the enemy to his front was one of the horns, then the 'Chest', which was certainly headed straight for Isandlwana, would eventually be behind him. The thought of being cut off from the rest of the battalion did not sit well.

As promised, Captain Mostyn and F Company soon arrived. They climbed up the slope just as the Zulus to Cavaye's left-front came under fire from Dyson's detachment. They were much closer now, just two to three hundred yards from their adversaries. The young officer's men were having much better success at finding their targets. However, despite the losses they were suffering, the Zulus were making no attempt to attack the company of redcoats, but instead pressing on towards the west.

Off to Cavaye's right, he had forgotten about the company of NNC on picquet duty. Their riflemen were firing wildly, burning through their paltry lot of ammunition and hitting nothing.

Captain Mostyn, meanwhile, was directing his company to fill the gap left between Cavaye and Dyson. His men unleashed a savage volley of musketry into them. The Zulus, losing men all the while, continued to move laterally, refusing to engage directly. This troubled the officers far more than if the enemy had attacked.

Cavaye's concerns about the Zulu 'Chest' getting behind him were soon shared by Lieutenant Colonel Pulleine. He was near the artillery, trying to observe the effects of their fire, when he realised the danger to his companies. With the *amabutho* of the 'Chest' now in full view, Henry knew that E and F Companies were at serious risk of being flanked and overrun.

"Ride like hell and get them back," he ordered Melvill.

The adjutant, realising the danger as well, galloped away with all haste.

"Mister Coghill!"

"Sir?" the young officer replied. Unable to walk with his injured knee, yet able to ride, he was anxious to do his part. The pain in his leg was temporarily forgotten.

"Ride to Captain Younghusband. Advance his company far enough forward to cover Mostyn and Cavaye's retreat. They will dress off C Company's right, once returned to the firing line. The NNC and Zikhali Horse will support."

"Very good, sir."

The soldiers of C Company had watched the departure of Mostyn's F Company and were concerned about their mates. It was about a mile to Mkwene Hill from where they stood. They could see very little, but the thunder of continuous volleys could be plainly heard. They then watched Lieutenant Melvill riding with all haste towards the forward companies. Reginald knew they would be withdrawing soon, and this was confirmed by Coghill's arrival.

"Captain Younghusband!" the ADC shouted, riding up to him. "Colonel Pulleine needs you to advance far enough to cover Mostyn and Cavaye's withdrawal, sir. They will fall in on your right, once returned to the main firing line."

"Thank you, Mister Coghill," the captain acknowledged before shouting, *"Company will advance three hundred yards!"*

While many of the officers were mounted, like Captain William Mostyn, Reginald Younghusband preferred to fight on foot. He was also very fond of his horse, Nikki, and the thought of her being killed by a Zulu musket did not sit well with him. He also wanted there to be no doubt in the minds of his soldiers that, should matters take a turn for the worse, he would fight and die beside them.

Given the need for haste, there was no formal marching order given, only a series of NCOs shouting, *"Follow me!"*

As he, Richard, Bray, and the others of their section followed Sergeant Edwards, Arthur's gaze was fixed on the hilltop to their direct front, over a mile distant. It formed the western edge of the Nyoni Ridge, and he could see bands of Zulus lurking in the saddle between the hilltop and the ridge. It was these enemy warriors they needed to supress in order to cover E and F Companies' withdrawal. They soon reached the Nyogane Donga and faced towards the saddle to the northeast.

"Mister Melvill!" Captain Younghusband shouted to the adjutant riding back towards them. "Inform Captain Mostyn that we are set. Once he reaches us, we'll bound by companies back to the firing line."

"Sir," Melvill acknowledged, turning his horse about once more.

Arthur nervously palmed his rifle, his hands sweaty from both the heat and apprehension.

"Load!" the captain ordered.

Arthur took a few deep breaths to calm his nerves. He opened the breach and shoved a round into the chamber. Like Bray had shown him, he kept the rounds in his ready pouch layered in rows with a folded cloth wrapping around each row. He quietly prayed for no jams or malfunctions from his weapon this day. His first battle, which had seemed all-consuming at the time, was little more than a schoolyard scrap by comparison. The Zulus here were far more numerous, and they were anxious for a brawl.

The sounds of firing kept coming from the north. Within minutes, Lieutenant Melvill came riding down the slope at a brisk pace. It was not just the two companies of redcoats retreating in the adjutant's wake. Charlie Raw, who had paused to help support the two companies, was leading his troop of Zikhali Horse, after their harrowing ride down the nine miles of ridges and hills. They were down to their last few cartridges and in desperate need of resupply if they were to do any more good that day. The Zulus surging over the ridge near Mkwene Hill spotted them. Sensing a ripe target, they were hurdling towards the company from the cover of the ridge.

"At four hundred yards!" Captain Younghusband shouted. *"Present..."*

Arthur quickly double-checked his sights and brought his rifle up to his shoulder. He shifted his feet slightly, bringing his rear foot back slightly. He slowed his breathing, allowing his front sight-post to rise and fall with each breath. He placed it around the centre of the mass of Zulus, who were now sprinting to the next piece of cover, hoping to flank Cavaye and Mostyn's companies.

"Fire!"

It was a relatively short distance back to the firing line, but the officers commanding the line companies were determined to keep close enough to each other that they could provide fire support as they retreated. Colour Sergeant Brown kept a keen eye on the situation, turning back frequently to make sure they were not being pursued as the captain led his men in the short sprint to their next position. Reginald raised his sword high, signalling the halt. Cavaye did the same, and both companies turned to face the Zulu threat. Captain Mostyn's F Company fired a single volley to keep the heads of the Zulus down for the moment. They then bounded past C and E Companies, continuing another fifty yards before halting. This tense, yet methodical means of extraction proved effective, as the Zulus were unable to pursue them without being subjected to murderous volleys of musketry.

Unbeknownst to the redcoats or their officers, two entire Zulu regiments now occupied the ground on either side of Mkwene Hill. The majority of the 'Chest' regiments were not yet in position, so they chose not to press the attack. The occasional volley from the withdrawing companies acted as a barrier the Zulus were not yet ready to break.

The uNokhenke had chased the bands of recoats from the rocks and high ground west of Mkwene. The *ibutho* was a very large one, with over 3,000 warriors, and there had been some confusion as to whether they should proceed to the right with the other regiments of the 'Right Horn' or press onward, directly towards Isandlwana. The *amakhosi*, who could not possibly hope to be everywhere at once, had to rely heavily on their *izinduna* to execute the Ntshingwayo's intent. Kwanele and the other *izinduna* had noticed a sizeable gap between the uKhandempemvu—the western-most *ibutho* in the 'Chest'—and the regiments of the 'Right Horn'. They therefore took it upon themselves to pursue this fleeing mass of redcoats, as well as the horsemen who had first come upon the *impi*, thereby closing the gap. And because they were headed straight for the northernmost spur of Isandlwana, it would be a fairly simple manoeuver for them to shift left and join the main attack, or right and skirt the backside of the mountain, linking up with the rest of the 'Right Horn'

"They're fleeing!" Kwanele shouted. "After them!"

Though they could see many straggling companies from the *amabutho* on their left making their way towards the Nyoni Ridge, the young *induna* decided the withdrawing force of redcoats was too great an opportunity to miss. The other *izinduna* echoed his commands, and soon a force of a thousand warriors was cresting the next rise.

To their horror, another company of redcoats had come up from the enemy camp. Their rifles exploded in a cloud of smoke and rolling bangs that echoed off the hills. Numerous warriors were shot down, leaving clouds of pink mist and torn flesh. Kwanele found himself sprayed with blood from an unfortunate young man whose throat had been shot away. There was a long donga to their immediate front, and warriors began spilling into it. The redcoats fired once more. From the edge of the donga, Kwanele watched in frustration as the companies of British soldiers ran back towards their main firing line. He was then filled with conflicting feelings of both hate and admiration for his enemy. They moved quickly, yet there was no panic visible amongst their ranks. Within minutes, their quarry had escaped, and they had nothing to show for their efforts but scores of dead and badly maimed friends. The piteous cries of the horrifically wounded made Kwanele's skin crawl. No amount of diviners' charms and enchantments could have prepared him for this kind of abject suffering and terror.

Chapter XXXII: Keep the Ammunition Coming

Isandlwana
22 January 1879
1.00 p.m.

Captain Edward Essex
Transportation Officer, No. 3 Column

Henry Pulleine was relieved to see his companies had successfully withdrawn from near Mkwene Hill, but he was harbouring deep concerns about the overall tactical situation. Foremost, the conical koppie left him partially blinded to what Durnford was doing. He found himself constantly looking east and southeast with his field glasses. He wasn't sure if the Zulus to his front were the entire army, or if there might be more of them out there. Melvill had relayed Charlie's Raw's assessment, that this was in fact the entire *impi*; however, he only had eyes on a small portion of it. The adjutant also informed Pulleine that the large force of warriors engaged by Mostyn and Cavaye were shifting to their left rather than engaging directly. This was also cause for concern, yet until he knew their intent, there was little Pulleine could do about them.

As for his own battlefront, he had Younghusband's C Company anchoring the left flank. They were butted up against the impassable steep slope of Isandlwana, securing their left flank for the moment. To their right were companies of iziGqoza NNC, supported by troops from Zikhali Horse, now collectively led by Captain George Shepstone. Mostyn, Cavaye, and Porteous' companies were to their right, followed by the two guns from N Battery, now under the charge of Major Stuart Smith. To Smith's right, the firing line angled gradually towards the southeast. Captain Wardell's H Company was formed up next to the guns, followed by the large force from 2/24th under Charlie Pope. James Lonsdale's iziGqoza were facing east towards the conical koppie. The ground there gradually sloped south and did not have nearly as many obstacles to slow the Zulus. The fate of their right flank was entirely dependent upon Durnford's No. 2 Column.

Pulleine remained mobile atop his horse, trying to personally keep an eye on how the battle was progressing. This was difficult, due to the size of their frontage, which was well over a mile from end-to-end, as well as the growing clouds of acrid smoke. In addition to Captain Gardner, Lieutenants Melvill and Coghill were acting as Pulleine's ADCs. Sergeant Major Gapp was overseeing the stretcher details, who were already ferrying those wounded by Zulu musketry back to Surgeon-Major Shepherd's hospital tent a half mile to the rear.

Frederick Gapp was a career soldier with twenty-five years in the ranks. He had previously served as the battalion's quartermaster-sergeant and had been colour sergeant of H Company at one time. He kept a sharp eye on the bandsmen / stretcher-bearers and would ride the line, shouting orders and pointing out any fallen soldiers. After the first thirty minutes, he returned to give a quick situational report to his commanding officer.

"What's the word on our losses, sergeant major?" Pulleine asked, as Gapp rode up.

"Regrettable, but acceptable, sir," he reported. "Four dead and about twenty wounded. The line is well beyond the effective range of the Zulu muskets, but there's so damn many of them. However, rest assured, we're giving it to them far worse than they are to us."

Along with the stalwart companies of imperial riflemen, the twin cannons of Curling's section were creating much havoc among the regiments of the Zulu 'Chest'. With just a few hundred yards separating the firing line from the heart of the Zulu onslaught, the explosive shells were proving to be particularly devastating. Swaths had been cut in the tall grass by the white-hot shards of metal. Scores of Zulus lay dead or maimed in their wake.

The Zulu 'Horn' manoeuvring off to the west, as well as the unknown status of Durnford's column to the east, certainly made their situation precarious. However, it appeared to Lieutenant Colonel Pulleine that the crux of the battle was going very much in their favour. The Zulu 'Chest' may have numbered ten to fifteen thousand men, yet the stretch of open ground between the Nyoni Ridge and the protective dongas was proving to be a murderous killing ground.

There was no mistaking that the Zulus were fanatically brave, but they were not the mindless savages the whites depicted, nor were they suicidal. Every warrior would fight with extreme valour, with the last ounce of his spirit, in order to soak his spear in enemy blood. Yet like their enemies, when it was all over, they wished to return to their homes and families, alive with only a few scars. A stalemate had occurred, and every time the Zulus attempted to surge out from behind the protective cover of the dongas and reverse slopes, savage volleys of musketry and cannon fire ripped the souls from the bodies of even more of their friends.

Henry Pulleine was keeping a close watch on the overall tactical situation, as were his ADCs and Sergeant Major Gapp. Thus far, they had held the Zulu *impi* in check. He allowed himself a half smile of hope. It was he, not Lord Chelmsford, Colonel Glyn, nor his counterpart, Lieutenant Colonel Degacher, standing toe-to-toe with the Zulu army. And despite being outnumbered at least 15-to-1, while fighting on open ground, with his battle line spread out further than he would have liked, there was a feeling of triumph that allowed itself to slowly form in his gut. The feeling that despite the overwhelming odds, he, Lieutenant Colonel Henry Pulleine, could win and bring an end to the war on this day.

Durnford's No. 2 Column now occupied the large Nyogane Donga, east of the camp. He had barely escaped the oncoming Zulu force. Several of his Basutos had not been so fortunate. Shot by enemy muskets or pulled from their mounts and stabbed to death, their screams echoed in the colonel's ears. His force frantically made their way back to a more defensible position. The donga was quite deep and very wide. More of a basin than a trench, the troops had little difficulty getting their horses down its slope.

Captain Bradstreet's Newcastle Mounted Rifles joined them and were on their left, just south of the wagon track. In addition to his two troops of horsemen, the colonel brought up Lieutenant Scott's mounted picquets from the conical koppie.

Last to reach them were the four survivors from the rocket battery. In their rage and desperation, the soldiers from 1/24th had managed to suppress their sorrow for the loss of friends for the moment. They replaced it with that frantic urge to stay alive. They regretted Major Russell's slaying, though Bombardier Goff was furious with his late superior for refusing to heed the warnings of the carbineers. He had led them straight into an entire Zulu regiment. And now the major, along with five of their mates, was dead.

James Trainer was particularly incensed with Durnford's asinine suggestion that they go back to retrieve Major Russell's body, and even more so for subsequently abandoning them. He had seen at least four or five rider-less horses among his troops. Instead of offering them up, the column had left the four soldiers to their fate. By a stroke of inexplicable luck, or perhaps divine intervention, the Zulus had paused long enough to allow their stragglers to catch up before continuing the pursuit.

The bombardier and three redcoats occupied the extreme right of the line, where a jutting boulder put some space between them and the Basutos on their left.

"If Durnford comes back this way, I'm playing dead," Johnson muttered, still catching his breath. Any amicable feelings he'd had for their column commander were now replaced by extreme bitterness

Harry Grant looked at Goff, who was wielding his pistol. "Bugger me, is that all you've got? The damned Zulus will have to be within ten feet of us before that does you any good."

389

"Give it some time, there will be carbines available soon enough," the bombardier replied morbidly.

The clouds of dust kicked up by their rampaging horses was still thick, and it gave the Zulus a fair measure of concealment for a time. But then, while at least five hundred yards from the donga, the dust cleared just enough for the carbineers and Basutos to mark their targets once more.

"At five hundred yards!" Durnford shouted.

While the short-barrelled carbines had a far shorter effective range than the Martini-Henry Rifle, the carbineers prided themselves on their superior marksmanship. It was the Basutos' demonstrated skill with their weapons that allowed Durnford to successfully requisition full allotments of ammunition, as opposed to the paltry five rounds per man Crealock had at first insisted on.

"Fire!"

The Zulu lines of the uVe regiment had been advancing in extended order, keeping six to eight feet per man in order to minimize the effects of the British firearms. The arrival of the iNgobamakhosi drove back the column of enemy horsemen, slaughtering their pathetic rocket force when rounded the conical koppie. But as their shared axis of advance forced them to merge, warriors of the *amabutho* ran into each other, and were compelled to cluster closer than their *izinduna* liked. This was maddening for Mehlokazulu, who kept shouting for the men to extend further left. This went either unheard or ignored.

They continued to run through the clouds of dust, with warriors now almost shoulder-to-shoulder. The loud crack of enemy firearms erupted somewhere to their front. Mehlokazulu heard the cries of several warriors near him, as their bodies were smashed by the heavy slugs. Their tumbling forms created additional tripping hazards, and their fellows, blinded by the billowing dust, stumbled and fell over them. As the dust cleared, they could see the long donga now lined with enemy carbineers and African troops. Three hundred carbines unleashed another salvo, felling another score of Zulus.

"Get down!" Mehlokazulu shouted to his men.

As a point of emphasis, one of his warriors doubled over when a bullet caught him in the guts. It burst out the back, leaving a large exit wound near the base of his spine. Despite being disembowelled, the man continued to writhe in agony for several minutes before he finally expired.

"Skirmishers, forward!"

Given the size of the British force in the donga, Mehlokazulu realised they could not simply sit back and wait for their own muskets to take their toll. Their adversaries were well-protected, by both the range, as well as the donga. The uVe and iNgobamakhosi risked being utterly defeated if they did not keep advancing. The *induna* knew that, no matter how brave, every man had his breaking point. Should too many of their companions be slaughtered, with the regiments unable to move forward, eventually there would be panic. Terror was contagious, and if even a single company broke, the entire 'Left Horn' could be undone. Mehlokazulu knew he *had* to keep the assault progressing forward!

Izinduna took charge of their companies, ordering them to move together, bounding from one protective terrain formation to the next. Whether behind boulders, brush stands, deep gouges in the earth, or simply lying flat in the open, the *amabutho* made their slow and painful advance towards their hated foes.

For the warriors of the uVe—one of the youngest regiments in the entire *impi*—it was especially trying. Men had arms shot clean off by the heavy bullets from enemy carbines, others' brains were smashed in, and still more had been their gut torn from their bodies. And for every warrior who lay dead or dying, at least three more bore various debilitating injuries wrought by these fearsome weapons.

The uVe had never been in battle, not even the brutal skirmishes that often erupted between their own rival regiments. All they knew of war were the dances, chants, calls to their valiant ancestors, tales of great heroism, and the medicines and spiritual charms of the *izinyanga*. The true nature of war, with all of its suffering, overwhelming terror, and extreme physical and emotional trauma, was soul-shattering. As they crawled on their bellies, trying to get close to the donga, with friends dying or being maimed with each enemy volley, the young warriors cursed the diviners. Their magic was completely useless against this unholy onslaught of British firepower!

Knowing the outcome of the battle would hinge on keeping the line companies supplied with ammunition, Captain Edward Essex began grabbing men within the camp, who were not otherwise involved in the growing battle; excess artillerymen not on an actual gun crew, soldier-servants, any of the sick or injured who could still walk, bandsmen not on stretcher detail, and anyone else he could find. He then rode over to Lieutenant Smith-Dorrien.

"Horace," he said calmly, but with much tension in his voice. "Take these men and form an ammunition detail. 2nd Battalion's supplies are much closer, so take those first."

"Sir!" Horace gave a quick salute. "Alright men, you heard the officer. Let's get some fresh cartridges to the lads!"

Given how spread out the camp was, it took them a good five minutes to reach the wagons marked with red flags. Though a ways back from the battle line, the volume of fire from Zulu marksmen caused the young lieutenant to hunker down in his saddle. Musket balls kicked up dirt and bounced off rocks at an alarming rate. The men in the detail kept low as they raced over to the wagons. They were laden with boxes of Martini-Henry ammunition, designated to Lord Chelmsford and 2/24th as needed. Due to the safety precautions, however, their draught oxen were penned together, well behind the main camp. The young African voorloopers were nowhere to be seen either.

The cartridges themselves were stored in thick wooden boxes, banded together, with a rope handle on each end. The lid in the centre slid off and was held in place by a single screw. Designed to be water-tight, the boxes were bulky and cumbersome, yet protected the cartridges from both water and rough handling. Each carried sixty paper packets which, in turn, held ten rounds apiece. The boxes were heavy, weighing approximately eighty pounds each.

One in every six soldiers was issued a combination tool for the Martini-Henry that included a small screwdriver used to remove the screw holding the lid in place. In an emergency, the heavy butt of the Martini-Henry could smash open the boxes with very little difficulty.

"Here we are, boys!" Horace said excitedly. He practically leapt from his horse.

With no oxen yoked to the wagon, they had little choice but to grab what boxes they could and load them onto a small donkey cart nearby.

Tipped off by the commotion, Quartermaster Bloomfield came running around the far side of the wagon. "What the devil do you lot think you're doing?" He then said to Smith-Dorrien, "For Heaven's sake, man, don't take that; it belongs to our battalion!"

"Hang it all," the young lieutenant replied with exasperation, "You don't want a requisition now, do you?"

From his position, James Bloomfield could not see the seriousness of the ongoing battle. None of them knew Chelmsford's situation, and he would be committing a grievous error if he allowed his ammunition stores to be plundered, only to find his lordship in need of resupply.

Captain Essex rode over to them. "Thank you, Mister Smith-Dorrien. Head to the firing line. I'll join you shortly." He'd seen the dispute between the quartermaster and the lieutenant. The captain decided he needed to settle the matter quickly.

"Captain, I understand your man's enthusiasm and intentions. But this ammunition belongs to 2nd Battalion. It's my head if they need resupply and I have nothing left to give them. 1st Battalion has their own stores."

"I understand, but do you not see what's happening behind me? *We* are the ones facing the Zulu *impi*, not Lord Chelmsford. Even if you did try to resupply him, you wouldn't get a mile from camp before the Zulus chopped you to pieces. I'm sure Quartermaster Pullen will make good on whatever we take from your stores. If he weren't another half mile from the line, I would have gone to him first."

Bloomfield was beginning to understand the gravity of their situation. The spread out companies and Curling's two artillery pieces were engaged in a musketry duel with an ever-growing

393

number of Zulus. If there were more to the east, they were cut off from Chelmsford and the rest of the column anyway.

"Alright." He slapped one of the boxes. "Have at them!"

A stray bullet struck the edge of the cart, splintering the wood and causing both men to flinch. Bloomfield let out a relieved sigh and waved over the nervous men of the detail. Two men grabbed the handles on each box and lugged them to the donkey cart. Because there was only one animal on the cart, and the rugged nature of the terrain, the quartermaster recommended loading no more than ten boxes at a time. It didn't seem like much, but ten boxes amounted to 6,000 rounds and 800 pounds of weight.

"Come on fellas," the captain said. "Let's get these to the firing line."

"I'll have one of my boys send word to Pullen, and have him start bringing boxes over," Bloomfield said. "Rest assured, captain, this battle will not be lost due to lack of ammunition."

Those would be his last words. As he stood with a reassuring smile on his face, a musket ball smashed into his forehead. His eyes squeezed shut and blood trickled down the middle of his face. He stood rigid for a moment before collapsing onto his back. His body convulsed several times before it was still.

Essex, who was behind the donkey cart, helping push it along, saw the quartermaster fall and rushed back to him.

"Fuck...fuck!" was the shout from Quartermaster-Sergeant George Davis, Bloomfield's second. He rushed over and knelt next to the man he'd served with for the past six years. "Damn it all," he swore as he fought back his sorrow. He then gently placed a hand on Bloomfield's chest and whispered, "Goodbye, sir."

Captain Essex grabbed him by the shoulder. "I am sorry, but there is no time to mourn. I need you to go to Quartermaster Pullen. Let him know we need his ammunition here immediately."

"Yes, sir." Davis gave one last look to his old boss and friend before rushing towards Pullen's tent at a dead run.

Edward continued to help push the cart, while leading his horse by the bridle. As the column transportation officer, he had no duties of his own to perform, so instead, he took it upon himself to head the ammunition resupply efforts for the firing line. It was nearly a mile from Charlie Pope's G Company, 2/24th on the right, to Reginald Younghusband's C Company, 1/24th on the far left. As they reached each company, a pair of boxes were heaved off the cart and dropped about thirty feet behind the line, where sections of bandsmen waited to act as stretcher-bearers for the wounded. They were ordered to smash open the boxes and begin distributing cartridge packets to the line.

Due to the weight, they were only able to deliver a single box to each of the last two companies. Still, Captain Mostyn and Lieutenant Cavaye were especially grateful for the resupply. Their men were now down to their last ten or twelve cartridges. Essex promised to bring extra boxes for C and F Companies the next time around.

"Captain!" Lieutenant Raw shouted, rushing over to the cart. "My men are running out of ammunition; we need you to bring us a few boxes as soon as possible."

"Damn it, Mister Raw," Essex chastised. "These cartridges would blow apart the breaches of your carbines! If you need ammunition, I suggest you find your own wagons."

It was more of a rumour, rather than a proven fact, that the longer rifle casings, with its heavier charge of black powder, would blow apart the breach block of the Swinburne-Henry carbine. However, that was how Captain Essex had understood it. And besides, he reckoned that No. 2 Column had its own resupply, and it would behove them if someone located their ammunition wagons sooner rather than later.

Nearly thirty minutes had passed from the time they left Bloomfield's wagon until Essex and his volunteers reached Younghusband's company. He stopped and caught his breath for a moment before ordering his men back to the supply wagons. It seemed like a lot of ammunition had been delivered. In reality, it amounted to only fifteen or twenty rounds per man. For F and Companies, who had been given only one box each, this was simply not enough.

"Let's keep the ammunition coming, boys," Essex implored his already tired detachment. "Battles can be won or lost by logistics, and I will *not* have this battle be lost because we did not keep the lads on the line supplied with sufficient cartridges."

Ammunition box

Back at Mangeni, neither Lord Chelmsford nor any of the staff officers knew of the grave nature of the ongoing battle. They had heard the faint sounds of rifle fire, but it was uncertain whether it came from Isandlwana or one of the bands of men from their half of the column that were still pursuing pockets of Zulus.

"I think we've done enough chasing after the enemy today," Chelmsford said to Colonel Glyn and Lieutenant Colonel Crealock. "Have all forces assemble at Mangeni Falls. We will establish our new camp there."

The GOC went for a walk to where the four guns from N Battery were being limbered up and made ready to move. He was soon joined by Rupert Lonsdale, who had compiled some early reports from the fighting.

"My lord," he said. "We've counted approximately sixty Zulus dead, along with fifteen prisoners. Our own losses are as yet unknown."

"Sir, I feel I should let you know that I am certain it was Matshana I chased off earlier," 'Offy' Shepstone added.

"Chasing a man off is pointless," Chelmsford replied without missing a step. "Capturing or killing him is what matters."

Further conversation was interrupted when Lieutenant Colonel Harness walked briskly over to them. "My lord, a rather extraordinary report from Commandant Browne; it would seem

Pulleine has a battle on his hands…a real one. Not some minor skirmish like we've seen here."

To the far right of the Isandlwana battlefront, Lieutenant Colonel Anthony Durnford was relishing the utterly terrifying, yet exhilarating thrill of battle. They had occupied the Nyogane Donga; carbineers, mounted police, and Basuto horsemen all dismounted and lay prone along the edge of the donga.

The colonel rode up and down the line, shouting words of encouragement to his men. "Well done, my boys! Keep up your fire!"

"By God, sir!" One of the Basuto troopers shouted at him in English. "You should not be exposing yourself like this!"

"Nonsense!" Durnford retorted.

The man simply did not understand the sense of honour among Victorian officers, which precluded them from hiding from the enemy.

Though few in number, the men of No. 2 Column managed to halt the entire Zulu 'Left Horn' for the time being. Captain Bradstreet's dismounted cavalry had particularly helped to strengthen Durnford's line of defence.

There had also been a noticeable change in the colonel's demeanour during this crucible of battle. He at last felt the scourge of Bushman's Pass being cast down; the humiliation of being defeated and left crippled, the subject of gossip in upper circles about his abilities as a soldier, disdainful false rumours about his relationship with Frances Colenso, and even the distasteful talk about his very courage and manhood, were all being swept away in the acrid smoke of gunfire and the distant screams of the dying Zulus.

As Durnford rode down the line, he dismounted several times to assist with jammed carbines. At the rate they had been firing, not only was there a danger of them running out of ammunition, but the heat and fouling of their weapons was beginning to cause malfunctions. With only one good arm, Anthony still managed to clear at least half-a-dozen jams and get his men back in the fight.

And yet, for all that, the column's transportation officer, William Cochrane, found himself feeling uneasy about Durnford's demeanour. The look in his eyes went beyond courage; it was as if he had crossed over into madness. Cochrane hoped he was wrong. He prayed Durnford would not lose his head. The young lieutenant was also the first to notice the change in the tactical situation that made their position suddenly precarious.

The overall Zulu scheme of manoeuvre was masked by the terrain and clouds of smoke. Until they were within a half mile of their positions, none of the British defenders knew the 'Chest' had not advanced as a single entity. In their excitement, several regiments had outpaced their peers and engaged the core of the British lines without being fully supported. This ignorance led Durnford to have no concern with the large gap, perhaps 900 yards in all, between his position and James Lonsdale's iziGqoza NNC to his far left. But now, a fresh regiment of Zulus, numbering two to three thousand, suddenly appeared. They were skirting around both sides of the conical koppie and looked to drive a wedge between the two forces. If that happened, both the No. 2 Column, as well as the main firing line, would be flanked.

"Colonel!" Cochrane shouted, pointing and waving his hand frantically.

Durnford scowled when he saw the Zulus now threatening to cut him off from the rest of the defenders. "Ride to Stuart Smith," he ordered. "Have him detach one of his guns to cover me. And let Pulleine know I'll be needing infantry support."

"Sir," William said. He spurred his horse into a fast gallop, heading first to the artillery section about a mile distant.

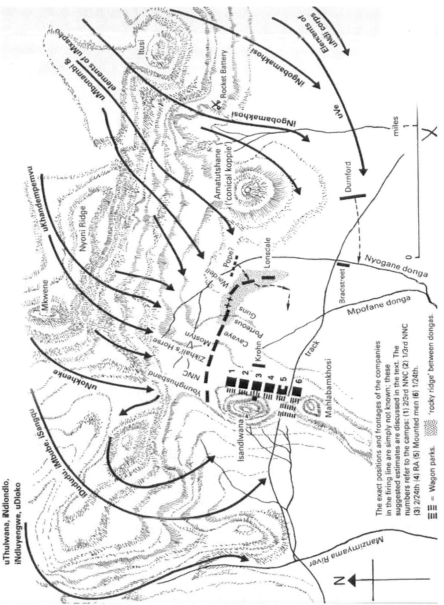

The tactical situation at around 1.00 p.m.

uThulwana, iNdlondlo,
iNdluyengwe, uDloko

iDudulu, iMbube, iSangqu
uNokhenke
uKhandempemvu
Nyoni Ridge
uMbonambi & elements of uKhandempemvu
Mkwene
iTusi
Rocket Battery
iNgobamakhosi
iNgobamakhosi
Amatutshane ('conical koppie')
Elements of iNgobamakhosi
uVe
Durnford
Pope?
Lonscale
Windell
Nyogane donga
Mostyn
Cavaye
Porteous Guns
Krohn
Zikhali's Horse
NNC
Youngshusband
Bracstreet
Mpofane donga
track
Isandlwana
Mahlabamkhosi
Manzimyama River

1 2 3 4 5 6

The exact positions and frontages of the companies
in the firing line are simply not known; these
suggested estimates are discussed in the text. The
numbers refer to the camps: (1) 2/3rd NNC (2) 1/3rd NNC
(3) 2/24th (4) RA (5) Mounted men (6) 1/24th.

▓▓ = Wagon parks.   'rocky ridge' between dongas.

miles
0   1

399

Chapter XXXIII: Untenable

Isandlwana
22 January 1879
1.30 p.m.
***

Pulleine also saw the new threat emerging from the east; however, he was deeply resentful that Durnford was giving direct orders to Major Smith and stealing one of his guns away. If Durnford wished to assume command of the camp's defences, so be it. But his insistence on fighting his own separate battle, while taking resources from the camp's defences, without any thought as to the tactical consequences, was intolerable. Therefore, when William Cochrane rode over with his next request from the commanding officer of No. 2 Column, Pulleine thought he might go mad.

"Colonel, sir," Cochrane said, with a quick salute. "Compliments of Colonel Durnford. He has tasked Major Smith with providing one of his guns for fire support. The enemy have brought up reinforcements and are threatening our left flank. Colonel Durnford also asks for infantry support."

"If Colonel Durnford was a tactical man, he would pull his men back and anchor off Lonsdale's flank," Melvill replied with agitated candour. Pulleine quickly held up a hand, silencing him. The last thing he needed was for his adjutant, however competent he may be, to risk injuring his career with a charge of insubordination.

"Mister Melvill, have Lieutenant Pope withdraw his force to the south of Lonsdale, where he can plug the gap between Durnford's forces and ours."

"Very good, sir," Melvill replied. Relieved to be given a task, he feared a reprimand might come later. Then again, given the precariousness of their situation, he would rather be dragged before the GOC for insubordination, rather than needlessly risk the lives of their entire command. Durnford's directive was poorly thought out, for he did not appreciate the overall tactical situation, nor was he even a part of the column. Melvill had always gotten on well with Durnford, who he personally liked and admired. Nevertheless, his singlemindedness and lack of tactical insight was adding

"A worthy foe, sir," the corporal leading the sharp-shooters concurred. "Just keep that ammunition coming, if you'd be so kind. I think we may need every last round if we're going to stop them."

It was an added thrill that Arthur was once again fighting alongside his fellow sharp-shooters. The high ground on the spur gave them a much better platform to fire from and kept them further out of range from return fire. The stretch of the donga their adversaries occupied was closer than the rest of the line, only about two hundred yards. The range and the dispersion of the redcoats' firing line made the Zulu marksmen largely ineffective. However, the company suffered its first casualty when Private Hughes, the annoyingly loud and unabashedly racist fellow, had been struck in the guts by a musket ball. Stretcher-bearers carried him away, though being shot in the stomach was almost always fatal, though it could take hours to die. At first Arthur thought, 'good riddance' to himself, but was then immediately shamed by it. The death of any one of Her Majesty's soldiers was a tragedy, even when it was an incorrigible bigot like Hughes.

The Zulu riflemen lay in the tall grass just beyond the donga, making them almost impossible to see from the firing line. Of course, the obstruction worked both ways. With their old, broken muskets, the Zulus were mostly shooting blind. In addition to Hughes, three other men had been wounded; two had their arms in makeshift slings and were attempting to fire their weapons with one hand from the sitting position. The other was struck in the leg and, after bandaging himself up, was also sitting and attempting to return fire. In order to break this stalemate, Captain Younghusband had dispatched Corporal Bellhouse and his skirmishers to the highest point, where they could best target the enemy marksmen.

"Damn it all, I can't see if I got him," Bill Johnson complained, having fired another round at a prone Zulu in the grass.

Bellhouse was looking through his field glasses, trying to confirm Bill's shot. "I can't tell if he's twitching or if it's the heat and the breeze on the grass…no, wait, you got him. I can see a nice, bloody hole in his back."

unnecessary risk to an already dangerous situation. That he was willingly risking his own life in the process was certainly brave, and the adjutant gave him credit for that. Melvill rode over to Charlie Pope's detachment, while hoping this would not prove to be their undoing.

"Charlie!" he called out over the din of musketry.

Pope's oversized detachment of his own G Company, plus the miscellaneous soldiers from 2/24th, gave him twice as many riflemen as any of the other companies. A haze of smoke clung to the battlefield. For the first time, Melvill could see the effects enemy marksmen were having. They may have been pinned down by the firing line; however, enemy firearms outnumbered theirs nearly three-to-one.

Bandsmen were carrying away those struck down by enemy bullets. The wounded were being ferried back to Surgeon-Major Shepherd's hospital tent. The dead were dragged about fifty feet behind the firing line, so their mates did not have to see them. Melvill quickly counted ten bodies behind Pope's formation, and it made his heart sink.

"Ah, Melvill," Charlie said, turning to face him. He was wearing his blue forage cap rather than his service helmet, and his revolver was smoking from being recently fired. "A splendid little thrashing we are giving these bastards!"

"I need you to shift to the south, at the double," the adjutant replied. He nodded towards the emerging force of Zulus coming around the conical koppie to the east. Major Smith had arrived with one of his guns, which was quickly being unlimbered south of James Lonsdale's position. "Set up just to the right of the cannon and plug the gap between us and Durnford."

"Right away," Pope acknowledged, before calling out to Lieutenant Godwin-Austen and Sergeant Carse, who was acting as G Company's colour sergeant.

This sudden move also compelled Captain Wardell's H Company to spread itself even further, in order to cover the gap left by Pope's detachment. James Lonsdale also attempted to help close the breach with a section of his NNC.

The lone cannon fired with a loud boom, rocking back several feet. The seven-pound shot flew in a high arc towards the advance elements of this fresh Zulu regiment. It burst just over the heads of their third and fourth company lines, tearing several men to shreds and leaving them bloodied, screaming, and dying in the trampled grass.

Horace Smith-Dorrien had just reached the end of the firing line for the second time, dropping off two more boxes to Younghusband and C Company. He took a moment to scramble up the northern spur of Isandlwana, occupied by a lone section of sharp-shooters protecting their left flank. The Zulus had reached the large donga about four hundred yards from the firing line, though at a heavy cost. The momentum of their attack appeared to have ground to a halt. The young officer was amused as he watched the *ibutho* across from C Company leap up with a loud shout of *'Usuthu!'*, only to be met by a crashing volley before they could charge a single step. The entire regiment fell to the ground. How many were hit and how many plainly dropped in terror was impossible to know.

From this position on the high ground the young officer caught his first glimpse of the main regiments of the Zulu 'Chest'. Far from being a simple rampaging mob, he could clearly discern their company lines advancing in extended order. Using his field glasses he could make out the presence of firearms carried by approximately one in every four warriors. This could be very problematic if the Zulus were allowed to get close enough to the camp. He had already seen, where the enemy was much closer, the effects of their incessant musketry.

Even at this distance, he could hear a strange murmuring; the light rhythm the Zulus beat on their shields, which kept in time with their low war chants. These were not the fierce battle cries emitted at the very end; but rather a low, almost musical cadence they used to propel themselves forward as one.

"Such discipline," he said, with a mix of fear and admiration.

Bellhouse then noticed a line of Zulus climbing out of the donga. They remained on their bellies, using the knee-high grass as concealment.

"Clever, clever," he said, with an appreciative laugh. He called out to the company below them. "Captain! Looks like our friends are slithering through the grass like bloody snakes!"

"Well we'll sort that one out," Captain Younghusband acknowledged. It was now apparent to all, for the field of grass was swaying from the numerous warriors crawling through it. Reginald grinned sadistically before issuing his next order. "Let's meet them like snakes, boys. Prone position, aim about ankle height, and we'll end this nonsense."

With the exception of the captain and Lieutenant Hodson, who stood with their pistols drawn, every last man on the company line dropped into the prone position. Even Colour Sergeant Brown and the other NCOs laid down with their men. A couple of rapidly-shouted commands, and a swatch of musketry cut through the tall grass. Only five or six Zulus were hit this way, yet the morale effects were devastating. Those less fortunate warriors were struck in the face, head, and shoulders leaving a horrific spray of blood, bone, and brain. A second volley, accompanied by well-placed shots by the sharp-shooters on the spur, forced the *ibutho* into a rapid retreat. Corporal Bellhouse reported to the captain that he counted another ten fresh corpses among those already killed.

A warrior lying in the tall grass near Kwanele cried out as he was struck by a rifle shot. The pain was overwhelming, and the man could not stop screaming. The bullet had smashed through the top of his shoulder, ripping the arm from its socket, and leaving a horrific wound full of bone splinters and blood. The entire regiment was descending into the throes of madness, unable to throw their might against the hated redcoats who were so close, yet shielded by a wall of rifle fire. Their own marksmen had only been marginally effective. The fear and frustration of the lead companies was threatening to undermine the entire assault. Knowing he was powerless to change the situation, Kwanele ordered his company to crawl back into the donga. None understood the desperate situation facing the British; all they knew was that there was a wall of ripping death that they could not get past. For Kwanele and his fellow *izinduna*, the situation was beginning to feel hopeless.

While 1/24th was more than holding its own against the stalled Zulu onslaught on the left and centre, on the extreme right flank, the situation was still very much in doubt. Not only were Durnford's and Bradstreet's men stretched incredibly thin, they were running critically low on ammunition.

Lieutenant Davies, whose troop was desperately trying to halt the advance of a large Zulu force that threatened to flank their position, as well as that of Charlie Pope's G Company, knew he had to notify Durnford. Davies mounted his horse and rode over to his commanding officer, who was observing the fire of his Basutos in the centre of the formation.

"Colonel, my men are almost out of ammunition!" Davies said, trying to maintain his composure. A Basuto sergeant then echoed the same concern.

Durnford acknowledged, quietly cursing himself for not having planned for this. "Take some of your men and bring up our ammunition wagon."

Davies called out the names of two of his section leaders. They and their men retrieved their mounts and rode at breakneck pace back towards the camp, approximately a mile away. They followed the wagon track until they reached the tents belonging to 1/24th and the No. 3 Column's mounted units. Davies suddenly realised that no one had told him where the wagons were, and he doubted that Durnford knew. The Zikhali Horse troop that had escorted their baggage in was engaged on the main battle line, along with Captain Shepstone and Lieutenant Raw. Feeling a trace of panic, the lieutenant spotted the ammunition wagon belonging to 1/24th. He rode over and quickly explained the situation to Quartermaster Pullen. He received a sharp rebuke.

"Damn it, lieutenant, have you lost your own ammunition wagon?" Pullen snapped.

"I'm afraid so, sir. Just, please, if we cannot get bullets to Colonel Durnford our right flank is finished."

"Wish I could help you," the quartermaster said consolingly. He then used the same explanation that Captain Essex had given to Lieutenant Raw. "These are Martini-Henry Rifle cartridges. They'll cause your carbine breaches to explode. I'm sorry, lieutenant. You'll have to find your own ammunition stores. And I suggest you hurry."

It was a terrible blow to Lieutenant Davies. He had his doubts about the infantry cartridges being incompatible with their own weapons; however, he knew it was pointless to argue. The wagon park extended along a mile of ground on the eastern slope of Isandlwana, and he had no idea which ones carried the No. 2 Column's ammunition.

"Scour the tents of the carbineers and mounted police," he ordered his men. He promised himself that any ammunition they stole, they would later pay back in kind. His troopers only managed to find a single opened box lying in one of the tents with about two hundred rounds. It was just enough to give each of his men a handful of cartridges. There was still no sign of their ammunition wagon, and it would take hours to search the entire camp with its hundreds of carts and wagons. Meanwhile, the Zulu 'Left Horn' kept pressing Durnford's position, which was quickly becoming untenable.

Chapter XXXIV: Charlie Pope's Stand

Isandlwana, the right flank
22 January 1879
2.00 p.m.

Lieutenant Charles d'Aguilar Pope
Officer Commanding, G Company, 2/24th

With remarkable speed and coordination, Lieutenant Charlie Pope's oversized detachment from 2/24th rushed south, past James Lonsdale's iziGqoza NNC on the right flank, and reformed in a long line, several hundred yards from where they had previously stood. They now faced east, towards the conical koppie that was less than half a mile distant. This was now swarming with Zulus, and entire regiment of several thousand warriors, rushing towards the gap between Lonsdale and Durnford's forces. Pope made a quick range estimate and raised his sword high.

"At six hundred yards!" He gave his men the briefest of moments to adjust their sights. *"Present…fire!"*

The crashing volley of one hundred and seventy rifles created a wall of flying lead that severely punished this newly-arrived Zulu regiment. At least a score of men fell dead or seriously maimed.

Facing this new threat, the Zulus became desperate to close the distance with the redcoats and overwhelm them with their massed numbers. But though they outnumbered Pope's small force nearly 20-to-1, the closer they got, the more fearsome the effects of the British firepower. For every fifty yards they sprinted, another volley sent more of their friends tumbling to the ground, their bodies ripped asunder. They attempted to bound by companies, with each man seeking cover. There was only a modest amount available; the occasional boulder, divot in the earth, or brush stand. It was simply not sufficient, with most of their warriors exposed in the open. Between Stuart Smith's lone cannon and Charlie Pope's volleys of musketry, the lead Zulu companies were being torn to pieces.

"Close intervals!" Charlie shouted to his men.

There was now only about three feet between each man. Pope not only wished to mass his firepower, with his men close enough to support each other once the enemy got within bayonets' reach, but the heat and fouling of their rifles was causing more frequent stoppages and jams. Soldiers were having to take their ramrods and slam them down the barrels, in order to extract bent or broken casings, at an alarming rate. Constant firing had rendered the barrels extremely hot. Without gloves, the men were compelled to use the sleeves of their tunics to grasp the burning metal as they cleared their weapons. But despite the unnerving frequency of these mishaps, his force was keeping the Zulus well at bay.

"Not so anxious to die for Cetshwayo, are they?" Sergeant Carse sneered venomously as he chambered another round into the smoking breach of his rifle.

Their attack stalled, the Zulus were attempting to use the rocky and broken terrain to their advantage. There was little integrity to their company lines at the moment, as individuals sought cover to protect themselves from the storm of bullets. There were many shouts from the *izinduna* for their own marksmen to get close enough to return fire.

Despite this early success at checking the Zulus, Pope's men, especially in close-order, could only cover so much of the right flank's frontage. There still existed a sizeable gap, at least 300 yards wide, between his force and Durnford's. And towards this sprinted a large band of Zulus.

Between weapons malfunctions and exhaustion of cartridges, the volume of fire from No. 2 Column in the donga had tapered considerably. The Zulus sensed this, and with a loud *'Usuthu!'* they charged. A distance of four to five hundred yards could be covered by a sprinting, blood-boiling Zulu in less than two minutes.

Without sufficient firepower to stop them, Durnford knew his position was unsustainable. *"To the horses! Retreat!"*

Panicking troopers fled to their horse-holders. The survivors of the destroyed rocket battery watched in horror with renewed feelings of abandonment as men scrambled aboard their mounts and rode away. The three privates from 1/24th were among the few who'd been able to keep a reasonable rate of fire in the faces of the Zulus, while Bombardier Goff had retrieved the carbine and bandolier from a slain Basuto shot in the head by an enemy marksman.

"Oh, bloody fuck, they better not be leaving us again," Private Johnson snapped.

As carbineers and Basutos hurried into their saddles, the redcoats noticed some were attempting to lead away the rider-less horses.

James Trainer rushed over and slapped away one trooper. "You sodding twats are not leaving us to die again!" He brandished his rifle menacingly. Goff and the other two privates similarly acquired mounts. The Zulus were now swarming the donga. Durnford's column fled up the far side and back towards the camp. Bombardier Goff and his companions galloped their horses due south, following the donga for another mile. Goff could ride readily enough, and James Trainer was a fair horseman. Johnson and Grant, however, found themselves struggling to control their bucking and bewildered mounts. Fortunately for them, the Zulus either simply did not notice them, or decided to instead pursue the bigger prize of Durnford's column.

The donga was calf-deep in water from the incessant rains, and their horses kicked up clods of mud as they splashed along. They soon reached a place where another donga merged from the northwest. With no enemy warriors in pursuit, the four men climbed their mounts carefully up the western side of the wide trench. They were now about three miles south of Isandlwana. In the distance they saw thousands of Zulus converging on the southern end of the camp.

"What was it they call the Zulu attack?" Grant asked, his voice shaking. Like his mates, he was famished and trembling from exhaustion.

"The 'Horns of the Beast'," Goff replied.

"Then from what I can tell, we were battling the 'Left Horn'. Which means the 'Chest' and 'Right Horn' are somewhere out there, to the north."

"So what the hell do we do now?" Johnson asked. He looked at his two friends, both of whom had come from C Company, 1/24th.

Trainer responded with a question of his own. "What can we do? We had no time in the camp. We don't even know where anyone is; Lord Chelmsford, Colonel Pulleine, our mates from C Company…hell, even Colonel Durnford has disappeared."

"Well, that's it then, lads," Bombardier Goff spoke up. "We've done our bit. If we go north, towards the camp, we die. I don't know about any of you, but I didn't make it through that shit-farce with the rockets and Colonel Durnford abandoning us twice, just to commit suicide now." He paused, seeing anguish on the soldiers' faces. All were fresh-faced boys not long out of recruit training. "I'm sorry lads, but you've done all you could. Your boys in the 24th are some of the best shots in the Empire, and they're letting those heathens know it. If anyone can survive this hell-storm it's them."

"We have two more companies, D and G, coming up from Greytown," Johnson recalled. "They should have reached Helpmekaar by now."

"Alright then," Goff said. "We'll make for Helpmekaar and join up with the rest of your battalion. If that was the 'Left Horn' we were facing, then the 'Right Horn' is probably crawling all over the trail to Rorke's Drift. We'll have to cut across country, but I know of another drift we can cross about ten miles south of the ponts. Let's move out."

410

William Cochrane had joined Harry Davies and his small element of fifteen men, when they spotted the breach in the lines. A horde of Zulus was rushing into the gap left between the 2/24th detachment and where Durnford's broken column had once stood. The first band, only about forty warriors in all, was driving a small herd of cattle and attempting to use them as cover.

"Oh, bugger me!" a trooper shouted. "The Zulus are in the camp!"

Adding to the rapidly unfolding disaster, Durnford's entire column was now in full retreat from the donga. Davies and his troopers quickly scrounged up all the cartridges they could carry and began to fire at the enemy warriors rampaging through the tents belonging to 1/24th and mounted troops. There would be no ride back to the donga. The remnants of No. 2 Column were now crowding in among the tents, while their officers attempted to restore order. Adding to their frustrations was Quartermaster Pullen with wagons full of ammunition, yet being told the thousands of cartridges he had available were useless.

Davies saw Durnford dismounting. He was attempting to reform his men into some semblance of a firing line. His orderly stood close by, holding the reins of his commander's horse. Despite the ongoing struggle all around him, it appeared as if Lieutenant Colonel Durnford was completely alone. The scene then turned surreal for Harry Davies. The sky above him began to grow dark, casting a deep shadow on Durnford and the entire battle.

The gradual blocking of the sun began around 1.00 that afternoon. With it came feelings of dread and superstition to all on the battlefield, both Zulu and British alike. William Cochrane, who had noted the pending solar eclipse in his diary that morning, felt the hairs on his neck stand up. Less than a quarter of the sun's glaring light remained, and even that was obscured by the incessant clouds of acrid smoke. It did not make the day seem as night, exactly, but rather overcast with thick clouds.

"God cannot bear to look upon the pain that man inflicts upon himself any longer," Cochrane said to Davies.

With growing feelings of hopelessness, the two men continued to fire. They knew the situation was rapidly collapsing, even though the redcoats on the main firing line were still holding their own.

Unless Durnford managed to pull off some sort of miracle, the right flank would soon collapse and the Zulus from the 'Left Horn' would close in behind them. Many of the NNC infantry, having few firearms between them and lacking the numbers to make a decisive stand against the Zulus, were in full flight. Only the indomitable iziGqoza and Durnford's Basuto horsemen remained steadfast.

"How many cartridges do you have left?" Cochrane asked Davies.

"Five…you?"

"Two. Bugger all, there isn't much left we can do, is there?"

"Not with the NNC fleeing and Durnford about to be overrun," Davies remarked. He hefted his carbine. "And this damn thing makes for a lousy club. Fuck it…"

It was a rare show of profanity coming from an officer, even a non-regular colonial. Yet Harry Davies was completely exacerbated and his nerves near the breaking point. With only seven shots between them, they had little left to offer except their own bloody corpses. Cochrane had already made up his mind and grabbed the reins of his horse.

"I can't very well continue to perform my duties if I'm dead. Are you coming?"

A force of twenty Zulus was now rushing towards them, pointing their spears and shouting furious war chants.

"Yeah."

Mehlokazulu could not even begin to describe the feelings that kept his stomach tied in knots; fear, anger, sorrow, hatred, determination, the urge to flee…all conflicting with each other in equal measure as he and his warriors rose up to attack. The cacophony of emotions soon merged into a cauldron of pure hatred. Finally, a chance for retribution!

His own lead company had taken a severe punishing. Twenty were dead, another fifty badly injured. Over half his closest mates since the day their *ibutho* had been raised were, over the course of an hour, either slain or crippled. It was the terrible price they paid for leading the iNgobamakhosi's attack on the British camp.

But now, the enemy's mounted troops were in full retreat. Anxious to pursue, the *induna* stood and raised his spear, ordering his warriors after them, *"Emva kwabo!"*

Their attack was no longer impeded by the rifle and carbine fire of their foes, and with a shout of 'Usuthu!' his men leapt to their feet and charged. Waves upon waves of warriors from iNgobamakhosi surged around the conical koppie. As they reached the donga, which they knew as 'Nyogane', they saw another opportunity for blood-letting; one far more promising than the fleeing cowards on horseback.

"There they are!" a warrior shouted, pointing with his spear. "Redcoats!"

Durnford's retreat, necessitated by the exhaustion of ammunition and the incessant pressing of the additional Zulu forces on their left, rendered Charlie Pope in an extremely precarious position. His G Company and all of the 2/24th attachments were on the verge of being completely cut off.

"Damn him!" a soldier shouted.

They could clearly see Durnford leading his fleeing troops back towards the camp. "We come out here to support him, and the bastard and leaves us!"

"Steady lads." Pope tried to reassure his men. Heat and sweat were making his eye-glasses fog. He removed them for a quick wipe down.

With nearly 170 men under his charge, Pope could not be everywhere at once, and he'd directed section leaders to control the fire of their men. The battalion soldiers who attached themselves to his company were hastily thrown into sections with whatever NCOs were directing their volleys. They were still being hard pressed to their immediate front, with greater numbers of Zulu marksmen returning fire. With Durnford's column now in retreat, and the majority of James Lonsdale's NNC losing courage and running,

Pope needed to organise a rapid withdrawal, lest his men be taken in both flanks.

"Lieutenant Godwin-Austen, Sergeant Carse!" he shouted.

The officer and NCO rushed over to their officer commanding.

"We're about to be flanked. There's a donga about a half mile behind us. Dash by sections, and keep the fire hot."

The two men quickly returned to their places on the line. Godwin-Austen had taken the left, consisting of mostly attached soldiers. Sergeant Carse took the right. Pope oversaw the entire force from his place in the centre. Four of his men were dead and fifteen more wounded. The wounded he had taken to the donga with all haste. With regret they left the slain. Two of the wounded were hit in the legs with musket fire. Each required a pair of their mates to assist them. The others had various injuries to their arms and torsos but were able move under their own power.

At the commands of Lieutenant Godwin-Austen and Sergeant Carse, sections rushed back towards the donga, reloading as they ran. They only went ten to twenty yards each time before turning back and firing into the Zulus, providing cover for the rest of their men to hustle past them. While trying to keep his entire force together, Pope also kept an eye on the Zulus to the south, who were chasing after Durnford's column. Then another entire regiment materialized from around the southern tip of the conical koppie. The warriors shouted and pointed with their spears, having spotted the prize target that was the 2/24th's detachment.

"Refuse the right flank!" Pope shouted to Sergeant Carse, who echoed the order to his men. Thirty soldiers pivoted, forming a right angle off the main line which now faced this new, oncoming threat.

The Zulus continued to rush in their company lines, as the *izinduna* struggled to keep their men from blindly charging on their own. It was no small credit to their discipline that only a handful of warriors broke ranks and rushed head-on at Pope's company. These men were quickly ripped apart by British volleys, compelling their companions to maintain formation and seek cover as they advanced.

The battling forces were now within two hundred yards of each other. The redcoats felt a growing sense of desperation, only held in check by their stalwart discipline and the calm reassurance of their NCOs. Minus the losses already suffered, Lieutenant Pope still had around 150 men in the fight. The Zulus, now advancing on their front and right flank, numbered in the thousands. The attacking hordes were closing the distance faster than the 2/24th soldiers could withdraw. Within a hundred yards, the accuracy of the Zulu musketry improved. The poor quality of their weapons and complete lack of marksmanship training meant that maybe one in every fifty shots found its mark; but with so many firearms coming into action, soldiers all along G Company's line were shot down. The few who were killed outright were the fortunate ones. Those badly injured and unable to be saved by their friends could only cry out in agony and terror. They were swarmed and cut to pieces in the wake of the Zulu onslaught.

Near the donga north of the wagon track, well behind the place where Durnford made his initial stand, Pope ordered his men to close ranks and fix bayonets. Soldiers were tearing into the paper packets of ammunition in their reserve pouches, feverishly trying to keep their rate of fire constant.

With his small command now concentrated, Pope took control of the line. *"Present...fire!"*

The company was now in a square, with the two officers standing in front of their men near the centre of the coming onslaught. A large band of Zulus, who had been assaulting the camp itself, broke off to try and strike them from behind. Heat and fouling of their Martini-Henrys was causing a growing number of jams and misfires. One in five weapons was constantly down, as their owners fought to clear them.

In addition to Zulu muskets, showers of assegais began to rain down on the company. These proved far more effective and lethal. Soldiers suddenly sprouted throwing spears from their chests, guts, and various appendages. With a loud cry of *'Usuthu!'* the hordes charged them on all sides. Firing from the trapped redcoats all but ceased. They were now forced to do battle in close quarters with the bayonet.

Drill and instinct took over. The soldiers fought shoulder-to-shoulder in a desperate attempt to keep the Zulus from utilizing their overwhelming numbers. They had this band of British soldiers trapped, but the *amabutho* would pay a fearful toll overwhelming them. With their vastly superior reach, the imperial soldiers held a decided advantage in one-on-one combat. Many a warrior paid a painful price for his valour. Bayonets punctured ribs, guts, arms, legs, and necks. One man screeched as he was stabbed through the eye socket.

But Pope's small command could not hold indefinitely. Though they continued to inflict much suffering on their assailants, their own men were now falling rapidly. Soldiers were badly wounded or slain; their mates tried to close the gaps, only to find them exploited by the Zulus, who were now able to kill more effectively with their short stabbing spears.

Pope and Godwin-Austen continued to fire their pistols, with one stepping back to reload while the other kept shooting. A Zulu *induna* shouted for a score of his men to follow him and he rushed the officers. Godwin-Austen had just stepped back to the line and raised his pistol when a musket shot smashed into his neck. His eyes bulged, and his weapon dropped from his hand.

"Fred!" Charlie shouted.

His friend slumped to the ground. His eyes glazed over, as his body convulsed in the final throes of death. Gouts of blood came from his mouth and the terrible wound.

Pope saw the *induna* rushing for him. He only managed to reload three cartridges and fired as fast as he could. He grazed the warrior leader on each cheek, with the last shot striking his leg. The *induna* stumbled. A chunk of flesh was torn from his leg, yet he maintained his footing. Pope tried to reload his revolver as the *induna* flung one of his assegais. It buried itself in the lieutenant's chest. Charlie screamed with rage. Suppressing the excruciating pain, he tried to pull the weapon from his body. Before he could do so, the *induna* hobbled forward and thrust his stabbing spear into Pope's guts then once more into the side of his neck. Charlie grabbed him by the shoulder for a brief moment before slumping to the ground next to his friend and fellow officer.

The remnants of his force fought bravely on. But as more gaps opened in their lines, the formation collapsed completely. Sergeant Carse, standing over the bodies of several wounded men, managed to fire off one more shot from his rifle before a trio of thrown assegais to the chest and stomach slew him.

The wounded were shown no more mercy than their mates, who had tried to protect them. All were stabbed repeatedly, until nothing was left of G Company and the 2/24ᵗʰ detachment except a slew of bodies covered in disembowelled guts and pooling blood. The scores of dead and badly injured Zulus among them was a testament to their bravery and defiance in the face of death.

Chapter XXXV: Murderous Destruction

The uNokhenke Donga, north of Isandlwana
22 January 1879
2.30 p.m.

Zulu warrior in ceremonial dress

There was a rousing feeling in the air for Kwanele and the survivors of the uNokhenke regiment. Their *inkosi* had sent two-thirds of their number to the right, to re-join with the 'Right Horn'. They were now sweeping around behind Isandlwana and threatening to cut off all roads of escape for the whites. However, the great *inkosi*, Mkhosana, had ordered the remaining companies to stay in place to support the uKhandempemvu. They had, by far, taken the severest amount of punishment in the entire 'Chest'. Exposed the longest to the onslaught of British musketry, many of their lead companies had been shot to pieces. The bodies of hundreds of dead and dying men lay strewn about the slope the *ibutho* had swarmed.

Kwanele was eager to finally engage the redcoats in hand-to-hand combat. He'd been taught to respect their skills. The rifle and bayonet had a far greater reach than their spears, and the imperial infantryman drilled infinitely more with his weapons than the Zulu warrior. But now he no longer cared. All that mattered was closing with their enemy, rather than continuing to take the murderous punishment from their rifles, with little to no recourse. '*Soon*,' he told himself.

On the high ridges, the senior *amakhosi* watched as the crashing wave of their regiments foundered. They were stalled in the dongas and saddles no more than three hundred paces from the British lines. They seemed unable to go any further. Overlooking the north side of Isandlwana, Ntshingwayo and Mkhosana stood grim-faced, as the uKhandempemvu and uNokhenke regiments refused to advance out of the long donga.

"The left regiments of the 'Chest' are pressing hard on the British right," Ntshingwayo observed. "But if these men who now lay on top of each other in the donga do not exploit this, the entire *impi* will be undone."

"Let me handle this, *inkosi*." Mkhosana reassured him. "They will not falter now, not when their king and nation so depend upon them."

Hefting his shield and stabbing spear, he bounded down the slope towards his paralysed force. Oblivious to the bullets that struck all around him, he reached the lead companies, huddled behind the embankment. He could see the terrible price they had already paid in this battle. Scores of men were dead, with many more bearing terrible injuries wrought by the British bullets. Refusing to allow his courage to fail, he gave a great roar and leapt to the far embankment. He faced his warriors as rifle fire from the redcoats continued to pelt the earth around him.

"*Uhlamvana ubul'mlilo ubaswe uMantshonga no uNqelebana kashongo njalo!*" he bellowed, holding his spear and shield high. It was a praise of the king that each warrior knew by heart. "*The Little Branch of Leaves, that extinguished the great fire kindled by the white men, gave no such order as this!*"

The words filled the men of the *amabutho* with shame and rekindled determination. Those who had loudly proclaimed they would be hailed as members of Cetshwayo's heroes, the *abaqawe*, during the ceremonies before the king, were most moved by the *inkosi's* fierce speech. With a roar of '*Usutu!*' they scrambled out of the donga.

Pleased with his men and determined to lead them in this last charge, Mkhosana turned to face the enemy, his spear pointed at them and ready to let loose his own cry of *'Usutu!'* It was not to be. In that moment a British bullet smashed into his head above the right eye. The back of his skull exploded, showering his nearest warriors in blood and brain. Their beloved *inkosi* fell dead. Yet rather than despair, this enraged them further. They were determined to avenge him or join him in the afterlife.

Pulleine's ability to see the larger picture of the battle had been impeded since the first shots were fired. Captain Gardner was now missing, and he was saddened to hear that Sergeant Major Gapp had fallen somewhere near Wardell's company. Thankfully, he still had Melvill and Coghill to act as his ADCs and messengers. Their main mile-long frontage was socked in with smoke, making it difficult to see his soldiers or the attacking Zulus. As Durnford's column retreated into the camp, it became abundantly clear that his line was stretched too thin and was too far in front of the main camp. In the haze and growing swarm of enemy warriors, he could no longer see Charlie Pope's 2/24th detachment. He feared the worst.

"Mister Melvill," he said, realising what he must do. "Find the bugler, have him sound *'retire'*. Then inform all officers commanding that companies are to compress their formations and reform on the camp."

"Yes, sir." In addition to what Pulleine surmised, the adjutant noted that unless the firing line was withdrawn back towards the mountain, the entire force of Zulus following in Durnford's wake would roll up and take the battalion from behind, having first overrun the ammunition wagons. Though Captain Essex and Lieutenant Smith-Dorrien's valiant band of volunteers had done an admirable job of keeping a steady flow of ammunition to the firing line, the situation would be rendered hopeless if the Zulus overran the wagons.

Melvill glanced briefly over his right shoulder at the southern stretch of Isandlwana. The firing line had been hammering the Zulu 'Chest' while Durnford battled the 'Left Horn'. This meant the

'Right Horn' was still out there, most likely somewhere behind Isandlwana. As he rode towards James Lonsdale's position, the adjutant concluded there were roughly five thousand Zulus they had not even engaged yet.

By the time Melvill reached Lonsdale's iziGqoza companies it was too late. The line companies of the 24th were retiring, in heed to the bugle calls. None of the NNC knew what the bugle notes actually meant. Instead, they saw the falling back of the redcoats as a sign that the general retreat had been ordered.

Among those now fleeing was Prince Sikhotha, Cetshwayo's brother, whom the British had hoped to use as a pretender to control the Zulu populace. The retiring of the redcoats and the retreat of the iziGqoza proved too much for most of the NNC. All order was soon lost. They dropped their weapons and fled, many tearing off the red arm and headbands that identified them as British auxiliaries.

One *induna* refused to leave the field. His name was Gabangaye, an old warrior who had fought against Cetshwayo at Tugela River. He would not flee in defeated disgrace again! His spear held high, he shouted *'Mani buya! Return to the fight!'* and marched bravely forward to meet his fate. About fifty iziGqoza returned to stand by his side, their honour not allowing them to quit the field. They would make many of their Zulu cousins bleed before it was all over.

Despite the harrowing and increasingly desperate struggle, Surgeon-Major Peter Shepherd maintained his ever calm, stoic demeanour. At this point, most of the wounded who reached his aid station had received their injuries from Zulu musketry. Fortunately for both surgeon and patient alike, the wounds caused by enemy gunfire paled in comparison to those inflicted by the Martini-Henry.

'Wash, stop bleeding, fix parts in natural position without delay'. This was Shepherd's axiom for dealing with battlefield injuries, and this day was no different. The homemade bullets, inferior burning powder, and the great range from which they were fired meant the Zulu firearms lacked the power necessary to kill or seriously maim in most cases. Torn muscles, ripped flesh, and the

twisting of bodies upon impact were the most common injuries the surgeon and his orderlies dealt with.

Peter Shepherd worked tirelessly on the growing number of wounded soldiers, oblivious to all other concerns. Broken bones were splinted, musket balls extracted, and wounds cleaned and bound with bandages. Whenever possible, soldiers who could still stand and make use of a rifle were sent back to their companies. But as the afternoon wore on, the sun slowly being masked by the solar eclipse, the volume of wounded men became overwhelming. At least three stretcher-bearers were missing and feared to be dead, having sacrificed themselves trying to save the wounded. And with Sergeant Major Gapp dead, there was no one left to organise them.

"Surgeon-Major!" a frantic voice shouted. Horace Smith-Dorrien burst into the hospital tent.

"What is it, Mister Dorrien?" the doctor asked, extracting a musket ball from the side of a badly wounded carbineer.

"The Zulus are in the camp, sir. We have to evacuate at once!"

Shepherd was so intent on performing his duties and saving lives, he paid almost no attention to the rapidly degrading battle going on all around him. In disbelief, and thinking this boyish officer half his age was panicking needlessly, Shepherd emerged from his tent, wiping his bloody hands on a rag. His eyes grew wide when he saw the hellish chaos unfolding. He understood.

"The wounded!" he shouted at his orderlies still in the tent. "Get them aboard wagons at once!"

He knew he could not possibly save all the injured men, and it wrenched Peter's heart. There simply wasn't time. The companies on the firing line were retiring in good order, keeping their volleys constant. The right flank, however, was in tatters, and the entire camp was now in chaos. As a doctor, Peter Shepherd had but one duty, to save as many lives as he could.

It was an arduous task, heaving each of the wounded men, especially those unable to walk at all, onto the wagons. There was only one which was limbered up and ready. It bore a large red cross on a white flag on the side and was much smaller than the large, ox-drawn wagons most of the column utilised. This one was hauled by half a dozen mules, along with a young Natal voorlooper and an African driver. Both were wide-eyed with terror, shouting at the whites to hurry, in their local tongue.

Within minutes ten men were loaded into the back. The driver gave a shout and the braying mules lurched the wagon away. Surgeon-Major Shepherd, his lieutenant of orderlies, and a few fortunate souls with horses, mounted and galloped away. Those without mounts grabbed whatever weapons they could. They were unable to make any sort of stand, as a wave of unchecked Zulu washed over them. They and the wounded left behind were quickly rendered into bloodied, eviscerated corpses just outside the hospital tent.

As the wagon bounded away, Lieutenant Harry Davies rode up beside, hoping to offer whatever support he could to the wounded. They rounded the southern tip of Isandlwana, with the wagon bouncing on the road and the wheels settling into the ruts. A terrifying sight ahead awaited them.

The regiments of the Zulu 'Right Horn', up to this point completely forgotten, emerged from dongas and streambeds to the west. The road to Rorke's Drift was completely cut off. Companies of warriors advanced quickly, seeking out what they knew would be easy prey.

Davies fired a shot from his carbine before veering his horse to the left, making his way southwest towards the river. Scores of others were doing the same. He stopped for a moment and looked back in anguish as the hospital wagon was swarmed by Zulus. They spared neither the patients nor the black driver and voorlooper. In their fury they even killed the mules. Lieutenant Harry Davies, and any who could find a horse and escape, began to forge their own trail of fugitives, hoping to escape the murderous onslaught threatening to destroy the entire camp and everyone within.

At the cannon, Lieutenant Curling had switched to canister shot; tubes filled with dozens of lead balls. When fired, they went off like a massive shotgun blast at close range. Were all six guns from N Battery present at Isandlwana, they could have perhaps held indefinitely; much like the famed Captain Mercer at Waterloo sixty-four years before. But two seven-pounders, even with the horrific mauling of canister shot cutting massive and bloody swaths through the Zulu ranks, was simply not enough. And with the bugles sounding 'retire', Wardell and Porteous had pulled their companies back into the camp. The artillery was now exposed.

Major Smith, whose gun had re-joined with Curling, was shot in the left arm, which he now kept tucked in his jacket. One gunner was shot through the wrist, another in the side. Another man was dead after taking a musket ball to the head.

"Fire!" Smith shouted.

The cannon erupted once more. At such close range, more than twenty Zulus were torn to pieces. Yet, there would be no 'Mercer stand' with the guns here. The enemy were too many and very nearly on top of them.

"Limber up, save the guns!"

The cannon were hastily connected to their limbers as the crews scrambled aboard. One gunner was stabbed in the back before he could climb onto his seat. With no time to mount, the remainder fled on foot. The horses towing the guns scrambled away. Stuart Smith's intent was to withdraw as far as the camp, a half mile behind them, and establish a new firing position. It was just a matter of outrunning the Zulus.

"Fix bayonets!" Colour Sergeant Brown bellowed.

Despite the long hours spent at drill, in actual combat one only drew their twenty-two inch triangular spike and fixed it to the end of their rifle when the situation became terribly desperate.

"Up the slope, lads!" Captain Younghusband shouted. "Easy now. Keep your weapons towards the enemy!"

It was a quick yet measured pace which C Company retreated up the northeast side of Isandlwana. Section leaders continued to control the volleys of their men. The Zulu companies were in disorder at the moment, and those who tried to close with them were felled by brutal salvos of lead. The redcoats were now in close-order, with only a couple feet between each man. A bristling wall of bayonets protruded into their enemies' faces.

Between volleys, brave bands of Zulus would rush forward. Despite their overwhelming urge to plunge their spears into the guts of the whites, the redcoats and their fearsome bayonets were too close together. Bayonets clattered against shields. Valiant young warriors attempted to push past the wall of spikes. Some still had throwing spears and used these to good effect. Several men from C Company were cut down with the blades plunged deep into their chests, limbs, or guts. As the men were felled, their bodies were viciously stabbed by the oncoming warriors. Their comrades, compelled to abandon them, shuddered in horror at the agonising screams.

Arthur deliberately picked his feet up as he stepped backwards, lest he trip over a protruding rock or bush. He was fumbling for another cartridge when he heard a howl of pain next to him. Richard was struck in the left shoulder with a musket ball. He was struggling to regain the grip on his rifle when a throwing spear plunged into his thigh.

"Richard!" Arthur screamed.

His friend called his name back, as a Zulu warrior rushed in and thrust his spear deep between the stricken soldier's neck and shoulder. Richard fell to his knees, eyes at first scrunched shut in pain, then open and vacant. He sputtered his last breath in a weak spray of blood and spittle as he collapsed into a twitching heap.

"No!" Arthur fired his weapon, not bothering to bring it up to his shoulder. The kick almost wrenched it from his hands. Tears of sorrow from watching his friend be brutally slain were compounded by the realisation that his shot had missed. A hand grabbed him by the shoulder and drug him up the hill. He recognised the voice of Sergeant John Edwards.

"Come on, Wilkie! You can't help him, he's gone!"

Up and up they continued. Controlled volleys were no more; men fired whenever they managed to get a round loaded without being impaled by the persistent Zulus. Still, others fell. By the time the ground abruptly flattened out along a short step, just sixty of C Company's original ninety soldiers were among the living.

Unfortunately for the companies of 1/24th, the fleeing NNC and the compressing of their own ranks left wide gaps between formations. Only Captain Younghusband on the extreme left had been able to utilise the terrain, a narrow stretch between the impassable cliff side of Isandlwana and the obstacles created by the rows of tents, to make his way up to the nek of the mountain. For Wardell, Mostyn, Cavaye, and Porteous there was no blocking terrain to use. They were completely exposed and on their own. With Charlie Pope's entire 2/24th detachment completely annihilated, it now fell to each company to make their own last stand and attempt to save their men.

While Pope's men were being surrounded and slaughtered, Captain Wardell and his colour sergeant, Frederick Wolfe, knew they had to act quickly if they were going to make it back to the camp.

"We cannot all move together, sir," Wolfe stated plainly. "Go. I will keep one section here and hold them long enough for you to get the rest of the company set."

There was no time to come up with a better plan. The captain nodded and called for the rest of the company to follow him. Colour Sergeant Wolfe ordered the remaining section of twenty men to close ranks. He called his fire commands as fast as he was able, but it wasn't long before he and his men were surrounded.

"Halt!" Wardell shouted, raising his sword high. He turned back, intent on covering the withdrawal of Wolfe's detachment, only to see it was too late. He watched the colour sergeant fall, stabbed through the heart. The rest of his men fell soon after. The captain was filled with both sadness and pride. Not one man attempted to run. He quickly formed the remnants of his company into a square. Colour Sergeant Wolfe had bought them some time, and he hoped it would be enough.

Captain George Wardell
Officer Commanding, H Company, 1/24th

As George Wardell and Frederick Wolfe made their defiant last
stand, Bombardier Goff and the survivors of the rocket battery
forded their way across the uMzinyathi River, ten miles south of
Rorke's Drift. It had been a harrowing crossing, yet was mercifully
devoid of any pursuit by the Zulus. Goff and his companions then
began making their way northwest, towards the road that would
eventually take them to Helpmekaar.

James Trainer decided to ride to Rorke's Drift first, to warn the
garrison. He felt they needed to know there was a terrible battle in
progress, and that the Zulu *impi* was much closer to them than
anyone had suspected. And the sooner they brought the companies
from Helpmekaar forward the better.

James approached from the south, following fairly close to the
river until he could see the lines of tents belonging to B Company,
2/24th. He was near the camp when he heard a voice.

"Hold, friend!" The soldier was a private named Thomas Cole.
Twenty years of age, though his boyish face made him appear much
younger, he had served with B Company for the past two years.
Cole immediately noted James' fearful appearance; his soaked,
filthy uniform, matted and dishevelled hair, face covered in soot and

grime; and above all, his tired, bloodshot eyes that seemed completely lost.

The two had never met, but Cole recognized the '24' on Trainer's epaulettes. "Where the devil did you come from?"

He was momentarily confused, for this man had clearly not crossed at the main Drift.

"Rocket battery, Durnford's column," James replied, his exhaustion suddenly overwhelming him. "The camp at Isandlwana has come under attack. We were cut off from the rest and lucky to escape with our lives."

"We?"

"There was me and two others from the 24th, plus a bombardier. Sadly, Major Russell is dead, as are the rest of the lads assigned to his battery."

Cole didn't know what to think of him. His wretched state could very well collaborate his story. If he were a deserter, he certainly wouldn't have ridden up to the station. "Do you need anything, friend? Food? Water?"

James shook his head. "No, I just came here to warn you that the Zulu *impi* is at Isandlwana. They slipped behind Lord Chelmsford and most of your battalion, who went chasing after them early this morning. I don't know if the camp can hold or not. We're headed to Helpmekaar to find two of our companies."

"Ah, yes," Cole said, with a reassuring smile. "They were supposed to have been here by now. Major Spalding left this morning to see where the devil they are."

"Looks like I'll be reporting to him, then." As he turned his horse about, he said hoarsely, "Keep your eyes and ears open. If our lads cannot hold the line at Isandlwana, there is nothing between you and the Zulu *impi*."

James then rode away. Private Cole was joined by Sergeant Henry Gallagher, who stared at the bedraggled man riding away.

"Who was that, Cole?"

"I don't know, sergeant. He didn't give his name, only that he had been part of the rocket battery, Durnford's Column."

"Yes, I recall some lads from the 24th were attached to them. But what in the hell is he doing here?"

428

Cole shook his head slowly, eyes still fixed on the mounted soldier. "He said the camp at Isandlwana was under attack by the main Zulu *impi,* and they had gotten behind Lord Chelmsford. Poor fellow looks to be completely mad."

"Might be a deserter."

"I don't think so, sergeant. He crossed at least several miles further upriver, possibly more. He would not have ridden here if he were deserting. He said he and some other lads were headed to Helpmekaar to join their other companies. I told him Major Spalding had left this morning to see what their delay was, and he said he would report to him."

"Hmm, well the good major can sort him out then," the sergeant remarked, before beginning his walk back into the main camp.

Chapter XXXVI: Flee or Die

Isandlwana
22 January 1879
2.45 p.m.
***

When the Zulu 'Left Horn' rolled up to the camp at Isandlwana from the south, most of the civilian drivers and indigenous voorloopers had already fled in the direction of Rorke's Drift. They did not know that the 'Right Horn' was soon coming into action. Those not quick enough to get past before they closed the proverbial trap would find themselves slaughtered by assegai, knobkerrie, and musket.

For Charlie Raw, the man who first laid eyes on the Zulu *impi*, his world was rapidly collapsing. The men from Younghusband's C Company were retiring in good order. The same could not be said, however, for Raw's own troop of Zikhali Horse. His men were running critically low on ammunition, and many had nothing at all. They had seen the *impi* in all its terrible glory and knew better than any other soldier on the field that this battle could no longer be won.

"Damned natives are fleeing like cowards," Raw snapped. He rode over to Captain Shepstone whose face was impassive.

"Do what you can," George said, his voice surprisingly calm. "If, indeed, all is lost, then save yourselves. Live to fight another day."

"What about you?"

"I am Colonel Durnford's political advisor and have acted as his senior staff officer. My duty is with him. Now go."

In appreciation of the captain's courage under these most dire of circumstances, Charlie Raw saluted before riding back to try to restore some order amid the chaos. In truth, there was little he could do. Even if the Zikhali wished to continue to fight, without any ammunition resupplies they were rendered completely useless. Many of his troops were now fleeing through the camp. Others rode around the backside of Isandlwana in hopes of finding the road to Rorke's Drift still open. Raw was among the few who recalled that the Zulu 'Right Horn' was still out there and would likely be on the field at any moment. As much as it shamed him, he knew there was little left to do but heed the captain's words, *'Live to fight another day'*. Yet those who fled from the disintegrating battle would soon face their own hell-storm of terror.

While the troops of his column attempted to rally themselves into a viable stand, Lieutenant Colonel Anthony Durnford rode into the camp, hoping to find Pulleine. If he could be supported by a company of redcoats, and if someone could find his damn ammunition wagons, they might be able to halt the Zulu onslaught. Though unable to find Pulleine in the confusion, he did happen upon Captain Nourse, whose NNC company had accompanied the rocket battery. Only four of his men remained with him, the rest had already fled or killed.

"Captain Nourse!" Durnford called out. His face was etched with concern, and an air of confusion and disbelief surrounded him. "You were escorting Major Russell and the rocket battery. What has become of them?"

Nourse was unaware that the colonel had already had the exact same conversation with the four survivors from the rocket battery, so he was not as alarmed by the question as he would have been otherwise. Nor did he know those same four soldiers had fought beside Durnford's troopers in the donga before they were abandoned again.

"Major Russell is dead, sir. I think some of his men escaped, but most were killed. I'm sorry I was not able to do more to protect them."

Durnford gritted his teeth, his gaze distant, beyond the savage chaos of the ongoing battle. His next words brought consternation to the captain. "I do not think I shall survive such a disgrace." He then wheeled his horse about and rode back to his column.

Anthony knew his attack had failed. And if the camp should be overrun, he was the most likely scapegoat Chelmsford would place the blame upon. Whatever mistakes Durnford made that day, he had done so with the best of intentions, based on the intelligence he had in that moment. His mind was thoroughly addled, and there was but one thing left for him to do; reform his men, and whomever else he could find in the bedlam, and make a final stand. He cared not whether he survived this day, his only personal concern was what would become of his reputation once he was no longer alive to defend it. And yet it mattered not. Whatever Chelmsford would later say about him, Lieutenant Colonel Anthony Durnford was determined to live and die as was befitting of a British soldier and gentleman officer.

He reached his column, which was now joined by men from the pioneer section, as well as John Chard's engineers, and a few other stragglers and volunteers. Durnford dismounted his horse for the last time.

A voice called out, *"Colonel!"*

With an appreciative smile he saw Captain George Shepstone, the loyal officer Durnford thought he had seen for the last time. "By God, George, I was not sure we should ever meet again."

"Zikhali Horse has broken," Shepstone reported. "Lieutenant Roberts is dead. Lieutenant Raw is trying to salvage what he can, but I already instructed him that if he cannot, he is to save himself and as many others as he can."

"But you did not think to save yourself," Durnford noted.

"My place is with you, sir. Whether I live or die this day, it will be by your side."

"The 'Right Horn' is still out there," the colonel remarked in a brief moment of clarity. He then pointed towards the southern spur of Isandlwana. "I need you over there. Whatever happens, do not let them flank us!"

The captain gave a grim nod and saluted, knowing he was seeing his commanding officer for the last time. With one troop of Natal Native Horse that had not fled the battle, along with roughly a hundred stalwart iziGqoza, he made his way over the spur.

"Colonel Durnford!" It was Quartermaster Pullen. "I thought you might like some help in turning the enemy flank."

The logistics officer, who had barely escaped with his life when his ammunition wagons were overrun, was carrying a Martini-Henry Rifle. He was joined by about thirty men, mostly pioneers. There were a few bandsmen, as well as several orderlies who had escaped the slaughter at the hospital. All were armed with pouches full of ammunition. Durnford nodded in appreciation, his confidence

432

returning. Whatever happened now, he was glad to have such valiant men by his side. He was also joined by Lieutenant William Vereker. Having lost his horse, he decided his luck was up and he should stand with his friends. Captain Bradstreet had rallied as many of his men as possible, roughly thirty carbineers, who also joined the fray.

The remnants of Lieutenant Colonel Durnford's No. 2 Column, along with Quartermaster Pullen and his volunteers, stood firm in anticipation of the coming onslaught.

It was one of the iziGqoza warriors who first caught glimpse of the approaching warriors from the Zulu 'Right Horn'. Fresh from the slaughter of numerous Natal wagon drivers and voorloopers, they sought to soak their spears in the blood of the white soldiers and their hated African allies.

"Yima ngomumo, amabhungu!" George Shepstone shouted, ordering his men to stand ready, as he drew his pistol.

The captain stood in the centre of the iziGqoza, who were arrayed into two ranks. Rider-less horsemen and anyone else with a rifle or carbine formed up on the wings. While they fired the last of their cartridges in rapid succession, the warriors of the iziGqoza began to beat their spears and clubs against their shields, while humming a rhythmic chant in time with the cadence.

"This is a day of reckoning, for both iziGqoza and Zulu," one of the leading warriors said in heavily accented English to Shepstone.

George gave an appreciative grin as he checked his revolver, which he'd loaded with his last four rounds. As he raised his pistol to fire, he realised at that moment that there was no other place he would rather die. The discipline and extreme courage of these brave warriors was beyond measure; they were the finest men he had ever known!

Despite the chaos surrounding them, coupled with the darkened skies and enveloping clouds of acrid smoke, Anthony Durnford's last command was holding its ground. There were numerous dead and dying Zulus, lying torn and broken in the grass and on the rocky slopes around them. The colonel was methodically firing his pistol, while his remaining officers and NCOs directed the fire of what little ammunition they had left. For the briefest of moments, with all of his thoughts fixed on this one engagement, Anthony thought that perhaps they might turn the tide of this battle after all. It was then that Captain Bradstreet pointed to his right in alarm.

"Dear God, they're behind us!"

A regiment from the Zulu 'Right Horn' emerged from behind the southern slopes of Isandlwana, symbolically cutting off all hope of escape. A few carbineers and mounted police, who had come to their commanding officer's aid, found themselves unable to link up with Durnford due to the emerging force of Zulus. With nowhere else to go, they turned and fled southwest, away from the battle. A bitter irony that the arrival of the 'Right Horn' saved the lives of a few whose horses could outrun the Zulus now in pursuit.

Durnford grimaced as he noted that the enemy was now emerging from where he had dispatched George Shepstone. His sorrow was tempered with pride, for he knew in his heart that the young officer had died a proper soldier's death; defiant in the face of the enemy, and contemptuous of his pending annihilation.

Lieutenant Edgar Anstey
Subaltern, F Company, 1/24th

All semblance of order had collapsed within the camp, as each company fought for its own survival. Captain William Mostyn's F Company had been towards the centre of the battalion firing line. They managed to make good use of the confusion caused by Zikhali Horse's mass exodus from the battlefield to quickly pull back into the camp. It had still been a hellish retreat, with at least a dozen dead and badly injured left to the mercy of the Zulus. One of his subalterns, twenty-four year old Lieutenant Patrick Daley, was killed while trying to help an injured private to safety. His venerable senior NCO, Colour Sergeant Ballard, was missing and most likely dead. He and six other men were cut off from the main company during the retreat.

"Looks like we're in a bit of a spot, sir," his remaining subaltern, Lieutenant Edgar Anstey remarked. His face was covered with sweat, and he was holding his revolver, the barrel smoking.

"Make sure you reload, Edgar, there's a good man," Mostyn replied. He shouted to his surviving soldiers, *"Company...reform square!"*

"Sir, we cannot just stand here and take this," Anstey protested. "The Zulus are too damned many. We must try to extract ourselves." His words were cut short as the soldiers facing the main Zulu onslaught unleashed a thundering volley at their foes.

"Tell you what, Mister Anstey," the captain replied. "If I should fall before these dark savages do you in, you'll be in command of the company and can do what you like."

"Sir."

Knowing further protests were futile, especially with the enemy closing on all sides, the young subaltern took up his position in the centre of the formation and began directing fire towards the Zulus on their right. All the while, he kept looking for means of escape. Around the tents of the Imperial Mounted Infantry, nearest the wagon trail, appeared to be their only means of salvation. It was a pity the Zulus had overwhelmed 1/24th's tents and wagons, for there was no longer any means of getting ammunition from Quartermaster Pullen's supplies. Bloomfield's wagon from 2/24th was somewhere behind them, and even that was now being plundered by the rampaging hordes.

"Present...fire!" Captain Mostyn shouted. *"Reload!"*

He never got the chance to issue another command. A Zulu assegai flew over the ranks of his men and slammed into his throat. It had been part of an organized volley from a mass of Zulus who were making their way through the smoke. Four other soldiers had fallen dead, six more badly injured. It seemed every last man in the company was bearing some sort of wound. Their faces were covered in powder and soot, their tunics torn and filthy, all with numerous cuts, gashes, and bruises.

"Captain!" Edgar cried out, rushing to Mostyn's side. Blood gushed from his mouth and his severed windpipe, which sputtered with a last exhalation before life left his body.

The young officer now found himself in command of the company, or what was left of it. He had a lone sergeant, three corporals, and perhaps forty privates. Small bands of Zulus were now able close the distance with the depleted company and engage in hand-to-hand combat. With a surge of strength and fury, the redcoats beat them back with rifle fire and bayonet. The sun was still partially eclipsed and the complete lack of a breeze disallowed any of the acrid musketry smoke to dissipate, making it extremely difficult to see. Anstey, however, knew which direction safety was, and he was determined to save what remained of the company or die beside them.

"F Company, on me!" He raised his sword high. "Maintain formation and make for the road to Rorke's Drift."

The company kept as close together as they could, trying to secure all sides of the square and not allow any Zulus to penetrate their ranks. Anstey and his NCOs had to keep pulling back those in the lead rank who wished beyond measure that they could sprint away to safety. It was nightmarish trying to navigate through the camp. Tents, poles, boxes of rations and equipment, fallen men— both British and Zulu—littered the landscape. The men walking backwards had the most difficult time, often tripping over the various hazards and falling on their backsides. Terrified, they would get back to their feet lest they fall victim to enemy warriors seeking easy prey. On several occasions they had to fight off roaming bands of Zulus. Each time they repelled them with fire and bayonet; and each time they left more friends dead and dying on the field.

Near the edge of the camp, behind their own line of broken tents, they saw the Zulus of the 'Right Horn' coming down the slope to envelope the camp. They could also see the 'Left Horn' charging towards Lieutenant Colonel Durnford and his men, who were making their stand. While it seemed they had escaped the trap for the moment, Anstey knew the Zulus attacking the rear of the camp were but a portion of the 'Right Horn'. Their enemy was smart. With several thousand warriors in the 'Horn', doubtless there were throngs further afield, gradually making their way to the camp. Many of them were chasing down the fugitives who had already fled on horseback.

The narrowing terrain forced them into a column formation of two lines, with men constantly looking over their shoulders. They could see fleeting glimpses of the marauding Zulus. The valley channelled them closer together, and all they could make out were the slopes on either side. Men were gasping for air, their mouths parched. Whenever the Zulus appeared, those with ammunition would fire a volley towards them.

"Steady lads," the young officer said. "Stick together, we'll make it." His words were as much for his own benefit as those of his men. It was ten miles from Isandlwana to the uMzinyathi. At their current pace it would take them well over three hours; if they were not surrounded and annihilated first.

They were just over a half mile from the camp, when the sound of fighting came from their front. They had reached the Manzimnyama Stream. The parched soldiers wished to dive into the waters and quench their agonising thirsts, but there would be no time for that. The entire valley was overrun with Zulus from the iSangqu regiment. Having gone furthest afield in the sweep to get behind Isandlwana, their mission was no longer one of attacking the camp, but of destroying any who tried to escape. Many of the dead from this latest clash were NNC warriors and civilians, with a few carbineers and volunteers amongst them. Zulus were now converging on all sides of this small band of redcoats.

Lieutenant Anstey knew there was nowhere left to go. *"Form square!"* His men stood shoulder-to-shoulder, with only a handful able to fire at their charging assailants. A few Zulus fell, but they closed so fast upon them, that the fighting was now a fierce melee of spear and bayonet. In truth, the Zulus hated fighting against bayonet-wielding redcoats. Their exceptional skill and reach advantage made every encounter fraught with excruciating pain and oftentimes death. But with nearly a thousand Zulus closing in on all sides of the formation, where perhaps thirty men remained, the end result was never in doubt.

Anstey fired what rounds he had left in his pistol, taking satisfaction in seeing a more elaborately dressed Zulu, most likely an *induna*, tumble to the ground as he was shot through the chest and stomach. His men continued to stab with their bayonets, bashing any Zulu who got close enough with the heavy butt-stocks of their rifles. Their enemies were making just as violent a show of it in return, smashing with clubs and stabbing away with their bloodied spears. The lieutenant was now using his sword, smacking away on a Zulu shield, and cutting the shin of another with a backhand slash. A horrifying pain shot through his shoulder and neck, as a Zulu spear was plunged into his heart. So deep was the wound, he mercifully suffered just a few brief seconds before death took him.

As they attempted to re-establish themselves on higher ground, it quickly became clear to Major Stuart Smith that there would be no making another stand. The camp was quickly being overrun with companies of Zulus surging in between the companies from 1/24th, who were now formed into squares and fighting for their lives. The gunners and drivers who were still in the camp were being brutally cut down as they tried to reach the guns.

"Save those guns!" It was Colour Sergeant Brown up on the nek. He was pointing to the southwest, away from the camp.

"He's right, sir," Curling said. "There is nothing left we can do here."

"Alright," Smith accepted. He called to the men riding the limbers, "Hang on, lads, it's about to get bumpy!"

As they rode past the camp belonging to the mounted contingents, they saw the first wave of Zulus storming through the wagon park on the road back to Rorke's Drift.

"Can't get out that way," Smith said.

They followed a large crowd of NNC, who they assumed would know the terrain. This was a misnomer. Only the iziGqoza were familiar with the lay of the land, and they were fighting to the last alongside the 24th. The remnants of N Battery followed the western slope of the hill just south of Isandlwana, and for the first quarter of a mile they made excellent time, for the ground was covered in tall grass but relatively flat. Soon, however, the land became gouged with a series of gorges and dongas that all led into a stream. It was here the limbers became hung up, and the gun section ground to a halt. Men and horses alike screamed in terror as the Zulus surrounded them. The animals were butchered without mercy. The drivers and gunners were yanked from the limbers and hacked to pieces. Smith fired his revolver into the face of one assailant, before managing to ride away. A dozen enemy warriors were rushing after him in pursuit.

For Henry Curling, there was little left he could do. Spiking the guns, thereby rendering them useless, was no longer an option. He could only hope the Zulus had no knowledge of how they functioned or, if they did, they would over-load the guns and have them blow up in their faces. The lieutenant kicked his horse into a gallop, riding with all speed along a series of natural formations that were being followed by others who sought escape from the scene of death. Of the seventy gunners and drivers left behind at Isandlwana that morning, only ten managed to free horses from the limbers and ride away.

Galloping away from the horrible scenes of death, Surgeon-Major Peter Shepherd was assailed by feelings of guilt. He felt more should have been done to save the wounded. It was a blessing that he did not witness the slaughter of his patients in the hospital wagon. He soon found himself with a trio of carbineers who had made a break for it once their ammunition was spent. Shepherd's horse, being fresh, was able to outrun theirs. As they hopped from one rocky and broken point to another, they could hear the chants and beating of weapons on shields coming from the Zulus.

Suddenly, there was a loud cry.

Another man shouted, *"Doctor!"*

Peter reined in his horse and saw a carbineer lying on the ground, a thrown assegai protruding from his side. His two companions stopped their horses and were frantically looking back at the oncoming mass of Zulus. Without a second thought, Shepherd dropped down from his horse and rushed over to the badly injured man.

"We'll help you get him on his horse," one of the troopers said, as he started to dismount.

Peter held up his hand and shook his head. "The poor fellow. Too late…too late!" He ran back to his horse, but only managed to put one foot in the stirrups when another flung assegai embedded itself in his back. His mouth open, eyes squeezed shut in pain, he froze in place.

"Doctor Shepherd!" one of the troopers cried out. Feelings of remorse overcame him, as he blamed himself for the surgeon-major's demise.

There was nothing they could do. The two surviving carbineers galloped away as Peter Shepherd, a man who had dedicated his life to healing and saving others, was murderously gutted and butchered by the Zulus.

For Mehlokazulu and the iNgobamakhosi regiment, their day of suffering was far from over. While a third of their number attacked the square of redcoats led by Lieutenant Charlie Pope, the remainder continued in their pursuit of Durnford's mounted troops, anxious to exact their revenge. The uVe regiment, who also suffered terribly at the hands of these soldiers, joined the iNgobamakhosi for the final charge.

The mounted troops, now devoid of their horses, were not finished yet. They had reformed with a number of soldiers from within the camp and were firing into the Zulus. There was much smoke and dust; as well as the intermingling of the fleeing Natal warriors, contrasted with those who were fighting to the bitter end.

440

With no cover or concealment available, and carried by the unstoppable wave of warriors behind them, Mehlokazulu and his men gave a loud battle cry and charged.

For the first time in many years, Anthony Durnford's mind was at peace. He found it fitting that so many of those now standing by his side were from the Natal Carbineers; the very unit that abandoned him at Bushman's Pass. This day they and Durnford alike would find redemption and reconciliation, in a crucible that could be best described as *'Brutal Valour'*.

"And now, my men," Durnford said, reloading his pistol with his good hand. "Let us see what you can do."

The carbineers, along with Pullen and his men, were firing as fast as they could reload their weapons. The attacking Zulus outnumbered their small force at least thirty-to-one. And despite the killing effect of their relentless volleys, it was now a numbers game. Troopers flung their empty carbines at their assailants, while those with pistols fired what rounds they had left. And even as the Zulus swarmed them, bitter hand-to-hand fighting commencing, they refused to yield. Knives were drawn, and men continued to kill with unbridled fury.

With their shields and stabbing spears, the Zulus now had the advantage. Despite their courage, the carbineers and other troops were rapidly cut down. Men were stabbed repeatedly and split open by Zulu blades. It took three warriors to bring down Quartermaster Pullen. He had fixed a bayonet to the end of his rifle and was using it to fearful effect. Finally, a pair of Zulus stabbed him in the sides. Another plunged his weapon into the quartermaster's throat.

While the savage killing unfolded, Durnford fired all six shots from his pistol before taking a step back to reload once more. Using his good arm and wedging his revolver into the other was a skill he perfected years before. With six fresh shots in his weapon, he stepped forward and began firing again.

He only got two off before a musket shot smashed him in the face. Another struck him in the chest, sending him sprawling backwards. He briefly lost consciousness, his pistol flying from his hand, as he fell onto his side. Before he could fully regain his senses, an enraged Zulu filled with blood-lust slammed his spear into the colonel's heart.

Whatever his mistakes, and regardless of what Lord Chelmsford or his contemporaries would later say about him, Lieutenant Colonel Anthony Durnford died as a Victorian officer should, beside his men, with his face towards the enemy.

Chapter XXXVII: Saving the Colours

Isandlwana
22 January 1879
3.00 p.m.
***

Lieutenant Colonel Henry Pulleine knew that it was only a matter of time until the end came. With Mostyn's company having attempted to extract themselves, Cavaye and Porteous fought in one large square that was receiving the most ferocity from the Zulu onslaught. George Wardell and Charlie Pope's formations collapsed, their men presumably dead. Only Reginald Younghusband's C Company was managing to hold its own from the small plateau up by the neck. All of the mounted troops were gone and Durnford's command wiped out. Roving bands of Zulus were now ransacking the various camps along the one mile stretch.

The commanding officer for 1/24th had lost his horse earlier, not that he would ever consider riding away from the field. Such thoughts would never even cross his mind. His adjutant still had his mount, and in Pulleine's mind, there was but one duty left to perform.

"The colours," he said. His expression was calm, but was his voice shaking. "They are your charge, Mister Melvill. Use them to rally the battalion; if not here, then at Rorke's Drift. Wherever you take them, the 24th will stand."

"Sir," Melvill replied with a humble nod of acknowledgment. He knew what he had to do.

For Henry Pulleine, there would be no leaving the battlefield this day. Commanding officers did not abandon their men, no matter the cost to themselves. This was why, even though every last captain and lieutenant in command of the line companies had a horse, they all dismounted and stood beside their men until the last. For Henry Pulleine, it was a simple matter, one he had been aware of since he first acquired his commission; in battle, he either won or he died.

For Teignmouth Melvill, it was not quite so simple. He was in charge of the Regiment's Colours. More than just ornate pieces of cloth, the colours were the sacred standards of the regiment.

In practical terms, they were used on the battlefield to rally units in distress, as was certainly the case with 1/24th. But more than that, they embodied the soul of the Regiment, generations of traditions and past glories. It was indeed the very symbol of a regiment's loyalty and devotion to Queen and Country. To lose them was an inexcusable disgrace. Thankfully, the Regimental Colour had been left at Helpmekaar and was safe. But the Queen's Colour of 1st Battalion was currently in the adjutant's tent.

Melvill's charge was clear; if he could, he was to bring the colour to the nek of Isandlwana and rally what remained of the regiment there. If, as Pulleine suspected, all was indeed lost, he was to save the colour and raise it at Rorke's Drift. 'Gunny' Bromhead's company was, hopefully, by now reinforced by the two companies coming up from Helpmekaar.

He emerged from his tent with the colour still rolled up in its protective case. He scanned the smoky field. Zulus were flooding in from every side. There would be no last stand here. He mounted his horse and rode along the eastern slope of Isandlwana, the colour tucked in his lap, reins in one hand, and his pistol in the other. The colour and the seven-foot pole were heavy and unwieldy, let alone with the case of thick leather used to protect it from wear and weather. Melvill, however, was a very skilled rider. He shot one Zulu in the face as he passed the wagon park filled with empty wagons that would no longer be making the return trip to Rorke's Drift.

Neville Coghill was in a near state of panic when he found Pulleine near the tents. He was on foot, his helmet gone and his pistol in hand. He looked tired and defeated, yet accepting of his fate.

"Five days," he said, shaking his head in disbelief. "Can you believe that, Mister Coghill? I've waited my whole life to command a battalion of my beloved 24th. I've held my command for five days, and this is how it will end." He sighed and looked over his shoulder. "You have no more obligations here, Mister Coghill. I've sent Mister Melvill to Rorke's Drift with the Queen's Colour. Find him, and help the 24th rise again."

"It's been an honour, sir," Coghill said, offering one final salute.

Pulleine smiled and raised his hand to return the courtesy. A
bullet then smashed into his upper chest, just below the throat.
Coghill heard the crack of the rifle a split second later. Pulleine's
mouth was open and his eyes wide. He dropped to his knees. Blood
flowed from the wound and out either corner of his mouth. His eyes
glazed over, and he collapsed to the ground. Neville gritted his teeth
and rode away, thankful the colonel did not suffer. Within seconds,
a dozen Zulus flooded the tent, plunging their spears into the dead
officer and splitting his guts open.

Though not among the very last to escape from Isandlwana,
Horace Smith-Dorrien only made his hasty departure when it
became apparent the battle was lost. At any rate, there were no other
duties to perform, besides what he knew would be a futile and
needless death. He passed by the wrecked gun carriages just minutes
after Stuart Smith, Henry Curling, and a small number of crewmen
escaped. As he followed one course that would eventually lead to
the river, he came upon Lieutenant Neville Coghill, who had left the
camp and was trying to find Melvill.

"Mister Coghill," Horace said. "I'm glad to see you still among
the living."

"For the moment," Neville replied candidly. "I need to find
Melvill. He has the Queen's Colour. Colonel Pulleine ordered it
taken to Rorke's Drift. 1st Battalion has two companies which
should have arrived from Helpmekaar. If so, and if we can rally
whatever survivors there may be from this bloody awful mess, then
we might be able to prevent the Zulus from invading Natal."

"God willing," Horace said.

"God?" Coghill looked at him incredulously. Shaking his head,
he added, "God has abandoned this field, my friend. We must save
ourselves this day."

He kicked his horse into a gallop, intent on finding Melvill and
completing his mission to rally at Rorke's Drift. With the Zulus still
in very close pursuit, Smith-Dorrien sprinted his mount towards
what he hoped was a viable route of escape. Given the broken
ground and numerous brush stands and gorges which one could not

see until they were almost on top of them, it was no small miracle he reached the river.

At the top of a steep cliff-face he came upon Stuart Smith, Henry Curling, their gunners, and a number of NNC warriors, both on horse and afoot. There was no time for words, and they carefully tried to make their way towards the bottom. When the Zulus came upon them, Horace noticed that they at first ignored the whites, focusing their wrath on the black Africans, regardless if they were NNC warriors, wagon drivers, or boy voorloopers. Less than half of those who made it to the cliffs survived the journey to the bottom. Stuart Smith was among the last to fall, having been pulled from his mount and several assegai plunged into his guts.

The Zulus scrambled down towards the river in pursuit, just as Horace and his mount plunged into the current. He clung to his beast's neck as Zulu marksmen opened fire. A few others began to swim across after him, though as Zulus were terrible swimmers, this was mostly futile. A couple were even sucked into the current and drowned.

There were a large number of men and horses escaping the slaughter; the lieutenant was certainly not alone. Every man was anxious to save his own life and had little interest in helping others who may have been swept from their mounts. Such happened to the young officer, as he was swamped from his horse. He took a quick breath and held it as he was pulled under the current. Swimming up to the surface, he fought to control his breathing, hoping to not be smashed against any hidden rocks beneath the surface.

As fortune would have, a rider-less horse came swimming past him. He grabbed hold of the beast's tail. The horse dragged him onto the Natal bank before Horace lost his grip, and the animal sprinted away. He lay on the sandbar for a few moments, trying to catch his breath; the sound of chanting Zulus ringing in his ears. He pulled himself up and stumbled up the hillside.

He soon came upon a trooper who had been kicked by his horse, and could not mount without assistance.

"Please, help me up, sir!" the man pleaded. "Help me, and I will find you a horse."

The lieutenant did so, offering his hands as a step for the injured man, who sighed with relief as he settled into the saddle. He then kicked his horse and rode away at a gallop, never looking back at the officer who, quite possibly, had saved his life.

"Oh, bugger me," Horace said. He sat on a rock facing the river and removed his boots, pouring out all the sand and river water. If the Zulus were going to slay him, he least wanted his feet to be comfortable.

The sound of gunfire drew his attention. To his left, about twenty Basutos were unleashing salvoes at the Zulus on the far bank, as well as those attempting to cross over. These brave souls, who could have continued to flee, were covering the escape of many of their comrades, black African and white European alike.

Horace sat open-mouthed, watching the spectacle and catching his breath. The Zulu assault across the river was temporarily halted. With the last of their companions across, the Basutos rode away. Smith-Dorrien reckoned they had given him just enough of a head-start to make his escape, even if it was on foot. He had no intention of heading to Rorke's Drift, for he was certain the Zulus would attack there next. He elected to make his way to Helpmekaar, a long and arduous trek, especially on foot. His boots squishing, he began to jog at a modest pace away from the river, hoping to find a horse. He wondered how Melvill and Coghill were getting on. Hopefully, they were well on their way to Rorke's Drift, and if not, perhaps they could meet up once more at Helpmekaar and try to sort out this awful mess.

Every fibre of Private Samuel Wassall's being was screaming for survival. Thirty soldiers from the IMI had been left at the camp. When it was plain to see that all was lost, Sergeant Naughton rallied what survivors remained to make their escape. Unlike the poor fellows Lieutenant Anstey tried to lead back to the river, the IMI were on horseback. It was still not enough for some. Several men were overwhelmed by rampaging Zulus who pulled them from their mounts, slaughtering them with their spears and clubs.

For those who remained, the ride was horrendous. The Zulu 'Right Horn' now blocked the trail to Rorke's Drift. They had to find another way, in a land that was completely unfamiliar to them.

The rough terrain channelled them down a long series of dongas. They splashed across the Manzimyama Stream, near where Anstey and his men had fought to the last, before following a long saddle at the southern base of Mpethe Mountain. To the north, on the far side of the hill, they could hear the sounds of pursuing Zulus.

Upon reaching the bank, Wassall plunged his horse head-long into the torrent. The river was faster-flowing than it appeared and nearly swept him from his horse. It was nearly eighty yards to the other side. The young soldier wasn't sure if he could hang on long enough or would be swept away. He could hear the muskets fire on the Zulu side of the river, and he knew they were aiming for him. He swore he saw the splash of a shot hitting the water not ten feet from him.

At length, he reached the Natal side, his helmet gone and his scabbarded carbine soaked, but at least he was still alive. He did not feel safe yet, however, with the Zulus on the far hillside continuing to shoot at him.

"Sam!" he heard a voice cry out. Wassall turned to see his friend, Private David Westwood. He'd been swept from his horse and was now floundering in the river.

"Sam!" the poor man cried out again, unable to swim, and scarcely able to keep afloat.

The natural instinct to survive made the notion of simply riding away tempting, but it wasn't an option for Private Samuel Wassall of the Imperial Mounted Infantry. He turned his horse around and plunged back into the swollen river; the Zulus firing at him be damned! His gaze was fixed on his friend, and the hope of saving him gave Sam renewed strength. In his peripheral vision, he saw the Zulus coming down the hill and heading towards the river bank. If he tried to pull Westwood onto his horse while still in the river, they would both be washed away. Instead, Sam made his way back to the Zulu bank as shots continued to fire. He hastily tied his horse to a tree before plunging into the river. He then heard what sounded like laughter. Were the Zulus were making sport of trying to shoot him and his friend?!

He forced the sense of outrage from his mind, as he could see Westwood's red-jacketed arms flailing about, his head barely splashing above the surface.

Sam grabbed him by the collar. "Hold on, I've got you!"

Westwood clung to Sam's waist, desperately trying to keep his head above water. Wassall swam for all he was worth. Completely exhausted, they pulled themselves onto the shore, but there was no time for rest. The crack of Zulu gunfire and a shot smashing a nearby rock drove them to get their feet once more. Westwood vomited up copious amounts of river water as they staggered to Sam's tethered horse. This was followed by the clattering of Zulu throwing spears. One struck the nearest tree. A branch splintered, smashed by a musket ball. Sam climbed into the saddle, and Westwood used the last of his strength to pull himself up behind his friend.

Thinking their quarry might escape, the Zulus rushed towards them, intent on gutting them with their assegais. Several Zulus with muskets were now within twenty feet; two of their shots went wide, and the third weapon failed to fire.

The tired horse, now bearing two riders, splashed again into the torrential river. Westwood clung to his friend, with both men hoping their brave mount would not flounder. Sam could no longer hear the crack of Zulu musketry, nor their taunting battle cries. Every yard the horse splashed felt laborious and painfully slow. At last they crossed onto the Natal bank. Only after they rode up the nearest ridgeline and were able to look back across the uMzinyathi did they know they were safe. Privates Samuel Wassall and David Westwood would survive Isandlwana. They couldn't help but think they were among the very few who fortune smiled upon that day.

Further upriver, near the drift, Melvill and Coghill were joined by Lieutenant Higginson of the NNC. He in turn had been following Durnford's transportation officer, William Cochrane; one of the few Europeans from No. 2 Column to escape. Melvill still had the Queen's Colour clutched in his lap.

"It seems it's every man for himself at this point, fellas," Higginson said grimly.

"Not for us, it bloody well isn't," Melvill scoffed. He nodded to Coghill. "We're getting out of this together or not at all."

"Come on," Coghill urged. "We can debate this later."

449

Much like Private Wassall and the IMI survivors, the three officers were being pursued by a host of Zulus. For this particular band of pursuers, it was about sating their bloodlust, rather than sport. The river was a teeming mass of men and horses trying to escape the pending slaughter. Most were mounted Africans from Basuto and Zikhali Horse, with a few European carbineers and mounted police among them. It seemed the only redcoat survivors were the handful of Imperial Mounted Infantrymen that Sergeant Naughton had managed to rally.

Coghill plunged first into the river, followed by Higginson whose horse soon hung up on a large submerged boulder. He was pulled from his mount by the deceptively strong current, his carbine and ammunition bandolier dragging him under. Melvill swam his horse along, trying to keep a firm grip on the colour. He saw Higginson surface, having discarded his weapon and ammunition. He was clinging to a protruding rock, crying out for someone to stop a young African boy from stealing his horse on the far bank.

Melvill continued to drive his horse on. He managed to see Coghill make it to the far side, still mounted; a fortunate stroke of luck for him, as his injured knee made walking all but impossible. Melvill's relief was short-lived. He was swamped from his horse and pulled beneath the current, his helmet ripped from his head. His left hand still clutched the Queen's Colour, but the protective case was quickly filling with water. Within moments it became like an anchor.

Melvill gasped as he lurched up to the surface once more. He was floating straight towards Higginson, who was still against his rock. The pursuing Zulus, meanwhile, had reached the river bank. Some were firing their muskets. A surprising number leapt into the current, intent on swimming over to Natal to catch their prey.

"Higginson, grab the colour!" Melvill pleaded. He felt them slipping from his hand.

Higginson did so, but the force of the current wrenched him from his rock. The two men were now floundering further downriver. It was a terrible personal tragedy for Melvill, once he realised he could either swim or keep hold of the colour, but not both. The casing was now completely filled with water. As they became submerged, Melvill's exhausted grip gave way.

"No!" he shouted. "Damn it all!"

450

"Come on!" Higginson pleaded. "There's nothing more you can do. Someone *will* find them."

They heard a shriek as Coghill's horse was shot by an enemy musket. Keeping his vow that they would survive together, he had ridden to where the two men floated downstream, and was coming back into the river to help them. He was flung from his stricken mount, pitching headfirst into the river. All three were now compelled to swim the rest of the way to the Natal bank. They pulled themselves out of the river, completely spent. They knew they were not out of danger. Despite their inability to swim, and innate fear of drowning, scores of Zulus were crossing the river, intent on not allowing any white man to escape.

Far from a simple climb, the Natal bank of the river was extremely steep and rocky, with gigantic boulders strewn about. It would be a feat of strength for any man, let alone one in a state of total exhaustion, or coupled with an injured knee.

"Come on, Neville, you can make it," Melvill said, as he helped pull his friend to another rock outcropping.

As they reached the very top, their strength failed, and they found themselves unable to go any further.

"Here they come," Coghill said, dejectedly.

A pair of Zulus who had been first to cross over were rushing in for the kill. Higginson was in a panic. He no longer had a weapon. But he noticed both his companions still had their pistols, soaked with river water as they were.

"For God's sake, fire!" he shouted. "You both have your revolvers!"

Such was the state of their fatigue, both men had forgotten they were armed. Summoning another surge of desperate strength, the two officers drew their weapons and fired. One Zulu was struck in the chest, the other in the face. The second let loose an ear-piercing scream and collapsed, his hands clutching away at his shattered face. He thrashed about, begging for death.

"I think I am done up," Melvill said, as the dying Zulu's cries subsided.

"I certainly don't think I can go on any further," Coghill added, clutching at his knee while gasping for air.

"Wait here, I'll find us horses," Higginson said.

451

He pulled himself to his feet and stumbled up to the top, where he saw a number of Basutos. These men had provided covering fire for another group of survivors, including Horace Smith-Dorrien, Henry Curling, and a handful of his gunners and drivers. Higginson called out to the mounted Africans about two hundred yards away. They stopped their horses and waited for him. Just as Higginson reached them, a full company of Zulu raiders crested the ridge.

"I thought those bastards couldn't swim," Higginson said bitterly.

The Basutos fired one last volley before they were compelled to ride away. One was felled by a Zulu musket, and Higginson found himself forced to grab onto the tail of a horse and bound away. As the terrified beast kicked up clods of dirt and dust into his face, the officer was filled with abject shame, for he'd left Melvill and Coghill to their fate.

At the rock, Melvill still lay on his side, while Coghill had somehow managed to pull himself up onto his good leg. The Zulus were coming for them, and he was determined to face them standing. There was no hesitation from their adversaries, who charged with fury. Melvill managed to fire off three rounds, two of which struck a warrior in the chest and stomach. Coghill only managed a single shot. The river water and sand had gotten into the cylinder of his revolver. His shot had struck a Zulu in the shoulder, knocking him to the ground in terrible pain. Neville Coghill stood defiantly as a Zulu throwing spear plunged into his chest. Another buried itself in his left shoulder, and he fell onto his injured knee, the pain blinding him. He could hear Melvill cry out as he was stabbed repeatedly. Blood streaming from the corner of his mouth, Coghill collapsed backwards onto the body of his friend, his gaze fixed on the still-eclipsed sun as death took hold.

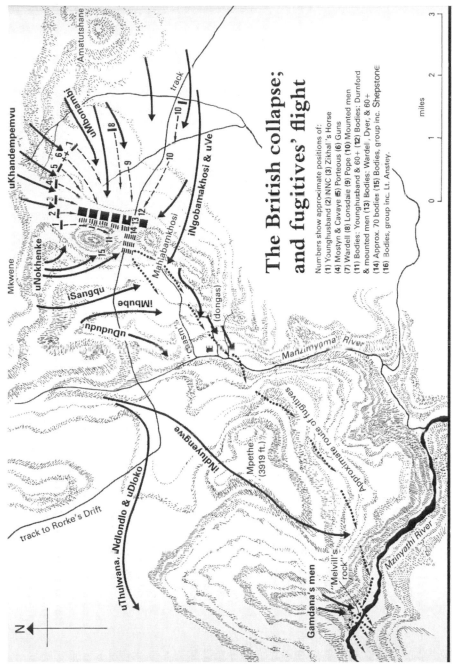

The British collapse; and fugitives' flight

Numbers show approximate positions of:

(1) Younghusband (2) NNC (3) Zikhali's Horse
(4) Mostyn & Cavaye (5) Porteous (6) Guns
(7) Wardell (8) Lonsdale (9) Pope (10) Mounted men
(11) Bodies: Younghusband & 60+ (12) Bodies: Durnford
& mounted men (13) Bodies: Wardell, Dyer, & 60+
(14) Approx. 70 bodies (15) Bodies, group inc. Shepstone
(16) Bodies, group inc. Lt. Anstey.

Flight of the Fugitives

453

Chapter XXXVIII: Stand firm, 24th!

Captain Younghusband's company, nek of Isandlwana
22 January 1879
4.00 p.m.
***

The shelf most of the men knelt on had provided excellent protection for what remained of Captain Reginald Younghusband's C Company, 1/24th. It was, in fact, an excellent position, giving them a commanding view of the entire battlefield. And now, for the first time since the Zulus appeared near Mkwene Hill, there was a momentary pause. Soldiers struggled to catch their breath, their collective demeanour having changed from one of berating mockery towards the Zulus, to abject horror. The battle had taken a savage turn, and now, their brimming confidence had changed to confounded disbelief. Each soldier's perspective had been very narrow and focused, never extending beyond the company's immediate battle-space. That the entire camp had been enveloped and overrun was unfathomable.

During this brief reprieve, Arthur took a moment to survey who was left. There was the captain, whose scalp was bleeding from where a Zulu spear skewered his forage cap from his head. Lieutenant Hodson and Colour Sergeant Brown had made it to the top. Sergeant Edwards was there, of course. He'd practically dragged Arthur the rest of the way up the slope. He was the only sergeant who remained. Arthur recognized Corporal Markham, who appeared to be regretting his decision to leave Brecon and volunteer for active service overseas. In that moment, Arthur was not so sure about his own decision to join the army, either. He saw neither Corporal John Bellhouse nor Lance Corporal Bill Johnson and could only assume they were among the fallen. He did take some comfort in seeing the ever-reliable Bray. Feelings of loss overcame him, for his dearest friend was no longer with them.

Richard Lowe, just eighteen years old, had been Arthur's closest friend since time began. A big-hearted lad from Shakespeare's home of Stratford-upon-Avon, he'd always had a soft spot for the ladies, especially sweet Molly McCormick. Molly would never know that

Richard died in terrible agony, thousands of miles and across oceans from home. All that was left of him was a bloodied corpse on a hill in some remote corner of the Empire that few back home knew or even cared about. Unless there was some sort of divine intervention, Arthur knew his own, and most likely agonising, death was not far away.

The eclipse reached its peak, the sun's light darkened to just a sliver of what it had been hours before. An ominous feeling came over every last man on that hellish battlefield, Zulu and British alike. God had, indeed, closed his eyes in sorrow and turned his back on the field of Isandlwana.

Kwanele's hand trembled. He gazed at the wide blade of his spear soaked in blood. He'd done it, he had slain a white soldier! The man was already injured, but it was Kwanele's spear that plunged down between his neck and shoulder, ending his life. And after the terrible losses his *ibutho* suffered at the hands of these red-jacketed murderers, it filled the young *induna* with lustful vengeance. And yet, another unexpected feeling crept into his mind. It was pity; pity for this young soldier who looked more like a boy than a man. Granted, he had brought war to the land of the Zulus, along with the rest of the White Queen's soldiers. He'd possibly killed one or more of Kwanele's companions. Still, he felt a strange trace of regret for taking the young man's life. He thought of all his brave friends, torn to pieces by the white man's firearms and bayonets. For many, their deaths were far more horrendous; arms and legs torn off, guts splayed onto the ground, others excruciatingly shot through the groin, throats torn away in a spray of blood…Kwanele had granted his victim a quick passing into the afterlife!

There was no time for further contemplation. Many of the soldier's friends had successfully scaled the heights and were now making a stand on top of the small plateau near the nek. And try as they might, the Zulus simply could not launch a successful assault on this naturally fortified position. The slope was too steep and rugged to launch a coordinated attack. And the few brave warriors who'd attempted to scale the heights had been bayoneted or shot at close range. Nearly twenty men lay dead or badly injured near the summit.

Zulu marksmen, a number of whom now carried captured Martin-Henry Rifles, began firing at the heights. The redcoats stayed too far back from the edge, or behind the big rocks, for the bullets to be effective. There was also some confusion as to how these new rifles actually worked. At the moment, only a handful of warriors were able to use them; and when they did fire, the kick was horrendous.

Watching this exchange of gunfire, the *induna* grinned, for he'd seen one white soldier fly backwards, struck by a well-placed shot.

"Bray!" Sergeant Edwards shouted.

The old private was knocked backwards, practically into Edward's lap. The ever-stoic NCO was fighting to control his emotions. He held the stricken man's head; clasping Bray's shoulder, he helplessly watched blood gush from the grave wound in his chest. The old soldier's breathing was ragged. His body convulsed.

"I'm sorry, John," he whispered, to the man he'd known since before he lost his beloved wife, and who'd been as much a friend as section leader to him. Arthur swallowed hard, wanting to rush over and comfort the man who had been like a brother to him. And yet, he could not. There were still Zulus trying to get at them. He fired his rifle at one who tried to crawl up between two boulders. The warrior disappeared, and Arthur knew not whether he hit him.

"Nothing to be sorry for," Edwards said, consoling the dying man. Bray's eyes were now closed, and his breath was becoming far more laboured. The sergeant nodded slowly, and said quietly, "Give Jennie our love."

Private Jason Bray gave one last smile. The sergeant's words provided him one final moment of comfort before he breathed his last. Edwards patted him on the shoulder and stood. His stoic demeanour returned at once.

"What are your orders, sir?" he asked the captain. With most of their NCOs fallen, Lieutenant Hodson and Colour Sergeant Brown had taken it upon themselves to control what sections remained. Though Corporal Markham had great administrative skills, as a line NCO he'd never shown much potential. As such, he had been relegated to simply another rifle on the line.

"Boys, it looks like we aren't the only ones still left in the fight," the captain announced, tipping his head to the right. At least one company was formed up in a square, fighting for their lives. Many of the tents were torn down, and hundreds of Zulus were ransacking the camp. The smoke was thick and with the sun partially eclipsed, it was difficult to see beyond that single company perhaps 500 yards away.

"Think we can make it over to them?" Reginald asked.

Colour Sergeant Brown shrugged. "Even if we can, will there be any of them left in a few minutes?"

"No sense just sitting here waiting to die, trapped like filthy rats," the captain remarked. His men were down to their last few cartridges. Some had none at all. As soon as the Zulus realised this, they would swarm over the crest.

Reginald Younghusband, however, was determined to die on his own terms. He cautiously stepped to the edge of the escarpment, his hand up near his chest, palm facing outward. The Zulus below seemed to understand the gesture. Their marksmen ceased shooting. He saw a warrior dressed far more elaborately than the others. A leopard hide was draped over his shoulder, and large feathers came out from his headband. He was much older than his companions and appeared to be the one giving orders. Reginald surmised he was an *inkosi*. The captain stood tall, gestured back to his men, and then pointed to the Zulu leader. The man nodded and shouted some orders to his warriors. They stood and reformed their battle lines. The captain turned to address his men.

"C Company, on your feet! Stand firm, 24th!"

His soldiers instinctively stood and came to attention. Without him saying it, every last one of them knew his intentions. The time for sorrow and lamentations over the loss of friends, as well as their own pending fate, was over. Now was the time to stand tall, as proud soldiers of the British Empire. They would meet their fate, giving their lives for Queen and Country with heads held high and defiant.

The Zulus below watched in rapt silence. Many smiled and gave nods of approval at what the captain did next.

He walked down the line, shaking hands with each of his men, exchanging a few quick words with them. When he got to Arthur he said, "Private Wilkinson, I regret you did not have more time with us. You did well, son, and you would have made a fine NCO someday."

"Thank you, sir," Arthur replied, clasping the captain's hand. "It is an honour to have lived…and died at your side."

Reginald deliberately waited to shake Colour Sergeant Brown's hand until the very last. He gave a partial grin. "We're a long way from Brecon."

"I think our spirits can find the way home, sir."

The captain returned to the centre of his company and drew his sword. He locked gazes with the Zulu chief and nodded. The *inkosi* nodded in return and began to slowly beat his spear against his shield. His warriors did the same. Though sounding a chant none of the British could understand, the meaning was abundantly clear. Despite the slaughter and horrors they had inflicted upon each other, and the dance of death that was to come, there was no hatred between these warring men… only respect and admiration.

"Hate not your enemy," Arthur whispered. He hefted his rifle and waited for his captain's final command.

"Bayonets!" Reginald bellowed, his eyes wide and ferocious.

"Rah!" the men of the company shouted as one, levelling their weapons, a wall of bristling spikes protruded towards the enemy. The Zulu chant grew louder, the banging of spears on shields harder and faster. The captain took a deep breath, his eyes focused and filled with ferocity as he gave his last command.

"Charge!"

The men gave a collective howl that echoed above the din of battle. Blood rushed through their veins, and their spirits soared as they charged valiantly to their fate.

Kwanele stared in disbelief, his eyes not believing what he saw, nor his heart what it felt. These men, these white soldiers in red jackets, they were not hiding behind rocks, nor cowering and begging for mercy. They knew their death was at hand, and they charged in defiance without fear or hesitation. These were the Zulus' mortal enemies; and they were some of the bravest men the young *induna* had ever seen. He knew he had to face one of them in single combat.

The British, who numbered no more than sixty, were bounding down the slope at angle away from Kwanele. He shouted for his warriors to follow him and sprinted towards a pair of wagons in the soldiers' path. They were in the midst of the British camp. Tents, both standing and torn down, creating a series of hazards and obstacles. Near the wagons, Kwanele stopped and raised his spear.

"Yeka!" he shouted. He and his small band of warriors turned to face the charging redcoats.

Kwanele settled into his fighting stance, his eyes fixed on one particularly young soldier. The masking of the sun by the eclipse and the haze of smoke made everything seem utterly surreal. The redcoat's eyes were now locked with his. Both men gave a loud battle cry as they charged.

With each passing moment, with every foot-fall and yard sprinted, Arthur expected to die. The world slowed around him as a Zulu came at him. Arthur jammed his shoulder into the man, who was subsequently impaled by Sergeant Edwards' bayonet. The section leader was immediately cut down as half a dozen spears plunged repeatedly into his body.

Their enemies, having suffered immeasurable torments during the course of the battle, swarmed the white soldiers, slaying them with the same frenzy they would a lion or other fearsome beast. A mark of honour among the Zulus, which their British adversaries would never understand, was the repeated stabbing of an enemy warrior after he was slain. Known as *ukuhlomula*, it was an acknowledgement of their enemy's ferocity, as well as allowing all warriors to soak their spears in blood. Macabre and horrifying to look upon, the soldiers of C Company, 1/24th were stabbed a dozen times each as they fell. It was both to make certain they would not rise up again, and as a chilling testament to their bravery.

When they reached the wagons, Arthur could not believe he was still alive. As best he could tell, it was just him, Colour Sergeant Brown, and Captain Younghusband who remained. Lieutenant Hodson, Corporal Markham, and several of their men had been quickly surrounded by maddened enemy warriors. To their credit, they killed or badly wounded half-a-dozen. Hodson fired the last round from his pistol into the face of an *induna*, before his own face was smashed in by a knobkerrie. The rest were soon slaughtered; the screams of the dying echoed across the valley.

Arthur smashed the butt of his rifle into the face of one charging Zulu, while the captain fired the last rounds from his pistol into the mob. The officer then leapt aboard a wagon, where two soldiers and an African wagon driver lay butchered.

Arthur raced past him, his eyes now fixed on a lone Zulu. The soldier's body tingled with anticipation. Simultaneously they gave a battle cry and charged. Arthur's bayonet slapped the inside of the warrior's shield, knocking it away. He lunged forward and plunged the twenty-two inch spike into the man's chest. The Zulu cried out as the bayonet became stuck between his splintered ribs. The warrior slumped forward, and the rifle was wrenched from Arthur's hands. He was frozen in place, unable to move during the half-second it took for his dying adversary to thrust his spear in just below the ribs. The pain was beyond measure and Arthur screamed, his eyes shut.

Both men collapsed to the ground, Arthur letting out an agonising sob as he fell onto his back. Through blurred vision he saw Captain Younghusband standing atop the wagon, a Martini-Henry in his hands. He fired the weapon into the mass of Zulus surrounding the wagon. To the left Arthur saw Colour Sergeant Brown finally succumbing to a throng of warriors, who were stabbing him repeatedly. He dropped to his knees; yet refused to fall, until his body was subjected to another dozen spear stabs and club blows.

The Zulus appeared unable to get close to the officer. He'd managed to find a pouch with some cartridges, and was fighting a one-man war against the *amabutho*. He fired at least three more times and bayonetted two warriors, one in the arm and another in the guts. His head snapped back when he was finally shot through the skull by a Zulu marksman. He froze for a moment then pitched headfirst over the side of the wagon.

Arthur was struggling to breathe, fighting through the pain as blood gushed from his mortal injury. He jerked as he felt a hand reach over and clasp his. He turned to see the Zulu warrior he had impaled with his bayonet. He lay twisted, the bayonet having snapped and the Martini-Henry lying under his violently trembling body. His eyes were wide, his face covered in beads of sweat. His expression told Arthur all he needed to know, and he squeezed the warrior's hand; an exchange of mutual respect. Their hands still clasped with every last fibre of their fading strength, Arthur gazed up at the shadowed sun. If the blocking of the sun was indeed God shutting his eyes in sorrow, Arthur hoped the Almighty might at least hear his prayer, one he unknowingly shared with Kwanele kaMandlenkosi. With their shallow, gasping breaths, each quietly gave thanks to the divines for having died at the hands of a brave man.

Arthur's head slumped back, and he saw the eclipse of the sun slowly pass. Perhaps God had heard him after all. His mind was fading, and he focused the last of his will on one last, final thought of profound sadness and regret.

"Elisa...my love," he whispered. *"Please forgive me..."*

Chapter XXXIX: Echoes of Pain and Savage Glory

Isandlwana
22 January 1879
4.15 p.m.

Last of the 24th, by Richard Thomas Moynan

The cave was at the foot of the impassable cliffs that jutted skyward. No more than a gouge in the side of the mountain, it was just large enough for a man to lie down. A line of boulders screened the front, making it an ideal defensive position. It was also very claustrophobic, and reeked of piss from whatever creatures used it as a temporary home.

The man who lay within was a filthy and frightful sight. His red jacket was covered in burns and grime and was torn in many places. The stitching from the crossed rifle badge on his cuff was coming undone, and the lone chevron on his right shoulder was smeared with dirt and dried blood. The only sounds were his own breathing and the chanting coming from the triumphant Zulus below. Even if he wanted to hide, they would find and disembowel him sooner or later. Instead, he wanted to make them pay for the gruesome deaths of his friends.

The bang of his rifle firing echoed even louder within the tiny cave, leaving his ears ringing and his senses disoriented for a brief moment. The cave filled with smoke. He coughed uncontrollably, and tears streamed down his face. He jerked the lever down, opening the breach. His ammunition pouch lay next to him, and he counted another fifteen rounds within. He had long since given up any hope for salvation. All that mattered now was the pain and savagery.

The ground below was teeming with Zulu warriors. They scrambled when his weapon fired again. Because of the stifling conditions, the smoke did not dissipate quickly enough for him to see if he struck his target. But, he was one of the best shots in the regiment; at least that's what the torn patch on his cuff said. Most of the Zulus who now ransacked the camp appeared to be ignoring his presence. It was only those well within range of his shots that were concerned. His hearing was now nothing more than a constant ringing in his ears. Yet he could sense someone climbing up the slope. The loose earth nearest the boulders was shifting, as if being pulled down by a groping hand. The foolish warrior allowed his spear point to be seen by the lone survivor. And just as his prey's head came into view, the soldier fired. At such close range, the round smashed through the forehead, blasting the entire back of the skull away.

The man wanted to speak, to call to his enemies to take him and finish what they started. His head was pounding, his mouth parched, and his tongue tasted nothing but the bitter residue of burnt black powder. The ringing in his ears had faded to a dull hum. He could scarcely hear anything at all. Even when he next fired his rifle, he felt the sound and the harsh kick of the weapon's recoil more than he heard it.

His mind was now completely addlepated; he struggled to focus on anything except working the action on his rifle. Memories seemed to fade, as if the only reality he had ever known was the cave and these feelings of torment. These black creatures that were trying to kill him, what were they? Were they men? He was no longer sure what men were or even what he was. Time was non-existent, and he had no concept of anything, except what his hands instinctively did with this weapon of destruction they held. In those moments, where the entire universe was confined to a cramped and enclosed space, clouded in smoke, he could not even remember his own name.

His hands, working of their own volition, without any conscious thought from the man, tried to open the breach to the weapon once more. But the lever was stuck, the casing wedged into the breach. Expressionless, he crawled forward and pulled himself onto one of the rocks. His hand reached out for something, but what was it? He could barely see and could no longer hear. He wasn't even aware of the musket shots that ended his torment, ripping what remained of his soul from his body.

The guns had stopped. With a gradual slowing of the chants and war cries, it became apparent that the Battle of Isandlwana was at last at an end. Not one white man, be he soldier, wagon driver, or civilian volunteer remained alive in the camp. A special kind of hatred had been unleashed upon the iziGqoza and cowardly Natal warriors who were unable to escape the slaughter. And what a slaughter it was!

Mehlokazulu slowly walked along near the wagons, where he witnessed what may have been the last organised stand of the British redcoats. He had heard the single shots coming from above the nek of the mountain afterwards. That was a half mile from where he stood, and he paid it no mind. His gaze was fixed on the British officer who lay sprawled on the ground, eyes wide open, the back of his head shot away. A warrior from the uNokhenke had already sliced his guts open, freeing his spirit. The same would be done for all of the enemy dead. Any warriors slain by the Zulu were split open down the middle, so their spirits might return to the home of their ancestors. Another gruesome tradition the whites found utterly repellent. To fail to do so was to keep the spirit trapped, which could then come back to haunt his killers.

Pieces of clothing from the enemy dead had to be worn until the cleansing ceremonies could take place. Ostensibly, this was supposed to be taken by the warrior who killed his enemy combatant, however, in the heat of battle, the *amabutho* storming through the camp until the last redcoat had fallen, this was simply not practical. The warrior who shot this particular officer had claimed his tunic. He was the last to fall and now only in his shirtsleeves. Mehlokazulu contented himself with taking the jacket from a slain soldier near the place where their *inkosi* had been slain.

His eyes fell for a moment on a dead warrior of the uNokhenke and a white soldier. Their hands were clasped as if in friendship, eyes still wide. It may have seemed unreal or perverse to some, but to Mehlokazulu it made perfect sense. He walked over to the dead officer, whose last stand he had watched with rapt fascination and respect.

"This was a brave man!" he shouted, pointing to the slain captain with his spear. "He came down the nek, ever onward, even as his warriors fell. And he died unflinching, with his face to his adversaries. Honour him, and return him to his men!"

Wordlessly, twenty Zulus came forward. They took the shield from the last warrior Captain Younghusband bayonetted and placed the officer's bloodied corpse on top. They closed his eyes and folded his arms across his blood-soaked chest. He was carried on their shoulders, warriors all around chanting and raising their weapons repeatedly, just as they would for one of their own slain *abaqawe*. There were ten dead redcoats near the mutilated body of Colour Sergeant Thomas Brown, and it was here the Zulus laid Captain Reginald Younghusband. They raised their weapons once more and gave a loud ovation to his ferocity and bravery.

"May your spirit find its way home," Mehlokazulu whispered, offering his own final salute.

A rather despondent Commandant Browne had helplessly watched the final destruction of the camp at Isandlwana. The starving and exhausted men of his 1/3rd NNC had been unwilling or unable to press onward. And even if they had, their numbers,

465

coupled with extreme fatigue, would not have changed the course of the battle, except to maybe add a few hundred more corpses to the field. His immediate superior, Rupert Lonsdale, had ridden ahead earlier. Still suffering from the late effects of his head injury, he had obtained the GOC's permission to return to Isandlwana and rest for a few hours. 'Maori' could only assume that Lonsdale was dead.

The hour was late, and Browne heard the sound of horses coming up the road behind him. He turned to see Chelmsford, accompanied by most of the column staff. His face was etched with what could have either been irritation or concern, yet there was no sense of urgency about him. Nor were there any soldiers with him besides a handful of escorts from the IMI.

"What are you doing here, Commandant Browne?" the GOC asked in surprise. "You ought to have been in the camp hours ago."

Browne shook his head, his countenance pale. "The camp has been taken, sir. Did you receive none of my despatches?"

Chelmsford's face turned red with anger, and he quickly lashed out at the commandant, "How dare you tell me such a falsehood? Get your men in line at once and advance."

Dejected and utterly defeated, Browne ordered his officers to make the battalion ready to advance. He knew not that Chelmsford had never received his urgent despatches earlier in the day and had only heard scant reports about a battle at Isandlwana. As these had come from colonial officers, whose word he mistrusted, lacking in sufficient detail, he had paid them little mind.

"Seven hundred starving natives and a handful of staff officers against the entire Zulu army," Browne muttered to himself as he led his battalion on.

Approximately two-and-a-half miles further on, the ground opened up and offered a very clear view of the camp. Even without his field glasses, Chelmsford could see the columns of smoke and knew something terrible had happened. He quickly rode over to 'Maori' and placed a hand on his shoulder.

"On your honour, Commandant Browne," he said gently. "Is the camp taken?"

"The camp was taken this afternoon, sir," Browne replied, his frustration boiling over. "Even now the Zulus are burning some of the tents."

"That may be the quartermasters' fatigue burning debris of the camp." Chelmsford's expression betrayed his realisation. Disaster had befallen the camp, and he did not believe his own words.

"Quartermasters' fatigues do not burn tents, sir," Browne countered. He then offered his field glasses to the GOC, that he might see for himself.

Chelmsford shook his head and simply said, "Halt your men at once." He then rode back to the staff officers and gave a hasty order, "Send word to Mangeni. All forces are to converge here at once."

While the GOC gave his urgent orders to the confused staff, Commandant Browne was surprised to see a lone figure walking up the road towards him, leading a pony. The man was in a daze, yet 'Maori' grinned at the first bit of good news he had witnessed all day. It was Rupert Lonsdale, escaped from Isandlwana.

"By Jove, Maori, this is *fun*." His voice dripped with sarcasm. "Did you know the camp has been taken?"

"I don't see the fucking humour, Rupert," Browne retorted. "But go and tell the staff, if you wish. They won't believe me."

Lonsdale's mind was befuddled, from his injury as well as fatigue and lack of sleep over the past couple days. The destruction he had witnessed was beyond description. It did not seem real to him. Yet he knew his eyes did not play tricks. The scene of carnage and death was very real; Dante's description of hell could not have had a more profoundly sorrowful impact. He led his pony over to where Chelmsford was giving detailed instructions to one of the staff officers, ordering him to 'ride like hell' back to Mangeni.

"Commandant Lonsdale," he said, noticing Rupert for the first time. "I am glad, sir, to see you among the living."

"Very kind of you, my lord," Lonsdale replied.

"Tell me, have you been to the camp?"

Rupert nodded.

The GOC swallowed hard and asked, "Is it true?"

"I approached the camp," Lonsdale explained, "but being half asleep I didn't notice anything amiss until I was well inside. The first thing that truly woke me up was a Zulu coming at me with a stabbing assegai already red with blood. I glanced around me and was suddenly aware of what had taken place; the camp had been captured by the Zulus. I saw dead bodies, both Zulus and our own, all over the place, tents rendered into fragments, bags of flour cut

467

open and the contents strewn about, broken boxes of ammunition. Every hinge, in fact, was smashed and done for. Last but not least, Zulus with assegais still reeking with blood wandering about in all this incredible chaos. I saw it all in a flash, turned, and fled. My horse was as tired as I was. It is only by divine providence that I survived. So yes, my lord, it is true."

Chelmsford looked like a man utterly crushed. He had rushed off before dawn, thinking he was going to chase down and destroy the Zulu *impi*, only to find the Zulu army had attacked and destroyed the camp at Isandlwana. There could be little doubt that Durnford and Pulleine were dead, and God only knew how many of their command.

It was slowly starting to sink in. Half his command had been destroyed, along with all of their rations and equipment. The other half of his men were famished, and had only their basic load of ammunition, minus what they had already expended. There was only one thing left to do, they would return to Rorke's Drift. It was twenty-five miles back to Rorke's Drift from Mangeni. Even then it was no more suited for defence than Isandlwana. Was the supply depot and hospital now under attack by a victorious Zulu force? If so, they could not hold for long. If Major Spalding's command were destroyed along with Lieutenant Bromhead and Colour Sergeant Bourne's company, then what remained of No. 3 Column would be in ever more dire straits.

"I can't understand it," he said, slowly shaking his head. "I left a thousand men to guard the camp."

Chapter XL: Nightfall

Helpmekaar, fifteen miles from Rorke's Drift
22 January 1879
8.15 p.m.
***

Night had fallen, and it was pitch black aside from the occasional torch and lantern that lit the work details hurriedly establishing defences around Helpmekaar. The few who escaped the hellish slaughter of Isandlwana were awash in feelings of complete exhaustion, profound relief that they were still alive, and dark feelings of terror that the Zulus would soon be upon them.

Upon his arrival, Captain Edward Essex was surprised to find the site all but deserted. He was relieved to see his subordinate transport officer, Horace Smith-Dorrien and Durnford's transport officer, William Cochrane were still counted among the living.

"Captain, sir," Horace said, with a tired salute.

"By God, Horace, where the devil is everyone? There were supposed to be two companies guarding this place."

"About that, sir," Private James Trainer spoke up. He hobbled over to the officer and saluted. "Major Upcher and Captain Rainforth left late this afternoon when they heard what happened. I hope they make it to Rorke's Drift before it is overrun."

Essex nodded. "I want all horses turned loose. This is our stronghold, where we will fight, and, if need be, die like true soldiers. I'll not have any more cowards running away."

"If we're going to die, it'll be on our own farms!" the quartermaster from the Buffalo Border Guard snapped. "You fucking regulars can stay here and die if you want."

With a few more shouts and profanities many of the volunteers promptly fled into the night.

Essex shook his head in frustration. "Filthy cowards." He then called for all officers and NCOs to get a tally of their men and weapons.

There were a handful of volunteer officers who remained, including Captain Nourse and Lieutenant Raw. All of their African troops had abandoned them. Even the gallant Basutos and Zikhali

Horse had broken. A few of the carbineers escaped, including Lieutenant Higginson and Sergeant Major Williams. However, as Higginson had no weapon, he excused himself and rode off into the night. In his shame, he said nothing about leaving Melvill and Coghill to an almost certain death. Though they had failed to save their guns, Lieutenant Curling and Sergeant Costello from N Battery escaped with their lives, as did eight of their drivers and gunners.

The first to arrive had been Bombardier Goff from the rocket battery and the three attached privates from 1/24th. They each still had their rifles and Goff his acquired carbine. They warned the garrison and prompted Major Upcher to make for Rorke's Drift immediately. The men had offered to accompany him, but in their battered and exhausted state, the major told them to remain and watch the stores.

There were ten survivors from the Imperial Mounted Infantry detachment; Sergeant Naughton, Corporal McCann, and eight privates. Like the privates from the rocket battery, Corporal McCann was originally from 1/24th, as were Privates Davis, Parry, and Power. McCann had served with Captain Wardell's H Company and was completely shattered to think that he was the only one of his mates left alive.

But for all the sorrows and terror, the one soldier from the IMI they could not stop talking about was young Private Sam Wassall. His selfless act of re-crossing the uMzinyathi River in order to save his friend, Private David Westwood, was a supreme act of valour; one of the few deeds of heroism from that terrible day that didn't end with the brave man slain.

Two bandsmen had also escaped, as had Colonel Glyn's orderly, Private Williams, who stated repeatedly that he owed his life to Lieutenant Coghill, whom he hoped had made it.

All told, Captain Essex had forty-eight men rallied at the tiny station of Helpmekaar, though only twenty-eight had rifles. The officers had pistols, and most of the artillerymen were unarmed.

"At least we have plenty of ammunition," the captain said.

He then formed a work detail to wheel the wagons into a barricade between the three iron sheds and two supply huts. Bags of mealie and oats were piled beneath the wagons, and in short order they had established a viable set of defences.

"Excuse me, Edward."

Essex turned to see his fellow captain, Alan Gardner. Originally from the 14th Hussars, he had been serving as one of Colonel Glyn's staff officers. Though he'd acted as one of Pulleine's ADCs earlier in the day, he'd lost his horse and only managed to escape with the mount belonging to a slain Zikhali trooper. He was still numb with shock, like everyone else. Of the entourage who left that morning from Mangeni to oversee the packing up of the camp at Isandlwana, only he remained. He had watched Major Stuart Smith die, as well as Lieutenant Francis McDowell. Henry Dyer and Thomas Griffith were missing and most likely dead.

"Alan," Essex said. "What do you need?"

"If the Zulus are seeking out other concentrations of British troops, what's to stop them from attacking Colonel Wood's column? Last I knew, they were only about twenty-five miles north of Isandlwana; a distance the Zulus can run in just a few hours. Someone needs to warn them."

"I'll ask for volunteers," Edward conceded, "but after what this lot has been through, I doubt anyone will accept."

When no one offered to ride into the pitch black of night, not knowing if the Zulu *impi* had crossed into Natal, the exhausted Captain Gardner mounted his horse and rode off in hopes of somehow reaching the upper drift, crossing back into Zululand, and finding the No. 4 Column before it, too, was wiped out by the Zulus.

The defences completed as best they could manage, the survivors settled in for what they knew would be a sleepless night. Clouds blotted out the stars, and it was impossible to see beyond a few feet. Gazing to the northeast, Private Sam Wassall noticed an unmistakable glow.

"Captain!" he called in a hushed whisper.

Essex came over. Even at this distance, he could clearly see what could only be described as 'red with fire' on the horizon.

"God save us," he said. "Rorke's Drift burns."

Historical Afterward

The Battle of Isandlwana was the most terrible defeat ever inflicted on the British Empire by an indigenous army. Of the 1,700 men Lord Chelmsford left in the camp, including Pulleine's forces and Durnford's No. 2 Column, over 1,300 were killed. The British public greeted the news with cries of mourning, national embarrassment, and a demand for retribution. Eventually, Sir Henry Bartle-Frere and Lord Chelmsford were sacked and both replaced by Sir Garnet Wolseley, who demanded they be called to account for starting an illegal war that led to an ignominious defeat and terrible loss of life. But first, British honour had to be restored, and large numbers of reinforcements were sent to Natal. Chelmsford's personal mission became to end the war successfully before Wolseley replaced him.

Zulu losses were equally horrific. Because they never kept any written records, exact numbers are impossible to know. By their own accounts, the *amabutho* suffered a terrible mauling before they closed the distance to engage in hand-to-hand combat. It is generally accepted that at least a thousand were killed outright, though the actual number is probably much higher. Due to the savage injuries inflicted by the Martini-Henry Rifle, the bayonet, and artillery shelling, coupled with the primitive medical practices of the Zulu people, at least another thousand died of their wounds. Add to that another two to three thousand more wounded, the Zulu *impi* suffered as many as 5,000 total casualties; a terrible price paid for what historians would consider their nation's greatest victory.

Perhaps the best indicator of just how terrible the Zulu losses were comes from when the *impi* returned to Ulundi and paraded before the king. Cetshwayo, sensing there were vast numbers of men absent, asked where the rest of his regiments were. When told that they were dead, the king prohibited his people from the traditional celebrations following such a victory. Instead, he called for a time of mourning and is quoted as saying, *"A spear has been thrust into the belly of our nation…there are not enough tears to mourn the dead."*

And while Cetshwayo wished to fight a purely defensive war, so he might be seen as on the side of right, his brother, Prince Dabulamanzi, dashed these hopes when he disobeyed the king and crossed into Natal. Eager for glory, and within hours of the victory at Isandlwana, the 4,000 warriors of the Undi Corps launched an attack on the tiny garrison at Rorke's Drift…

Appendices

Appendix A: The Victoria Cross

The Victoria Cross is the highest military decoration in the British Armed Forces, awarded for valour and extreme courage, beyond that normally expected of a British soldier in face of the enemy. It is first in the order of wear in the United Kingdom honours system, taking precedence over all other orders and decorations, even the Most Noble Order of the Garter. First established in 1856, it has been awarded just 1,358 times (as of 2016). Three of these were bestowed to soldiers who fought at Isandlwana; only one lived to receive the honour.

The Victoria Cross
Lieutenants Teignmouth Melvill and Neville Coghill

The following are the citations for the Victoria Cross, gazetted 15 January 1907, to Lieutenants Melvill and Coghill:

Lieutenant Teignmouth Melvill
On 22 January 1879 after the disaster of the Battle of Isandlwana, South Africa, Lieutenant Melvill made gallant efforts to save the Queen's Colour of his Regiment. He and Neville Josiah Aylmer Coghill were pursued by Zulu warriors and after experiencing great difficulty in crossing the swollen Buffalo River, during which time the Colour was unfortunately carried downstream, the two men were overtaken by the enemy. Following a short but gallant struggle, both were killed. The Colour was retrieved from the river 10 days later.

Lieutenant Neville Coghill
On 22 January 1879, after the disaster of the Battle of Isandlwana, South Africa, Lieutenant Coghill joined another officer, Teignmouth Melvill, who was trying to save the Queen's Colour of the Regiment. They were pursued by Zulu warriors, and while crossing the swollen River Buffalo, Lieutenant Coghill went to the rescue of his brother officer, who had lost his horse and was in great danger.

The two men were eventually overtaken by the enemy and, following a short but gallant struggle, both were killed.

Teignmouth Melvill's body, along with that of his friend, Neville Coghill, was found on 4 February, nearly two weeks after their deaths, by a patrol led by Major Wilsone Black and acting-Captain Charlie Harford. Black found Melvill's gold pocket watch still on him, which was sent to his widow, Sarah. They covered the bodies with stones and returned the following day with Chaplain George Smith, who read the funerary rites.

Harford and serveral others conducted a subsequent patrol downstream, where they located the leather case pooled with all sorts of military debris. A short ways further down, the colour was found. Though partially rotted from having been submerged in the cold waters for so long, Major Black carried them high as they returned to Rorke's Drift. Today, they hang in Brecon Cathedral.

Both of Melvill's sons followed him into the army; the elder, Teignmouth Jr, served in the 24th Regiment of Foot (South Wales Borderers) along with Henry Pulleine's son. The younger, Charles Melvill—who was just four months old at the time of his father's death—rose to the rank of major general with the New Zealand Military Forces. Coghill was unmarried and left no children behind. He has been commemorated with a leadership programme named in his honour at Haileybury College in Hertfordshire.

Because there was no provision at the time for a posthumous award, it was simply announced in the London Gazette that Melvill and Coghill *'would have been recommened to Her Majesty for the Victoria Cross, had they survived'*. Sarah Melvill and Coghill's father began a petition on their behalf that would last almost three decades. Finally, in 1906, the rules were changed, and on 15 January 1907, Melvill and Coghill were among the first posthumous awards of the Victoria Cross. In the 1979 film *Zulu Dawn*, they were portrayed by James Faulkner and Christopher Cazenove.

The Regimental Colour (right) along with the recovered Queen's Colour, which
Queen Victoria adorned with the 'Wreath of the Immortals'

The Victoria Cross
Private Samuel Wassall

The following is the citation for the Victoria Cross that was gazetted for Private Samuel Wassall. He was the only survivor of the Battle of Isandlwana to be recognised for his extreme valour:

For his gallant conduct in having, at the imminent risk of his own life, saved that of Private Westwood, of the same regiment. On the 22nd January, 1879, when the Camp at Isandlwana was taken by the enemy, Private Wassail retreated towards the Buffalo River, in which he saw a comrade struggling, and apparently drowning. He rode to the bank, dismounted, leaving his horse on the Zulu side, rescued the man from the stream, and again mounted his horse, dragging Private Westwood across the river under a heavy shower of bullets.

Appendix B: Historical Requiem – The Survivors of Isandlwana

Lieutenant Horace Smith-Dorrien became ill with a fever soon after Isandlwana. He was transferred to a hospital in Ladysmith; however, he discharged himself in time for the second invasion later that year. He returned to his duties as a transportation officer, this time with the newly organized 2nd Division, and was present for the climactic Battle of Ulundi.

He went on to have a long and distinguished career, returning to his regiment in 1882. He took part in suppressing the Urabist Revolt in Egypt, as well as the Sudan Campaign, where he was awarded the Distinguished Service Order for valour during the Battle of Ginnis in 1885. He continued to rise through the officer ranks, being promoted to lieutenant colonel in 1897, during the Tirah campaign in India, and later to full colonel while serving in Malta. He returned to South Africa during the Anglo-Boer War of 1899 to 1902, where he was subsequently promoted to brigadier, and later major general. Five years later he returned to England, where he assumed command at Aldershot as a lieutenant general.

In 1911 he was named aide-de-camp to King George V, was promoted to full general the following year, and knighted as a *Knight Grand Cross of the Most Honourable Order of the Bath* (GCB).

During the Great War, he commanded the II Corps of the British Expeditionary Force under Field Marshal Sir John French. French and Smith-Dorrien had a terribly strained relationship, and he resigned his command following the Second Battle of Ypres. He ended the war as Governor of Gibraltar.

General Sir Horace Smith-Dorrien retired from the army in 1922, having served for forty-six years. He was killed in a motor vehicle accident eight years later at the age of seventy-two.

General Sir Horace Smith-Dorrien

Captain Edward Essex maintained his small garrison at Helpmekaar in anticipation of a Zulu invasion which never materialized. In May, he was appointed Director of Transport for the 2nd Division during the Second Invasion of Zululand. He was one of the few survivors from Isandlwana to take an active role in the Battle of Ulundi. Ironically, one of the weapons captured from the Zulus was his own sword, which he had left in his tent prior to the Battle of Isandlwana.

He was promoted to brevet major in 1880 and served as Quartermaster General to the Natal Field Forces during the disastrous campaigns of the First Boer War. He survived the repulses at Laing's Nck and Ingogo, once again living up to the nickname 'Lucky Essex', which his friends gave him after Isandlwana.

He soon returned to England, serving as Instructor of Musketry at Sandhurst from 1883 to 1885. In 1886 he was promoted to lieutenant colonel, then in 1891 placed on the half-pay list. The following year he retired at the rank of full colonel, having last commanded the 2nd Battalion of the Gordon Highlanders. He lived a very long life in retirement and died on 10 September 1939 at the age of ninety-one, just seven days after Britain declared war on Germany to start the Second World War.

Captain Theophilus 'Offy' Shepstone Jr accompanied the first burial detail to return to Isandlwana on 21 May 1879. The extreme decay brought on by five months of exposure, compounded with many of the bodies being stripped of their clothing, made identification impossible for many of the remains. While searching for the body of his brother, George, 'Offy' did find the corpse of Anthony Durnford. He removed a ring from the body, which he sent to Durnford's family. However, he was later accused by some of Durnford's friends of having removed papers from his pockets, which would have proved damning to Chelmsford. This, however, was never substantiated.

During the second invasion, he took command of a reorganised troop of mounted natives, who became known as 'Shepstone's Basutos'. He took a very active role during the Battle of Ulundi on 4 July 1879, where both he and his African troopers were praised for their prowess and courage. His troop was disbanded later that month, just after the war's end. For his exemplary service, Shepstone was named a *Companion of the Most Distinguished Order of Saint Michael and Saint George* (CMG).

Five years later, and with his father's influence, he acted as an intermediary in Swaziland, between the local Swazis and white concessionaries, seeking the rich mineral resources. He was later criticised for his rather unscrupulous means of gaining commissions for himself, as well as financial irregularities. He left Swaziland in 1895. Captain Shepstone died of cancer in Johannesburg in March 1907 at the age of sixty-four.

Lieutenant Henry Curling remained at Rorke's Drift for the next few months. He was promoted to captain in August and given command of C Battery, 3rd Royal Artillery Brigade in Kabul, Afghanistan. He later served with the recently raised Aldershot Command, where he was promoted to major in 1885. Ten years later, he was given command of the Royal Artillery in Egypt and promoted to lieutenant colonel. He retired in 1902 as a full colonel. His wife had preceded him in death and Colonel Henry Curling died at his home in Ramsgate on 1 January 1910 at the age of sixty-two.

Lieutenant William Cochrane was given the local rank of captain, following George Shepstone's death, along with command of the Natal Native Horse. He served under Lieutenant Colonel Russell's cavalry, as part of Colonel Wood's newly reformed division. The NNH fought with distinction at the battles of Hlobane and Khambula in late March, while also taking part in some of the heaviest fighting at Ulundi.

After the war, Cochrane was appointed Assistant Adjutant-General to the Colonial Forces, and took part in the Basuto 'Gun War' of 1880 to 1881. He was made a substantive captain in June 1881, with a brevet to major the following February. That year he returned to service with the regular army, campaigning with Sir Garnet

Wolseley in Egypt. He later served as a staff officer in Hong Kong, Ireland, and again in South Africa, with his majority made substantive in 1886. In 1893 was appointed brevet lieutenant colonel, the same year he married a Chilean named Maria Carola.

Cochrane commanded a brigade during the Sudan campaigns of conquest, achieving the rank of full colonel as well as being named *Companion of the Most Honourable Order of the Bath* (CB). His final posting was to Belfast, Ireland, where he retired in 1903 at the rank of brigadier general. He died in October 1927 at the age of eighty.
(Note: The rank of brigadier general was phased out in 1921 and then brought back in 1928 in its current designation of 'brigadier'.)

Lieutenant Henry Charles Harford returned with Lord Chelmsford's forces to Rorke's Drift. The 3rd NNC was disbanded, and Harford was left at Rorke's Drift for the next several months. He was given custody of Captain Stevenson and Lieutenant Higginson, who were both accused of desertion. Higginson would later be acquitted, while Stevenson was found guilty. Harford continued his rather strange hobby of collecting insects, gaining the scorn of some of his fellow officers for using the gin supply from the Officers' Mess as a preservative.

On 4 February, Harford took part in the patrol, led by Major Wilsone Black, which found the bodies of Lieutenants Melvill and Coghill. A few days later they retrieved the Queen's Colour of 1/24th. In April, he re-joined the 99th Regiment, which had followed him to Natal and was now at Thukela. Ironically, the officer who replaced him as adjutant during his absence had been killed during the Siege of Eshowe. He later served with the 1st Division during the Second Invasion, yet they took no active role in the remainder of the war. Because of his fluency in Zulu, he was later utilised as an interpreter, and was present when Cetshwayo was captured in July.

Harford and the 99th were then sent to Bermuda for a short time, but quickly returned during the Transvaal Rebellion in 1881. They were posted to Cape Flats, near the place where Cetshwayo was living in exile. The king, who the regiment held in the highest regard, was often invited to attend banquets and other functions hosted by the regiment.

He remained with the 99th Regiment for the remainder of his career, rising to the rank of full colonel, having commanded each battalion at one time or another. In 1898 he married Florence Page, with whom he had one daughter. From 1902 to 1905 he commanded the 62nd Regimental District, and for two years after was Colonel in Charge of Records for the Yorkshire Grouped Regimental Districts. He retired in 1907, having been named a *Commander of the Most Noble Order of the Bath* (CMB). Colonel Harford died on 25 March 1937 at the age of eighty-seven.

Private Samuel Wassall returned to the Imperial Mounted Infantry (IMI), following Isandlwana. They participated in the second invasion of Zululand, including the Battle of Ulundi on 4 July 1879. Two months later, in Utrecht, he was presented with the Victoria Cross by Sir Garnet Wolseley, for his extreme heroism in saving the life of Private Westwood.

Wassall left the army two years later, and settled in Barrow-in-Furness, Cumbria, where he worked as a dockyard electrician. He and his wife, Elizabeth, had four sons and three daughters. On 26 June 1920, the Wassalls were invited to a special reception at Buckingham Palace, hosted by King George V and Queen Mary. It was his first trip to London, yet the third time he had met the king. He described the afternoon as one of the greatest experiences of his life.

Private Samuel Wassall died forty-eight years after the Battle of Isandlwana, in January 1927, at the age of seventy. He was buried at Barrow Cemetery with military honours. His Victoria Cross is displayed at the Museum of the Staffordshire Regiment.

Frances Ellen Colenso remained a staunch friend and defender of Anthony Durnford's memory. A fictionalised account of the debacle at Bushman's Pass, which Durnford had asked her not to publish during his lifetime, was released in 1880. Titled *My Chief and I*, Colenso wrote it under the pseudonym, Atherton Wylde. After Isandlwana, and in part due to Chelmsford's attempts to cast the blame on Durnford, she became a more harshly outspoken critic of Chelmsford, Bartle-Frere, and their disastrous policies in South Africa. She further accused those who found Durnford's body of hiding documents found on him that would have been damaging to Chelmsford.

In October, Frances left Natal for England, where she befriended Anthony's brother, Edward. Together they collaborated on a book called *A History of the Zulu War and its Origins*, a severe critique of British policies, as well as an attempt to clear Anthony's name. She later returned to Natal, and with her father's help wrote a second book, *The Ruin of Zululand*, published soon after Bishop Colenso's death in 1884.

Frances would only outlive her father by a few years.

Having contracted tuberculosis nine years earlier, while tending to a sick British soldier, her health was rapidly declining. Even so, she and her sisters continued to work on behalf of the indigenous people of both Natal and Zululand, right up until her death in 1887 at the age of thirty-eight.

Appendix C: The Complicated Legacy of Brevet Colonel Anthony Durnford

One of the most complex and difficult to understand persons surrounding the Battle of Isandlwana is Brevet Colonel Anthony Durnford. In wake of the disaster, Lord Chelmsford—in no small part due to the influence of Crealock—felt he needed a scapegoat to take the blame off of him. And since Durnford was the senior officer present, this fell to him. Much bad press was directed at Durnford, where he was depicted as insubordinate and incompetent, who had disobeyed orders and run off seeking personal glory, allowing the camp and his own column to be overrun. This was expounded by other influential figures, such as Sir Theophilus Shepstone, who blamed him for the death of his son, George. This was met with much backlash by Durnford's friends, as well as those who felt Chelmsford was simply trying to cover up for his own incompetence. And one cannot help but wonder, if Durnford had not been present, would Henry Pulleine have been so ruthlessly slandered?

The most vocal critics of this character-assassination were Durnford's brother, as well as he dearest friend, Frances Colenso. Frances wrote a series of books on the subject, depicting Anthony as a brave and competent soldier, while decrying British policies in South Africa and their treatment of the indigenous people; echoing much of the same criticism levelled by her father, Bishop John Colenso. And a hundred years later, in the film *Zulu Dawn*, Burt Lancaster depicted Durnford as both heroic and of far greater competence than the other officers, particularly Chelmsford. Both Chelmsford and Colenso's depictions of Anthony Durnford are, however, very one-dimensional, and of course the truth is always far more complicated.

During his attempts to discredit Durnford, Crealock had stated that the orders written specified that Durnford was to 'take command of the camp'. Much to Crealock, and likely Chelmsford's chagrin, the actual orders were found, and no such directive to take control of the camp was ever mentioned. Given Chelmsford's rather heavy-handedness with him just a few days before, it is small wonder that Durnford was reluctant to assume command without written orders. It was also a logical conclusion for Durnford to draw, that Chelmsford had ordered him up to Rorke's Drift, and later to Isandlwana, with the intent of aiding him in the pursuit of what he thought was the main Zulu *impi*.

However, Durnford cannot be completely absolved here. Since we do not know Chelmsford's mind, perhaps he was simply being prudent by ordering the No. 2 Column to reinforce Isandlwana, and had no intention of Durnford linking up with him. If that was the case, then it was not necessary for him to specifically state whether Durnford should assume command. It was known to all that his rank of Lieutenant Colonel was substantive, whereas Pulleine's was only a brevet, making Durnford the senior officer. And even if there was a profound reluctance to assume command—only to hand it back a short while later—there should have been far better coordination between the two. Though neither would survive the battle, and therefore cannot justify their actions or inactions, there were witnesses who overheard what was said between them. Vague and uncertain would be the best descriptive terms.

In hindsight, Durnford's leaving the camp and venturing out on his own led to his committing a series of fatal errors. However, as no one in the camp even knew that the Zulu *impi* was so close, and would not until well after the No. 2 Column had departed (it was they, after all, who found them), one cannot decry his actions as necessarily reckless, given what they actually knew at the time. They had seen several thousand Zulus, and though their origins were unknown, it was never suspected they were part of the main *impi*. There was, however, a very real concern that they would head east and get behind Chelmsford and the rest of the column. Were this their actual intent, and Durnford had done nothing, the potential disaster would have been inexcusable. In reality, the Zulus did not know that Chelmsford had left, otherwise this may have very well been their intent. His actions did also fit within the narrative of what orders Chelmsford had given him; after all, he had neither directed him to stay at the camp, nor had he ordered him up to Mangeni. It was therefore a perfectly logical course-of-action to take his highly mobile force to prevent the Zulus from flanking the lead elements of the column.

Where Durnford committed his gravest folly was upon seeing just how large the Zulu army was, and deciding the fight them on his own. We'll never know if he thought he was up against was their entire force, or if he knew that this was simply the 'Left Horn'. Though Charlie Raw had seen the entire *impi*, he remained along the main firing line, several miles way, and he and Durnford never saw each other again. Regardless, with Raw and Roberts' troops split off, Durnford had just a few hundred carbineers and mounted rifles with him. Knowing that he was terribly outnumbered, to stay and fight crosses the boundary from bravery to foolhardy.

The other grievous command-and-control error made was not knowing where his supply wagons were. He had tasked one of his troops to escort their wagons in, yet gave no instructions as to where exactly they should place them. This proved to be crucial when Lieutenant Davies went back to find the ammunition wagon, and no one knew where it was.

From the accounts of survivors, Durnford seems to have suffered from serious 'tunnel vision' during the battle. He was so intently focused on the fighting at hand, that he completely lost sight of what was going on elsewhere. Much of this was possibly due to the scourge of Bushman's Pass, which he longed more than anything to rid himself of. There is, perhaps a bit of truth to Chelmsford's accusation that Durnford was eager for personal glory, though 'redemption' is probably a more accurate statement. One must also remember that Durnford was not an infantry or cavalry officer, but an engineer. Aside from Bushman's Pass, he had almost no experience leading combat soldiers into battle.

There can be no doubt that Anthony Durnford was extremely brave, that is motivations for chasing the Zulu were both noble and, given the information he had at that moment, tactically and strategically correct. However, for an officer of his rank, valour alone is simply not enough. When one is in command, and directly responsible for many hundreds of lives, calm calculations and cool-headed tactical savvy are even more important, as is situational awareness and knowing where your own resupplies are located. In this, he failed. However, to pin the blame squarely on him for the defeat at Isandlwana is both unfair and inaccurate. Henry Pulleine still maintained control of the camp itself, and could have taken measures to concentrate his forces, which were spread way too thin. During future battles, particularly the finale at Ulundi, Chelmsford's theory that a wall of musketry, from soldiers in multiple ranks standing shoulder-to-shoulder, would prove impenetrable for the Zulus.

As an aside, one must also credit the Zulus for their triumph at Isandlwana. It is far too easy to brush it off as simply a disaster brought on by arrogance and incompetence from the British. The Zulus, far from being a disorganized mob of 'barbarians', were highly disciplined and extremely well-organized. Yet theirs was not a flawless attack either, as there were many errors committed, and in fact they had not wished to fight that day at all. Warriors became overzealous, with regiments charging forward without waiting for support, which doubtless contributed to many of their casualties. In the end, though, it was still a triumph of coordination and tactical prowess. Ntshingwayo had an army of upwards of 25,000 warriors, covering a massive battle front, which extended miles. The warriors in the 'Chest' and 'Horns' could neither see nor coordinate with each other as the battle wore on. And yet, despite the errors committed and the terrible loss of life, in the end they still prevailed. The Battle of Isandlwana was as much a Zulu victory as it was a British defeat.

Both Bishop John Colenso and his daughter would remain stalwart defenders of Anthony Durnford's honour. John died in 1883 at the age of sixty-nine. Frances Colenso would only outlive her father by a few years, before succumbing to tuberculosis in 1887, at the age of thirty-eight.

To this day, the subject of Colonel Anthony Durnford's legacy is still one of much debate and controversy. The Royal Engineers have taken up the mantle of defending Durnford as one of their own; a man, who though deeply flawed, was one of honour and extreme courage, whose intentions were noble, both before and during the war against the Zulus.

(Note: Though he was brevetted to full colonel in December 1878, and is thus usually referred to as 'Colonel' Durnford in historical sources, the orders bearing this promotion did not reach Natal until after his death. Hence why in the narrative of this story he is still referred to by his substantive rank of Lieutenant Colonel.)

Appendix D: Glossary

Note: All terms from the isiZulu language will appear in italics

Assegai – Term used to describe a Zulu spear, though it does not appear in the isiZulu language. Their actual name for the short stabbing spear is *iklwa*. Assegais usually referred to the throwing spears, though it was often used to describe all spears carried by the Zulus.

Battalion – British Army unit designation, consisting of eight line companies, plus battalion staff officers. Commanded by a lieutenant colonel, with the sergeant major as the senior non-commissioned officer.

Boer – From the Dutch term meaning 'farmer', refers to all Dutch-speaking settlers in South Africa.

Bombardier – An artilleryman, roughly equivalent to an infantry lance corporal, except a bombardier was rated as a full non-commissioned officer, while a lance corporal was not. They wore a single gold chevron on their right shoulder.

Boy – British army rank given to those who were underage. The minimum age was fourteen, and they served as buglers, bandsmen, and officers' servants. Upon reaching the age of eighteen, they were given the option of enlisting onto the roles as a private. Contrary to the myths depicted in both art and film, the youngest boy at Isandlwana was sixteen.

Brevet – A temporary promotion given to officers who were filling a billet above their substantive rank, as well a reward to those who had performed exceptional service. Though they would wear the insignia and be addressed by their brevet rank, they were still paid at their substantive grade, and were always subordinate to substantive officers of the same rank. Example: Henry Pulleine was a brevet lieutenant colonel, yet he was still paid as a major, and was subordinate to Antony Durnford, who was a substantive lieutenant colonel.

Captain – Commissioned officer, just above lieutenant and below major. Most often given command of line companies, and in some cases used as battalion staff officers.

Colour Sergeant – The senior non-commissioned officer within a company, responsible for day-to-day training, drill, discipline, and logistics. He was the equivalent to a modern Company Sergeant Major (British Army) or First Sergeant (U.S. Army). He wore an insignia of three gold chevrons, with two crossed flags and a crown above, on his right shoulder.

Company – British Army unit, consisting of up to a hundred soldiers, including officers and other ranks. Commanded by a captain, with a colour sergeant as the senior non-commissioned officer. Note: Companies on overseas service were notoriously understrength, with seventy to eighty total soldiers being the norm.

Corporal – First of the non-commissioned officer ranks in the British Army. They acted as assistants to the sergeants, and were sometimes given command of their own sections or specialty units, such as company sharp-shooters. They wore two white chevrons on their right shoulder.

Drift – A natural river crossing, more commonly known as a 'ford' in modern times.

***Ibutho* (plural *amabutho*)** – A term used to describe a Zulu regiment. Each *ibutho* was age-based, with the king raising new regiments around the time young Zulu males turned seventeen to twenty, based on the needs of the kingdom. They served as the chief labour force, at the king's pleasure, in addition to their military responsibilities in defence of the kingdom. Zulu men were considered youths up until they were allowed to marry, which was usually around the age of thirty. At which time, and with the king's permission, they would take wives-often marrying en mass together-and be allowed to take charge of their own households. Married regiments were exempt from labour and menial details, and were only assembled during times of war or national emergency.

Impi – The name given to a large Zulu army, consisting of numerous *amabutho*.

***Induna* (plural *izinduna*)** – An officer within the ibutho, selected by his peers. Most often given charge of roughly a hundred warriors, they were roughly the equivalent to a captain in the British Army.

***Inkosi* (plural *amakhosi*)** – A Zulu chieftain, sometimes referred to as a 'baron' by the British, for their titles came by birth right, rather than appointment. In war they commanded the *amabutho*, with the older and more experienced *amakhosi* placed in charge of the younger regiments.

Inyanga (**plural** *izinyanga*) – Diviners, also derogatorily referred to by Europeans as 'witchdoctors'. They oversaw all spiritual ceremonies for the Zulu *impi*, as well as serving as herbalists and healers.

Iqawe (**plural** *abaqawe*) – Zulu warriors of great renown, who had shown extreme bravery and prowess in battle. Those elevated to the *abaqawe* were regarded as the most valiant heroes of the Zulu Kingdom.

Koppie – Comes from the Dutch term, 'kop', which literally means 'head'. It is used to describe a small, stony hill that stands out on an otherwise flat landscape.

Kraal – Though not a Zulu term, it came to describe local African homesteads. Typically, they consisted of several huts surrounding a central cattle pen. Kraals that belonged to the nobles of the *amakhosi* could hold dozens, or even hundreds of huts, with thousands of residents. The Royal Kraal at Ulundi is said to have had several thousand huts, with numerous cattle pens and arena pits.

Laager – A term used by the Dutch to describe encircling wagons as a means of defence. Can also be used to describe temporary wood or stone fortifications.

Lance Corporal – An uncommon British Army rank, just above private. Though not officially a non-commissioned officer (a status which changed in 1961), they are often given leadership responsibilities and used to assist the sergeants and corporals. They wore a single white chevron on their right shoulder.

Lance Sergeant – Another uncommon British Army rank, lance sergeants were corporals who were either temporarily appointed to a sergeant's billet, or who had displayed great leadership potential and were waiting for promotion to full sergeant. They wore three white chevrons on the right shoulder.

Lieutenant – Junior commissioned officer, most often used as a subaltern within a company, or staff officer at the battalion. Because promotions were so painfully slow during most of the Victorian Era, they tended to vary considerably in age, with older lieutenants often given command of companies while waiting for an eventual promotion to captain. *Note: While the U.S. Armed Forces pronounce* *the rank as it is spelled "lew-tenant", in British and Commonwealth Forces it is pronounced "left-tenant".*

Lieutenant Colonel – A commissioned officer, just above major and below colonel, it is the rank used by commanding officers at the battalion level.

Major – A commissioned officer, just above captain and below lieutenant colonel. Most often used as staff officers, there are two per battalion, each of whom can assume overall command if needed.

Ndabazitha – A Zulu term of reverence to their king, equivalent to 'your majesty'.

Nek – Refers to the lower ground between two high points. In modern times this has been mostly replaced by the term 'saddle'.

Private – Most common rank in the British Army, outnumbering all other combined ranks approximately eight-to-one, and given to all other ranks upon their enlistment and completion of basic recruit training. In a company, between seventy and ninety of the soldiers will be privates. They wear no rank insignia.

Quartermaster – A commissioned officer, tasked with overseeing all supply and logistics for the battalion. Though the equivalent of a major, because they are in the Support Arms (i.e. Commissariat / Transport / Medical) they technically cannot give orders to combat soldiers (i.e. infantry, cavalry, artillery). They are, however, still given the respect of their rank, and referred to as 'sir', by subordinates.

Quartermaster Sergeant – A senior non-commissioned officer, acting as chief assistant to the battalion quartermaster. Though nominally equivalent to a colour sergeant in terms of rank, they were considered to be senior, due to their position being a regimental appointment. They wore four gold chevrons on the right sleeve.

Sergeant – A non-commissioned officer, given command of a section, consisting of up to twenty soldiers. They answered directly to the colour sergeant, and were in charge of the daily drill, discipline, and welfare of their soldiers. Each sergeant usually had at least one corporal or lance corporal to assist him. They wore three gold chevrons on the right shoulder.

Sergeant Major – The senior non-commissioned officer within the battalion, he is responsible for the overall training, standards, and discipline. He also acts as a mentor to the younger lieutenants, even though they technically outrank him.

Subaltern – Term to describe the junior commissioned officers of a company, usually lieutenants, who were tasked with aiding the officer commanding. The senior subaltern would assume command in the captain's absence.

***Usuthu* (sometimes spelled *uSuthu* or *uZulu*)** – Refers to the uSuthu faction, who fought for Cetshwayo during the Zulu civil war of 1856. Following Cetshwayo's victory, it became the battle cry of all Zulus who fought for the king.

Voorlooper – An African boy used to guide the teams of oxen and draught animals.

Author's Notes

It was during the spring of 2011 that I first considered writing a novel about the Anglo-Zulu War of 1879. Like many, my interest stemmed from the 1964 film, *Zulu*, starring Sir Michael Caine in his first major role. Less-heralded, yet equally important was the prequel from 1979, *Zulu Dawn*, starring Peter O'Toole, Burt Lancaster, and Bob Hoskins. Given the age of the films, interest in the Anglo-Zulu War has waned considerably, especially in the U.S. Though Sir Michael Caine remains an extremely popular actor on both sides of the Atlantic, many of his American fans have never even heard of *Zulu*. I felt it was time to revive interest in this conflict, as it is crucially important to the history of both the British Empire as well as the Republic of South Africa. I also wished to pay tribute to those who fought and died in that terrible campaign nearly one hundred and forty years ago.

That summer I contacted the Regimental Museum of the Royal Welsh in Brecon, Wales. It was their predecessors in the 24th Regiment of Foot who fought the savage and tragic battles of Isandlwana and Rorke's Drift. The curator was a retired Regimental Sergeant Major named Bill Cainan, who over the subsequent years I forged a lasting friendship. Bill invited me to spend a few days at the museum, where I could conduct my research, with access to their archives and vast library of photographs. This would prove invaluable and set the foundation for this project. However, despite my growing enthusiasm, it would be another five years before I could finally put the proverbial 'pen to paper' and begin to tell this story in earnest. I was still in the middle of my Ancient Rome series, *The Artorian Chronicles*, which I was obligated to finish first. Bill became a fan of my works and even helped me with conducting research, including exploration of the ancient battlefields, for the final book, *Soldier of Rome: The Last Campaign*.

It was also through Bill that I met a gentleman by the name of Ian Knight in 2013. Ian is widely regarded as the most respected and well-versed historian on the Anglo-Zulu War, as well as South Africa's history both during and after the Victorian Era. He's written over thirty books on the subject, including his life-long work, *Zulu*

Rising, which is by far the most in depth and detailed look at both the war and the Zulu people in existence. Most years he also leads tours of the battlefields, which I highly recommend. I met with Ian at his home in southern England and had a great discussion about our respective works, as well as the Anglo-Zulu War itself. I explained to him that this was a future project, and not something I was jumping into immediately. He understood and offered to assist in any way he could. He appreciated that we both share a passion for telling history as it happened, while dispelling any lingering myths, many of which still linger from the Anglo-Zulu War.

It wasn't until three years later, during the early spring of 2016, that I was finally in a place where I could begin to tell this story. Though I still had one more book to finish in my trilogy about the Fall of Jerusalem in 70 A.D., I was in desperate need of a break. I had further become consumed by the stories of Zulus and Redcoats, and realised that now was the time. I once more enlisted Ian and Bill's assistance. They helped me keep the historical and cultural aspects correct, both of the British Victorian Army, as well as the Zulus, while attempting to amalgam it all together into an engaging story that readers will immerse themselves in. Through their kind generosity, I was given access to scores of photographs, maps, as well as original documents from the time. They further served as my chief beta readers, giving their honest feedback along with any corrections that needed to be made. For this I am truly grateful.

I would also be remiss if I did not thank my loving wife, Tracy, for her unwavering support. She has always been there for me with encouragement, whether I was absorbed in twelve to fourteen hour days of incessant writing, or those insufferable weeks where I was afflicted with seemingly incurable Writer's Block.

And finally, I wish to dedicate this book in memory of the soldiers of the 24th Regiment of Foot, and the warriors of the Zulu Kingdom, who made the ultimate sacrifice on the battlefield of tragedy known as Isandlwana.

James Mace
July 2016

500

Further Reading / Bibliography:

Bibliography

Castle, Ian and Knight, Ian. 1992. *Zulu War 1879, Twilight of a Warrior Nation.* Oxford: Osprey.

Horse Guards War Office. 1873. *Queen's Regulations and Orders for the Army - 1873.* London: Her Majesty's Stationary Office.

Knight, Ian. 2011. *Zulu Rising.* London: Pan MacMillan.

Knight, Ian. 1992. *Zulu, Isandlwana and Rorke's Drift 22-23 January 1879.* London: Windrow and Greene.

Snook, Lt Col Mike. 2010. *How Can Man Die Better: The Secrets of Isandlwana Revealed.* London: Frontline Books.

The story of the Anglo-Zulu War continues with:

Crucible of Honour: The Battle of Rorke's Drift

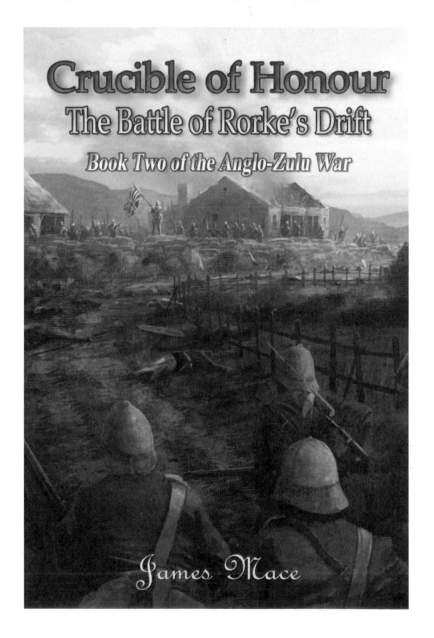

503

Made in United States
North Haven, CT
04 July 2023

38544811R00300